LAND SYSTEMS

AND

INDUSTRIAL ECONOMY

OF

IRELAND, ENGLAND & CONTINENTAL
COUNTRIES

BY

T. E. Cliffe Leslie

[1870]

REPRINTS OF ECONOMIC CLASSICS

AUGUSTUS M. KELLEY · PUBLISHERS
NEW YORK 1968

First Edition 1870
(London: Longmans, Green & Co., 1870)

Reprinted 1968 by
AUGUSTUS M. KELLEY · PUBLISHERS
New York   New York   10010

Library of Congress Catalogue Card Number
67-18570

PRINTED IN THE UNITED STATES OF AMERICA
by SENTRY PRESS, NEW YORK, N. Y. 10019

REPRINTS OF ECONOMIC CLASSICS

LAND SYSTEMS
&
INDUSTRIAL ECONOMY

LAND SYSTEMS

LAND SYSTEMS

AND

INDUSTRIAL ECONOMY

OF

IRELAND, ENGLAND, AND CONTINENTAL COUNTRIES.

BY

T. E. CLIFFE LESLIE, LL.B.

OF LINCOLN'S INN, BARRISTER-AT-LAW:

*Examiner in Political Economy in the University of London, and Professor
of Jurisprudence and Political Economy in the Queen's University
in Ireland, and Queen's College, Belfast.*

LONDON:
LONGMANS, GREEN, AND CO.
1870.

CONTENTS.

		PAGE
*I.	INTRODUCTION	1
II.	THE STATE OF IRELAND, 1867	5
III.	IRELAND IN 1868	34
*IV.	THE IRISH LAND QUESTION, 1870	57
V.	POLITICAL ECONOMY AND EMIGRATION	85
VI.	POLITICAL ECONOMY AND THE TENURE OF LAND	117
VII.	LORD DUFFERIN ON THE TENURE OF LAND	133
VIII.	MR. SENIOR ON IRELAND	151
IX.	THE LAND SYSTEM OF ENGLAND, 1867	160
*X.	THE ENGLISH LAND QUESTION, 1870	204
XI.	WESTPHALIA AND THE RUHR BASIN, 1868–1869	230
*XII.	WESTPHALIA AND THE RUHR BASIN, 1869–1870	254
XIII.	A VISIT TO LA CREUSE, 1868	265

CONTENTS.

	PAGE
*XIV. A SECOND VISIT TO LA CREUSE	283
XV. THE PEASANTRY AND FARMS OF BELGIUM, 1867.	294
*XVI. THE FARMS AND PEASANTRY OF BELGIUM, 1870.	341
XVII. APPENDIX: POLITICAL ECONOMY AND THE RATE OF WAGES	357

LAND SYSTEMS
&c.

INTRODUCTION.

ALONG with a republication of several essays in deference to many suggestions, this volume contains additional articles* on the Land Systems of Ireland and England, and on the industrial economy of La Creuse, Westphalia and the Ruhr Basin, and Belgium, founded on later study and local inquiry.

It appears to the author that the Land Systems of England and Ireland are best studied together. The two systems react in many ways on each other; their results present some striking resemblances, and where they differ most, the differences are instructive. They have a common origin and foundation. The first sentence in Mr. Furlong's standard treatise on the Law of Landlord and Tenant in Ireland is: 'The common law regulating the enjoyment of real property

---
* Marked with an asterisk in the table of contents.

INTRODUCTION.

both in England and in Ireland is founded upon and governed by the principles of the feudal system.' Their similarity of structure is the main cause why the Irish land system has remained intact down to the introduction of the Land Bill now before Parliament. This is so, not only because the landowners of England have been reluctant to permit interference with powers similar to their own, but also through the influence of the structure of the English land system on the ideas of other classes. Had there been in England a simple jurisprudence relating to land, a law of equal intestate succession, a prohibition of entail, a legal security for tenants' improvements, an open registration of title and transfer, a considerable number of peasant properties, the rural economy of England would long since have created unanswerable objections to the Irish land system in the public mind.

On the other hand, there are striking differences in the results of the two systems, which throw much light on both. The Land System of Ireland, for example, tends to suppress the existence of towns; that of England, on the contrary, to give to large towns undue predominance in our industrial and social economy. The English agricultural labourer, again, answers to the Irish small tenant-at-will. And emigration is the movement in the case of Ireland corresponding with immigration into large towns in England. The latter movement is moreover swollen by immigrant

INTRODUCTION. 3

poverty from Ireland; and there is a reflux of its own poverty into that island.

Both Irish emigration and English immigration into towns contrast curiously with an immigration from the country into the towns of France, arising from a very different cause, the economic and political effects of which are among the subjects discussed in the two articles on La Creuse.

Although the author has described effects of the Land Systems of France, Germany, and Belgium, he has, in doing so, simply recorded facts which have come under his own observation, and the genuine impressions made on his mind by careful inquiry on the spot. He has endeavoured also to indicate the influences of geological and other physical conditions on the industrial economy of the Continental localities of which a description is given in the volume. Without reference to such conditions, to history, and to positive institutions, the author believes it impossible for the economist to arrive at a true theory of the causes which govern the production and distribution of wealth.

It is right to acknowledge the obligations the author is under to the extensive and profound learning of his friend Mr. Francis S. Reilly for information and suggestion on many, but especially legal, subjects; although he ought to add that Mr. Reilly is in no way responsible for his conclusions.

Without the hospitable aid and instruction which he has received from M. Léonce de Lavergne during visits to La Creuse, it is improbable that he would have attempted a description of that singular department—the history of which, isolated as it is, has been strangely interwoven with the political and social history of France for more than two hundred years.

2 Stone Buildings, Lincoln's Inn:
February 21, 1870.

THE STATE OF IRELAND,* 1867.

STUDENTS of Irish history know how from time to time in its troubled course, after some overwhelming disaster, there has come a pause in misfortune, a tranquil interval, when statesmen, beholding the capabilities of the country and its people, and mistaking the signs of exhaustion for those of a new life of peace and prosperity, congratulated themselves upon the regeneration of Ireland in their own days. 'In the first nine years of King James,' wrote Sir John Davis, after three rebellions in the reign of Elizabeth, 'there hath been more done in the reformation of the kingdom than in the 440 years since the Conquest.' A still profounder statesman, Bacon, four years afterwards congratulated a Chief Justice of Ireland on his appointment at a time when 'that kingdom, which within these twenty years wise men were wont to doubt whether they should wish it to be a pool, is like now to become a garden, and younger sister to Great Britain.' A generation had not passed before these words were followed by

---

* Reprinted from 'Macmillan's Magazine' for February 1867. In the reprint of this and other essays in the volume, a passage here and there has been omitted. In other respects hardly any change has been made. But as the situation of things *has* changed in succeeding years, changes in the author's views may occasionally appear, owing to that cause, or to further inquiry and reflection.

another rebellion, suppressed in its turn in such a manner that Sir William Petty in 1672 expressed his conviction that the Irish never would rebel again, the more so, as they had never before such prosperity as then.* Political wisdom and sagacity are both supposed to have made great progress since the reign of Charles II., yet such has been the falsification of repeated hopes of Ireland's reformation that there are still to be found men who repeat the very wishes (doubtless ignorant of their antiquity) which Sir William Petty 200 years ago sternly rebuked, and of which nearly 300 years ago the poet Spenser exposed the folly.† The repetition of such sentiments in itself might merely prove that political and moral progress has been unequal in England as in Ireland, and be worth notice only on the part of those historic minds who find an interest in every living vestige of ancestral barbarism in either island. But it is connected not remotely with inquiries of more practical interest and importance, to which conflicting answers are returned; inquiries such as, What is really the present state of Ireland? Has it made any real progress since its last great disaster? Is the land, the people, or the law, the cause of its

---

* 'Political Anatomy of Ireland,' chaps. iv. and xii.

† 'Some furious spirits have wished that the Irish would rebel again, that they might be put to the sword. But I declare that notion to be not only impious and inhuman, but withal frivolous, and pernicious even to those who have rashly wished for those occasions.'—Sir W. Petty, 'Political Anatomy,' chap. iv. 'So have I heard it often wished that all that land were a seapool, which kind of speech is rather the manner of desperate men than of wise counsellors; for were it not the part of a desperate physician to wish his patient dead rather than to apply the best endeavour of his skill for his recovery?'—'A New View of the State of Ireland,' by Edmund Spenser, 1596.

long backwardness and misery? Can legislation do anything for its benefit?

The chief difficulty in answering the two first of these inquiries arises from the very different state of different parts of the island. Different counties and towns—adjoining estates, and even adjoining farms and houses—are very differently circumstanced, and would return a very different report; nor is it too much to assert that the man does not exist who could give a complete and true account of Ireland's present condition. Even the very same results may be produced in different places by opposite causes, and are of different import and omen accordingly. Of this a striking instance offers at once in the rate of wages; an instance of great importance in itself, because it touches the root of the whole Irish question, as for brevity it is sometimes called. Great stress is laid by some on the advance in Irish wages as a proof of a proportionate increase in general prosperity, and of the benefit of emigration. As a matter of fact, the rise in wages is much less than those who take this view suppose; and, in truth, the bulk of the employers of labour below the landed proprietors are in no condition to pay such a price for it. The demand at such a price as has been stated could in most Irish counties be that of one small class alone; and such wages would therefore imply a much greater emigration of labourers and disappearance of farmers than has as yet taken place. But, moreover, those who allege a rise in wages as a conclusive proof of a proportionate increase in general prosperity, overlook the distinction between a

8 LAND SYSTEMS AND INDUSTRIAL ECONOMY.

home demand for labour and a foreign one, to which alone they refer it. If ten thousand labourers only were left in the island, they might earn perhaps more than a pound a day from the upper ten thousand; but would such payment be a proof of Ireland's great prosperity? Would it not rather prove that Ireland had lost one of the three great instruments of production, labour; and that the industry of Ireland had gone to develop American instead of Irish natural resources? The following table shows the rates of wages earned by agricultural labour throughout the year just closed in different parts of the island, as ascertained by personal inquiry:—

	s.	d.		s.	d.	
County of Antrim from	7	0	to	10	0	a week.
Down	7	0		10	0	,,
Armagh	7	0		9	0	,,
Monaghan	6	0		8	0	,,
Cavan	6	0		7	0	,,
Dublin	7	0		11	0	,,
Wexford	6	0		8	0	,,
Cork	6	0		8	0	,,
Mayo	6	0		7	6	,,
Donegal	6	0		8	0	,, *

From the foregoing table it appears that wages throughout most of Ireland do not average more than a shilling daily throughout the working year, which, though a great improvement upon former

* Even such rates as the above are not maintained in all the districts remote from railways: occasional wages of 2s. 6d. a day in the West are far from being a sign of agricultural prosperity and a permanent demand for labour. In parts of Mayo, for example, where oats and potatoes are commonly grown in alternation until the land is exhausted, there is a great demand for labour at spring-time and harvest (when wages sometimes reach 2s. 6d. a day) and very little demand through the rest of the year.

rates when constancy of employment is considered, is yet at present prices a low rate, and one which threatens or promises, as people may think it, a great additional emigration, if the home demand for labour be not greatly improved. And, in connection with this, it is an important point to notice that wages are highest in the localities where population, in place of decreasing, has increased—a point illustrative of the distinction between a home demand for labour and a foreign one. When wages rise by reason of the amount of profitable employment, the quantity and brisk circulation of capital, the wealth and consumption of large classes within a country, it is not only an advantage to the labourers, but a sign of general affluence; it is otherwise when it means no more than that labourers have disappeared. Happily it means the former in at least one-half of Ulster. In that vast system of manufactures which now stretches over several countries, it is around towns in which population has doubled in half a generation that agricultural wages are highest. This circumstance deserves the more attention since it has been lately persistently alleged that the want of coal and iron is the cause of Ireland's poverty, and a cause which must keep it always poor. Writers who persist in such statements can surely never have heard of Derry, Coleraine, Ballymena, Antrim, Newtownards, Lisburn, Banbridge, Newry, Armagh, Strabane, and many other manufacturing towns of Ulster, besides Belfast, to say nothing of the numerous factories which stud the rural districts of the provinces, or of the great amount of industry engaged in the domestic manufacture of the finer fabrics, which the power-loom cannot for many years compete with. Much of the wealth and usefulness of Belfast itself arises from the fact that it is the commercial centre of several counties; and were it overthrown by an earthquake to-morrow, the United Kingdom would have lost one of its best cities, but the looms of Ulster would remain numerous and busy. That the natural deficiency of coal and iron is not the chief obstacle to Irish wealth is indeed sufficiently established by the fact, that in Belfast manufactures in iron are successfully carried on. A fact of still greater significance is that Belfast has in one generation sprung to its present importance, through the land on which it stands becoming the property of its citizens, from being the property of a single proprietor hampered by settlements and incumbrances, and by no means brought up to industry. This is a fact which in itself might justify a presumption that the want of other than agricultural employment for labour in Ireland, and the consequent rush to a foreign demand, is due to no faults of the people or the island, but to the law.

A noble writer has recently described with graphic eloquence the long series of restrictions laid on almost every branch of Irish trade and industry by English legislation in less enlightened times than our own; and the importance due to such historical causes is proved by the different history of two Irish industries —the linen and the woollen manufactures. Almost at the same moment that Protestant manufacturers were flying from France on the Revocation of the Edict of

Nantes, to lay the foundation of the linen manufacture of Ulster, now one of the most flourishing industries of the world, woollen manufacturers, both Protestant and Catholic, were flying in thousands from Ireland to parts of the Continent where the industry they planted flourishes still, but in Ireland has only begun to revive. The history of Flanders affords a precisely parallel instance; the manufactures which the Spaniards drove from its provinces took lasting root in Great Britain, but only begin to reappear in the land of their birth.* The foregoing is not the only historical explanation of the exclusion from three provinces of Ireland of every industry but that of tilling land. It has been pointed out by Adam Smith, that whatever progress was made by England in rural industry itself, originated in the trade and freer institutions of its towns. In common with other philosophers, he has also remarked that in every part of Europe wealth and civilisation began upon the borders of the sea, where there was comparatively free and easy communication with the outer world, but in Ireland the English seized every important port; and Sir John Davis, early in the seventeenth century, asked, 'When the Irish might not converse or commerce with any civil men, nor enter into any town without peril of their lives, whither should they fly but into the woods and mountains, and there live in a wild and barbarous manner?' It was no more the policy of the age following than of the one preceding that

* When manufactures started up with steam in Belgium, it was in the Walloon provinces near mines of coal and iron they rose. Now, however, the Flemish provinces begin to count their growing manufactories again.

eminent statesman, to civilise and elevate the Irish; and the period of the Commonwealth was signalised by repeated orders to drive all Irish and Papists to a distance from every considerable town. When to this we add the blighting influence of the penal laws and the exclusive municipal institutions of a later time, we need hardly wonder that the Irish people clung with 'morbid hunger' to the land alone for their support. But why did the land afford so little support? why was their only industry so barren of results when starvation was frequently the penalty of failure? Why, as it has been often asked, did the English system of landed property, which has succeeded so well in England, fail so utterly in Ireland?

The first answer such a question ought to get is that the English system has not succeeded well in England, but has, on the contrary, proved a most disastrous failure. Agriculture, it is said indeed, has been carried in England to the greatest known perfection. If this were so, it would nevertheless be true that the proper test of any rural system is the peasantry, and not the beasts or herbs it produces; and that the English peasantry, descendants of a noble race, are a reproach to the name of Englishmen. But can agriculture really be said to have prospered when Sir Robert Peel in 1850 could describe it in the terms that follow, though favoured by the very circumstance the Irish cultivator lacked,—the contact and demand of wealthy towns? 'You will find,' the statesman wrote to Mr. Caird, 'immense tracts of good land in certain counties, Lancashire and Cheshire for example, with good roads, good markets, and a moist climate, that remain pretty nearly in a state of nature—undrained, badly fenced, and wretchedly farmed. Nothing has hitherto been effectual in awakening the proprietors to a sense of their own interests.'* Such was the state of English agriculture under the legislation of the proprietors of the soil for its especial benefit ; and the improvement since—an improvement far from general—is traceable to an opposite policy, the policy of commerce and of towns ; towns which have long been cities of refuge for the rural population while half the island is uncultivated.

But England at least *had* towns to receive and employ its landless population, while Ireland was without them. And thus, while the chief movement of population in England has been a migration from the country to large towns, in Ireland the chief movement has been emigration—to the towns of England and America. This emigration of the rural population of Ireland to America is no new phenomenon of this century ; it was the subject of treatises more than a century ago. 'What was it,' says a writer of 1729, 'induced so many of the commonality lately to go to America, but high rents, bad seasons, and want of good tenures or a permanent property in their lands? This kept them poor and low, that they scarce had sufficient credit to procure necessaries to subsist or till their ground. They never had anything in store, all was

---

* This description was more than borne out by the published accounts of Mr. Caird's tour, and in reference to many counties in addition to those particularly named by Sir R. Peel.

14 LAND SYSTEMS AND INDUSTRIAL ECONOMY.

from hand to mouth, so one or two bad crops broke them. Others found their stock decaying visibly, and so removed before all was gone, whilst they had as much left as would pay their passage, and had little more than would carry them to the American shore.'* It might have been urged then, as it is urged now, that the emigrants were but seldom evicted. Eviction was unnecessary—not even a notice to quit was commonly required. The broken down, the breaking down, and those who feared to break down, fled along with the evicted. Even farmers with capital, the writer adds, fled likewise, from the want of security for its investment on their farms. It has been lately maintained that the absence of leases cannot be the present cause of the distress and emigration of the farming classes of Ireland, since leases were 'almost universal in the eighteenth century,' when rural distress was as great as it is now, or lately was, before the worst cases of distress disappeared. But in the first place, the fact is not so; farming leases were not common in that century. Where leases to farmers existed at all, they were for the most part too short to permit of the permanent improvements essential to husbandry being made by the tenant; and the landlord never made them—what with settlements, charges, and mortgages, seldom could make them. The actual cultivators, however, for the most part had no leases and

---

* 'An Essay on the Trade of Ireland,' 1729. A beautiful edition of this and several other rare treatises on Ireland, including those of the poet Spenser, Sir John Davis, Sir W. Petty, and others, was published some years ago by Messrs. Alexander Thom, of Dublin, with great liberality, for private circulation.

were placed and displaced, as the Highlanders are to this day, at the whim of the landlord. Accounting for a decrease in the number of houses in Ireland, the writer last quoted observed in 1729 : ' Another reason I apprehend to be that from gentlemen's receiving or dismissing whole villages of native Irish at once ; and this is done just as gentlemen incline to break up their lands and improve them by tillage, or as they lay them down under grass and enlarge their sheep-walks ; and by this means the poor are turned adrift, and must remove to some other place where they can get employment.' And this was while Ireland had no Poor-law—the contrivance in England to prevent insurrections of the peasantry. But the middlemen, it is said, *had* leases, and long leases, yet cultivation did not prosper with them. The middleman, however, was a landlord, not a cultivator ; and it is for cultivators that security is demanded. It is not proposed to increase the security of landlords, otherwise at least than by making their titles more marketable and their tenants more solvent. The middleman lived in a world from which commerce and enterprise were banished ; his only ambition was to live like a landlord ; he was often deeply embarrassed ; his title was almost always defective ; but he had a famishing crowd round his doors offering rent, and a power of distress to take all they could give. The petty freeholders of a more recent date were not middlemen, it is true, and they had leases of a kind much better than none ; but they were made at random for political objects ; the measure of security allowed them came unattended with any other change to teach agriculture either by example or precept, or to furnish a market for their produce or any safe investment for their savings. What indeed are all such arguments against leases intended to prove? Is it that security is needless as a motive for investment? Do men of sense build houses or shops on other men's land without leases? Cases of actual confiscation of tenants' improvements may be rare; but a single such case as that of O'Fay and Burke alarms every tenant who hears it or reads it, and ill news now travels faster than ever. Does any one measure the mischief of an agrarian outrage by the injury to the victim, or the harm done by a Fenian by his personal acts of destruction? It is really not against his actual landlord that a tenant most needs security, but against all possible landlords; security in fact against the law, which is for him a law of confiscation. It is one of many examples of the tardy accommodation of human jurisprudence to justice, that 270 years ago the poet Spenser urged the necessity of legislative protection for the tenantry in Ireland in terms which apply to this day as well as to that at which they were written:—

'*Iren.*—There is one general inconvenience which reigneth almost throughout all Ireland : that is, that the lords of the land do not there use to let out their land for terms of years to their tenants, but only from year to year, and some during pleasure.

'*Eudox.*—But what reason is there that any landlord should not set, nor any tenant take, his land as himself list?

'*Iren.*—Marry, the evils hereby are great: for by this means both the landlord thinketh that he hath his tenant more at command to follow him into what action soever he shall enter; and also the tenant is fit for every occasion of change, for that he hath no such state in any his holding, no such building upon any farm, no such cost employed in fencing or husbanding the same as might withhold him. All which he hath forborne, and spared so much expense for that he hath no firm estate in his tenement, but was only a tenant at will, or little more, and so at will may leave it. And this inconvenience may be reason enough to ground any ordinance for the good of the commonwealth, against the private behoof or will of any landlord that shall refuse to grant any such term or estate unto his tenant as may tend to the good of the whole realm.

'*Eudox.*—Indeed it is great wilfulness in any landlord to refuse to make any longer farms unto their tenants as may, besides the general good of the realm, be also greatly for their own profit and avail. For what reasonable man will not think that the tenement shall be made much better for the landlord's behoof, if the tenant may by such good means be drawn to build himself some handsome habitations thereon, to ditch and inclose his ground, to manure and husband it as good farmers use? For, when his tenant's term shall be expired, it will yield him in renewing his lease both a good fine and also a better rent. And also it shall be for the good of the tenant likewise, who by such buildings and inclosures shall receive many benefits.

First, by the handsomeness of his house, he shall take more comfort of his life, more safe dwelling, and a delight to keep his house neat and cleanly, which now being, as they commonly are, rather swine-styes than houses, is the chiefest cause of his so beastly manner of life and savage condition. And to all these other commodities he shall in short time find a greater added—that is, his own wealth and riches increased and wonderfully enlarged by keeping his cattle in inclosures, warm covered, that now lieth open to all weather.'

This passage contains the whole political economy of the question of small farms. There is hardly any part of Europe, save England, better fitted for farms of the smallest description than the greater part of Ireland, excluding its waste lands; and even its waste lands could be made highly productive by Flemish cultivation. The soil of Flanders was once all waste; the spade of the peasant, as a Flemish proverb denotes, has turned sand into gold.* The soil of Flanders is, in fact, the creation of man; nature gave little but space for the exertion of his powers.

'Having visited Belgium,' says Dr. Mackenzie, of Eileanach, an expert in the management of small farms, 'by invitation of the Government, for the purpose of inquiring into the advantages of the *petite culture* there, I found much of the land of inferior quality, extremely light and sandy, yet, by force of liquid manure and intense care in weeding and stirring the soil, giving

---

* 'De spa is de goudmyn der boeren,'—The spade is the peasant's gold-mine.

wonderful crops of every kind.'* This description is true of the soil of almost every part of East and West Flanders,†—the provinces of Belgium in which farms of the smallest size are most numerous. But everywhere in Belgium, on rich and poor soils alike, wherever large and small farms meet in competition the former are beaten. Of the part of Belgium in which large farms are most numerous, Le Condroz, M. de Laveleye says: 'This is the region of Belgium which counts the greatest number of large farms; those which reach one hundred hectares, so rare in the Flemish provinces, are here met often enough. As soon as a farm is divided in Condroz, the land is better cultivated, and the number of cattle increases. The small proprietors who cultivate their own two or three hectares know no fallow; their crops are more varied, more carefully cultivated, and the produce is much larger. The too great size of the farms is thus one cause of the inferiority of cultivation in Condroz. But,' M. de Laveleye adds, 'there is another cause. To embark a considerable sum in an agricultural operation, always long and

* Letter to Lord John Russell on the State of the West Highlands, 1851.

† An error prevalent in England respecting the natural fertility of the soil on which Flemish spade husbandry is so successful, has arisen partly from its actual productiveness, and partly from the real natural fertility of *French* Flanders. The soil of Belgian Flanders for the most part is by nature little more than sand.—'Essai sur l'Économie rurale de la Belgique,' par Émile de Laveleye, pp. 1, 2. I have myself seen instances of this in M. de Laveleye's own family campagne, and elsewhere. Nor is the climate of Belgian Flanders so much drier than that of Ireland, as has been alleged. It rains there on the average by computation every second day. But, in fact, a moist climate like that of Ireland is the very climate for the growth of food for cattle, and therefore the very climate for the small farmer.

hazardous, at least in appearance, there must be a certainty that the cultivator shall reap the results of his sacrifices and efforts; and that certainty the contracts between landlord and tenant do not give.' Unfortunately, in Flanders, too, the customary contracts or leases do not give that certainty; they run only for nine years, and the small farmer, in spite of the excellence of his farming, is very poor. He is poor, not because he is a peasant proprietor, as is sometimes supposed, but because he is not; because he pays a high rent under a short lease for poor land which requires a great outlay of the produce to make it bear produce at all; and because he marries earlier and has more children than the peasant proprietor in countries where peasant properties prevail. His spade has thus become a gold-mine for his landlord, not for himself.

It is not then the soil or climate of Great Britain or of Ireland that prevents the success of five-acre farms, for which both islands have much greater advantages of nature than Flanders. 'I have seen,' says Dr. Mackenzie, 'three acres of land which I maintain to be quite inferior in many respects to much of our abused Highland soil, and cultivated far below what it might be, produce in the year 1842:—

		£	s.	d.
80 bushels potatoes, sold at 1s.	. . .	4	0	0
21½ „ wheat „ 7s.	. . .	7	10	6
44 „ oats „ 3s.	. . .	6	12	0
2 calves	. . .	5	10	0
423½ lbs. butter, at 10d. .	. . .	17	12	11
		£41	5	5

besides several pigs and poultry fattened by the buttermilk, and skimmed milk sufficient of itself for a large family. And I assert that no average family can cultivate properly by the spade more than five acres of arable land, and attend to the stock and manure upon it, without hiring extraneous labour.'* The figures of produce in this passage were recently shown by the writer of these pages to several agricultural experts, English, Irish, and Scotch (one of particular eminence), all of whom admitted their probability, all of whom too added the remark that, as prices now are much higher, the value of the produce of the three acres would be proportionately greater. The writer next inquired where the three acres were situated; and found to his surprise that they are on the estate of a friend of his own, a lady who has many similar acres under *la petite culture* in the south of England, succeeding as well now as did the three acres in 1842; as the reader may judge from what is stated below,†

* Letter to Lord John Russell, 1851.

† In reply to inquiry on the part of the writer, the lady referred to states: 'The little farm whose produce you mention was let to a man named Dumbril, and is still occupied by his son, who is doing well, in spite of the disadvantage of the situation, which is on the side of the chalk down and excessively steep. —— —— let several of these small farms: most of them have become absorbed in the large ones, but some are doing well. I spoke yesterday to our bailiff; and he says that if a man is industrious and can work a few acres with his own family, he is sure to make it pay, but not if he is obliged to hire labour or keep a horse. —— —— began the system of allotments here, and it succeeds admirably, and is a great boon to poor people. They are worked by labourers and small tradespeople, and give very good produce. To secure the rent, it is paid in advance most willingly. We have allotment gardens also at —— and at ——; and they *always* pay well and are greatly sought after; but the small farms are more doubtful, and success seems to depend in some measure on the situation, but especially on the industry and good management of the tenant.'—The date of this letter is December 19, 1866.

in addition to the fact that their rent varies from 5*l.* 10*s.* to 30*s.* per acre. Dr. Mackenzie answers a question put by myself as to the possibility of an Irish peasant living by his spade on a few acres as follows :—
'I know as surely as I write, that spade husbandry *must* succeed in Ireland and everywhere if properly pursued, and that land will *never* under horse labour give anything like the return it will give under spade and crofter cultivation. Who denies this?' To the same question a gentleman in the south of Ireland gives a different answer, but also a pertinent one :—
'The very small high-farming peasantry do not exist here, because the house-feeding and keeping, which is the soul and body of this system, is unknown to our peasantry. Not having ever housed themselves, they have no notion of housing a beast in comfort and cleanliness.' The remark is just, but Spenser, in the sixteenth century, went still deeper into the matter, when he showed why the Irish peasant has never housed himself, and why he had therefore no notion of housing a beast in comfort and cleanliness : *—' All which he hath forborne, and spared so much expense,

---

* That from never seeing a decent cottage on a five-acre farm the Irish peasant should have no notion of such a thing is not surprising, when, owing to the same circumstance, persons who are as much his superiors in knowledge as in wealth and station, have no more notion of such a thing. One of the ablest land-agents in Ireland, managing one of the largest and best English estates, commenting on the Bill introduced by the late Government in a letter to the writer, remarked : ' The Bill specifies no improvements, and simply refers to the improvements recited in a late Act, where they are called " suitable." Now what is a *suitable* house for a five-acre farm ? Mud, clearly. Is the landlord to pay for mud?' The Flemish five-acre farmer, nevertheless, and even the Flemish labourer with a much smaller plot, has a neat well-furnished cottage with three or four rooms.

for that he hath no firm estate in his tenement, but was only a tenant at will or little more, and so at will may leave it.'

From the foregoing evidence (and abundance of similar evidence is obtainable by any one who makes proper inquiry) it cannot be disputed that the landlords of Ireland might introduce the art of spade husbandry into the island with triumphant success, and make five-acre holdings more productive in many parts of it, even the barrenest, than large farms. It has actually been done in the highlands of Scotland, among a less sharp-witted peasantry than the Irish, but of the same race. 'I am factor on estates,' says Dr. Mackenzie,* 'where there are many crofters, who execute great improvements yearly without any aid from me beyond a fourteen years' lease; and next May, on one estate, I shall be renewing fourteen years' leases to some thirty such crofters, who cheerfully agree to pay about 1l. an acre for all they have added (by their own elbows) to their crofts of new land, worth nothing fourteen years ago. And all these are good regular rent-paying tenants, from 20l. down to 2l. crofts. I could get very few large farms let on these terms, so I value the crofters much as steady improvers of rental without any outlay on the part of the landlord; and really without outlay on *their* part beyond spare hours, *their* capital in bank. I could name many who use their crofters for thus improving their waste lands, and then turn out crowds of them, and throw their land

---

* In a letter to myself, December 19, 1866.

into large farms, on the plea of danger from increase in the poor-rates. Our towns and villages are packed with these poor ill-used people.'

Irish farms may be classified roughly as follows: first, those under fifteen acres, upon which no horse is kept; secondly, those from fifteen to thirty acres, upon which one horse is kept, but no hired labourer is regularly employed; thirdly, those from thirty to fifty acres, on which two horses are generally kept, and some labour is usually hired; lastly, large farms which require a considerable capital. To all the smallest of these classes of holdings, direct legislation cannot give stability. The only mode of subsisting upon a few acres by which the tenant's very existence is not precarious, is by the Flemish system of spade husbandry,—elaborate, minute, and scientific. But that is in Ireland a new and difficult art, irksome to learn, and not to be learned without supervision and instruction by peasants to whose customs, traditions, and habits of life it is foreign. A peasantry is proverbially sceptical of new systems; and so new is this system that the witnesses on behalf of tenants' compensation before Mr. Maguire's Committee never thought of it, giving it as their opinion that a tenant cannot live on a farm of less than from fifteen to twenty acres of good land. But in some parts of Ireland the land now occupied by the smallest holders is naturally too bad for the success of the Flemish system without great previous outlay of capital or labour; in others, from ill-cultivation, it is so exhausted that it would take years to restore it to fit condition. Time, therefore, is needed, and time would not be given by a Parliamentary lease; the tenant sometimes would fail in his rent, and be ejected for nonpayment. Even on the best soils Flemish husbandry would in Ireland be much stiffer work than it is in Flanders (because the soil is much stiffer), and therefore harder to learn; though it would also be more productive in the end, because the soil is naturally better. Practical obstacles of this kind are indeed effects, and not causes of the present and past state of Ireland; but they are effects not to be removed in a moment at the fiat of a law. It must necessarily be that the very causes which have thrown the bulk of the population of Ireland upon agriculture for support have thrust into the very smallest farms some who are naturally ill-adapted for such a business, though perhaps well-adapted for some other. In Ulster, for example, some were weavers by nature rather than farmers; the handloom has failed, or is failing them, and the power-loom draws them to towns. If legislation could keep such men in their holdings, it would only keep them in privation, and keep men who might succeed out of them.

The difficulty which surrounds legislation for small holdings, and the danger of its defeating its own aim, is exemplified by this fact, that the larger farmers with capital in Scotland are opposed to the landlords' right to distrain because it favours small farmers without it.*

---

* See the Evidence taken before the late Commission on the Law of Hypothec (analogous to the English and Irish law of distress) in Scotland. Dr. Mackenzie answers a question from myself on the subject as follows: ' Were the law of hypothec abolished, I could not give one hour's delay in payment of rent, and multitudes would thus be ruined

Indirectly however, legislation may assist *la petite culture*, if directly it cannot. It may abolish entails and sell incumbered estates, thereby introducing wealthier and more business-like landlords. It may teach the rudiments of agriculture in every national school, and have a model farm around each, which the boys might be encouraged to cultivate; and thus even their parents would learn that a constant succession of oats and potatoes must be a ruinous method of farming. The Anglo-Saxon Dialogues of the tenth century, called Alfric's Colloquy, are a model to this day of the sort of industrial instruction which may be easily given in schools even by book. Unfortunately the Government of Ireland has gone backwards of late years as regards agricultural instruction; not its only retrograde step respecting education.

The best service perhaps which legislation can render to the smallest holdings is to give legal security to the tenants of larger ones; thereby removing the present temptation to landlords to get rid of the former, to escape a number of future claims for compensation.

yearly. Now, every year I give delay to this or that tenant, who has had a squeeze and is not ready; always with gain to the landlord and the greatest relief to the tenant.' To myself the right of distress appears a clumsy and anomalous expedient. Nevertheless a speedy, cheap, and effectual remedy for the recovery of rent is undoubtedly beneficial to small holdings and poor farmers. So it is with other claims. One of the causes of the extortionate rate of interest often paid by the Irish tenant to the Gombeen man or local usurer, is that the Assistant Barrister's Court is a Court of Equity for defendants, but not for plaintiffs; and the money-lender charges in proportion to the difficulty of recovering his loan. The landlord's right to distrain is no doubt a cause of risk to the money-lender; but without it landlords would not let small holdings at all, or would require payment in advance, which would not improve the poor man's position.

The system of farming at present pursued on the larger farms, though defective as regards manuring, rotation of crops, draining, and buildings, is so chiefly for want of security, and needs only to be improved, not to be superseded by a new system of cultivation, like that of Flemish spade husbandry. Farms of fifteen and twenty acres may seem ridiculously small to the eye of an English or Scotch farmer, but they prosper in many parts of Ireland, and even in some backward counties are now prospering under present prices for butter and stock as they seldom prospered before, although their husbandry is imperfect and their dwellings are sordid. For at present it may be downright imprudence on the part of the farmer to farm well, or to have a comfortable house; a rotation of crops implies a certain duration of tenure, draining a longer one, and building one longer again. But a tenant may be turned out for voting as he thinks right, or because a new landlord comes in by succession or purchase, or because the present landlord desires to try a new system of farming, or to anticipate a long promised Act in favour of tenants. The very fact of an improvement may endanger a tenant, since this present outlay may make it harder to meet two or three bad seasons and to pay his rent to the day. Those who deny the right of the law to interfere in any case between landlord and tenant, forget that the history of the law of tenure is the history of successive interpositions to give security to the tenant, who originally was treated as the servant or serf of the lord of the soil, and whose work and improvements were then consistently viewed as done for his lord. The principle of proper legal security to secure proper cultivation is one which the law of emblements and of implied tenancy from year to year recognised and established before the necessity of a rotation of crops and of durable improvements in husbandry was known.* The doctrine of non-interference applies only to the production of commodities under free competition. When railway companies were established, they too claimed exemption from State interference as a violation of the principles of political economy and of the law of supply and demand; but the pretension was refuted by statesmen,† and set aside by the legislature. Not only is the supply of land strictly limited by nature, but the number of proprietors is limited by the law both directly and indirectly; its few proprietors moreover are given by the law a distinct motive for refusing to their tenants proper security, in order to control their political action. For these reasons the principle of the Bill of the late Government giving tenants a claim for compensation within a specified limit per acre, in the absence of a lease for thirty-one years, was clearly a sound one.‡ But to fix a uniform limit to compensation (or to the alternative lease) for

---

* For this remark I am indebted to Dr. Hancock, whose 'Impediments to the Prosperity of Ireland' and other writings are the real source of almost all the improvements in the law relating to landed property in Ireland in the last twenty years.

† See in particular Mr. Cardwell's speech, Hansard's Debates, Railway Bill, July 8, 1844.

‡ The Bill made, however, no provision for the registration of improvements after completion. Some such provision seems only just to landlords, and desirable to prevent disputes and litigation. The attorney is not the proper party to be benefited.

holdings of all sizes alike appears to me inexpedient, as tending to the artificial consolidation of the holdings of from fifteen to thirty acres, so numerous and important in Ireland. At least, for the farmers of more than fifty acres, a larger margin for improvement, or a longer lease, appears to be required. These latter may justly aim at a higher class of house and a higher scale of permanent improvement than smaller farmers would attempt or desire ; and to put all classes of holdings of fifteen acres and upwards upon the same footing would tend to the extinction of the smaller class. For if twenty holders of fifteen acres apiece might each demand the same compensation for his house as a single farmer of three hundred acres, it would be the interest of landlords to seize every opportunity to crush the small holders, and to extinguish small holdings for ever. Thus Ireland would lose in the end all that deserves the name of a rural population.

It is not only to the maintenance of a rural population in Ireland, however, that just measures respecting the ownership and tenure of land would conduce. They would tend likewise to augment the home demand for labour in towns, to find new employments for capital, and to open a new sphere for manufactures and trade. For in the natural progress of industry and opulence, as Adam Smith has clearly explained, towns, manufactures, and a brisk and flourishing home trade are the natural consequences of rural prosperity, because agriculture, after providing for the first wants of existence, creates both a demand for higher things and the materials and subsistence of those who supply it. This is especially true of a country like Ireland, where the bulk of the population is dependent on agriculture, and must furnish the consumption upon which home trade depends. The evidence of the last Committee of the House of Commons on the Tenure and Improvement of land appropriately ends :—

'Do you account for the competition for holdings in Ireland from the fact that there are, as a rule, no other means of livelihood in Ireland for the great mass of the people?—I think their livelihood, generally speaking, must be obtained from agriculture; there is no trade, or anything of that sort.

'And when there is a bad harvest, I suppose they do very little in the shops?—The shops feel it immediately.

'Therefore it is of great importance to render this great branch of industry as prosperous as possible?—Yes, undoubtedly.'

In the north-east of Ireland the country towns are rapidly increasing in population and wealth, because country and town react on each other, and the rural wealth—created by town consumption of food, and town markets for flax—finds its way back to the factory and the shop. In the south and west, on the contrary, the country towns are, in general, decaying, because the rural population is poor and declining, and the peasant must be content with home-made flannel and frieze. It is by no means only by its direct effects upon the agricultural classes, however, that the present land system tells upon trade and manufactures, and deprives the population of Ireland of a demand for their industry at home. 'Would you see what Ireland might have been,' Lord Dufferin urges, 'go to Belfast.' The instance clearly proves, what has escaped the noble writer, that it is not only by direct legislation against its trade and manufactures that England has impeded the prosperity of Ireland, but still more by the introduction of a system of landed property designed to make land an inalienable instrument of political power in a few families, instead of the great instrument of production of a commercial society. Belfast has become what it is by passing from the hands of a prodigal noble. Settlements are intended to prevent prodigals from ruining their estates, but it is by keeping them, not by parting with them, that they really ruin them. There might have been fifty Belfasts instead of one but for settlements and other legal restrictions on the transfer of land.* The first great factory in another flourishing town of Ulster was built on a bankrupt's estate. Recent statutes have attempted, with unintentional sarcasm, to mitigate the evil of feudal restrictions on the transfer of land by giving particular powers to present owners to improve their own land, or to let them to tenants for improvement: but such patchwork reform always defeats itself by creating costly formalities, and other impediments to its own object. No reform will suffice short of one, in the first place, giving ownership to each owner in turn, to deal with his land according to the circum-

---

* A remarkable example of the exclusion of manufacturing enterprise in Ireland by the law of real property is instanced in Dr. Hancock's 'Impediments to the Prosperity of Ireland,' chap. xix.

stances of his own time and case; and, in the second place, freeing landed property from incumbrances by its sale on the death of each owner to the amount of all charges and debts. The industry of towns, even more than that of the country, would be promoted by such legislation. It has been most unjustly alleged that the violence of the working-classes of Ireland has prevented the investment of capital and success of trade and manufactures in Irish towns. Those who desire evidence of what the character of the Irish working-classes really was—even before a Poor-law existed, or emigration had provided an escape from destitution at home—will find it in the Report of Lord Devon's Commission in 1841. In 1865 a Government Report showed that in all Ireland an average of only six persons per annum in the ten years preceding had been even charged with combinations to raise the rate of wages, and of this more than one-half had been acquitted; and, according to the latest information, there was not one person for trial for such an offence in 1863, 1864, or 1865. Every candid inquirer will find history, statistics, and practical experience confirm alike the testimony which Sir John Davis has borne at the beginning of his essay to the character of both the land and its people, 'endued with extraordinary abilities of nature,' and that with which his essay concludes:—' There is no nation under the sun that doth love equal and indifferent justice better than the Irish; or will rest better satisfied with the execution thereof, although it be against themselves; so as they may have the protection and benefit of the law when upon just cause they do desire it.' In the close competition of modern commerce, every country has become more than ever dependent upon its natural advantages, and the two great natural advantages of Ireland are its land and its people. It remains for legislation to remove obstacles to their combination created by the law, and to enable the people of Ireland to cultivate and improve the resources of the land of their birth instead of those of lands of their exile.

IRELAND IN 1868.*

Two economic currents are flowing in Ireland—a current of progress and a current of retrogression—of the character of each of which this article aims at furnishing some indication and some suggestions for promoting the former and arresting the latter. For both purposes something must be said of the only strong political current visible in the island at present, one rushing back to the dismemberment of the kingdom, civil war, and the dissolution of civil society. I speak here of Fenianism, not so much in its organised and criminal form, as in that morally blameless form, so far as many of its adherents are concerned, which it takes without any definite organisation, and spreading, as it were, in the air. Organised and criminal Fenianism, though it numbers more sworn members than seems commonly supposed, is by itself, or without aid from America, a destructive, but not a formidable power. The annual chapter of accidents includes in its catalogue a thousand times more suffering and disaster, yet does nothing to shake the foundations of the State, or to endanger the safety of the nation as a nation. But another kind of Fenianism is developing itself, under no specific name

* Reprinted from the 'Fortnightly Review,' of February 1868.

as yet, in declared antagonism to the integrity of the State; which would shortly leave, if it gained its point, but one of the two economic currents before spoken of flowing in Ireland, that of backwardness and ruin. Various motives and feelings are converging to form a combination of a great part of the people of Ireland to demand separation from England. Romantic and generous hopes of a great independent Ireland, old legendary Ireland resurgent in glory, derived partly from ancient tradition, and partly from the nationality movement on the Continent, blend with well-grounded discontent at the system of tenure and the consequent emigration, and with it must be added the selfish desires of some individuals or parties; but the chief source of this gathering movement is an idea that England is falling (an idea which mistakes the weakness of a Government for the weakness of a nation), coupled with a persuasion that an English Parliament will concede anything to force or fright, nothing to justice and policy, and that even separation may be extorted by demanding it loudly in menacing numbers. What sort of legislation would follow the establishment of a separate Irish Parliament, if any legislation at all, might easily be anticipated, had it not been distinctly foreshadowed in a tentative declaration of some Catholic clergymen, drawn with great ability for its purpose, and assuredly not put forward without the private sanction of higher authority than it claims. It is enough to say it is declared that political economy will not do for Ireland, that the Irish manufacturer cannot compete with the English, and that the natural energies of the Irish people must be developed, that is to say, properly speaking, repressed by protection and prohibition. But there would, in reality, be small time or heed for legislation. The inevitable, immediate result of separation would be a furious war of religions and races, in which the upper and middle class of Catholics would be placed in a position of cruel embarrassment and danger from both sides; both sides, moreover, would invoke foreign assistance, and to exclude any other occupation England would be driven to resume her former position by main force, after the island had become from one end to the other a compound of Mexico and the Campagna, with the anarchy of one and the desolation of the other.

There is indeed a sense to be hereafter referred to, in which (paraphrasing a foreign writer's remark) it were well that Ireland should be de-anglicised;* but in all other respects, what is especially desirable for the island, instead of separation, is a closer union with England. The greatest of all the calamities from which the Irish people suffered for centuries was not connection with England, but compulsory isolation, politically, socially, and commercially. For six centuries they were kept forcibly aloof from the nearest border

---

* Speaking of the lingering effects of Spanish law and misgovernment in Lombardy, M. Émile de Laveleye has observed:—'Le sort de la Lombardie fut semblable à celui des provinces flamandes: le joug de l'Espagne y arrêta toute activité commerciale et industrielle. Les fidéicommis et la main-morte s'étendirent rapidement. Les suites funestes se font encore sentir aujourd'hui. Ainsi que le remarque un économiste qui connaît parfaitement son pays, la Lombardie n'est pas tout-à-fait *désespagnolisée* (dispagnolizzata).'—*Les Forces productives de la Lombardie.*

of European civilisation and wealth ; down to the time of many living men, they were denied both equal political rights and social intercourse with the English and Scotch, and their descendants in Ireland itself; and placed by nature in the remotest part of Western Europe, they have only in the present generation begun to derive from the English invention of steam locomotion something like a commercial equality for half of the island with the rest of the British nation. In every country in the world, however advanced, England itself not excepted, there are localities which remoteness has kept to this day in arrear of general progress ; into which improvements common elsewhere have not found their way ; and where the inhabitants appear almost barbarous in their ways to people whose father's ways were precisely the same. Had England been a solitary isle in an untraversed ocean, could its inhabitants be much better than savages now? Deduct from English wealth and civilisation all that is derived from the little country of Flanders alone, and how small would the residue be! He must be a barbarian who does not feel that the glory of England is a glory to the whole human race ; but he must be a fool who does not see that it also belongs to the whole human race, and has come from every part of the world. Throughout its history the movement of both intellectual light and material progress has been one of diffusion, reaching the less accessible places last, and obstructed not only by distance, but by every moral barrier between country and country. England was by position an early receptacle of the movement in modern

Europe, and it would have passed rapidly over to Ireland, but for a cruel succession of accidents and crimes which kept two races apart, in the words of a great English philosopher, 'the most fitted of any two in the world to be the counterpart of one another,' * and two islands apart adapted by nature for the closest commercial connection. No stronger evidence of the truth of these propositions is needed than the fact that in spite of Ireland's calamitous history, in spite of a system of law most obstructive to the development of natural resources—a system not really English in origin, but imposed upon England also by conquest—in spite of political conspiracy and insecurity, a current of progress is nevertheless running in various parts of the island, distinctly traceable to a closer connection with England. Draw a line between east and west from Londonderry to Cork, and on the eastern side, the one nearest to English markets, English influence, and English example, it will be found that the main current is one of progress, though not without an opposite stream; while on the western side, though the main current is one which carries desolation along with it, there are yet scattered indications of improvement, come from an English source and wearing an English form.†

No one who has known the eastern half of the island for more than twenty years can have failed to perceive that a striking change has taken place in the life and

---

* 'Representative Government,' by J. S. Mill.

† In this description it is not thought necessary to take account of a temporary stagnation of the linen trade of Ulster, nor of a partial failure of crops last year in particular counties, balanced by good crops in others.

manners of the gentry, and that where the landlords are resident, prudent, improving, and trusted, the tenants are in many cases following the example of prudence and improvement. In a southern county on this side, not many years ago a backward one from its isolation, there is a locality comprising several large estates well known to the writer, which, within his remembrance, and chiefly within very recent years, has undergone a complete transformation. It was farmed, as most other parts of Ireland were farmed in his childhood; it is now farmed as well as any part of England, and a single dealer in a small town within it sells artificial manure to the value of 25,000*l.* a-year, who could probably not have sold a pound's worth to a former generation. From this locality a large proprietor, of English descent, himself the cause of much of the improvement he describes, and who used to define the Irish tenant as a creature to whom multiplication and subdivision come by nature, but to whom the art of man cannot communicate an idea of farming or forbearance from marriage, now reports :—' The twenty-acre men are holding on well, farming far better than formerly, and not involving themselves as formerly with wives and families as a matter of course. The farming of this class, Roman Catholics and indigenous Irish, is exceedingly improved ; their prudence in the matter of marriage still more remarkable ; their sisters and younger brothers, too, remaining frequently unmarried, as they will not marry out of their class, unless to better themselves. The condition of the country here shows rapid amelioration.'

Other instances of a landlord's good example being followed by his tenants, where English markets have come within reach, and English improvements in farming have become known, fell under the writer's observation in a recent visit to other eastern counties; and from one that was not visited a farmer, loud for tenant-right, writes:—'Farming in general is greatly improving in this district and the neighbouring ones. Here farmers are to some extent able to compete with the landed proprietors at agricultural shows and the like.' To compete with the landed proprietors at agricultural shows and the like! From what quarter has this competition come if not from England, and what sort of competition has it superseded in Ireland? With their fathers would it not probably have been a competition in the dissipation of their fortunes? In other counties, such as Cavan, and even Roscommon, new crops—flax, artificial grasses, and rape—are appearing, and land may be seen turned up by spade or plough in December, which not long ago would have been left untouched until the end of January. It is, again, English markets, English manufacturing towns, and English wealth that enable the Irish farmer to eke out in any way the scale of wages on the eastern side. No fallacy has more tended to hide the real condition of Ireland and the remedies it requires, than one into which writers of authority have fallen, that emigration must steadily raise wages in Ireland in proportion as it diminishes the number of labourers. The base of the fallacy is an imaginary 'aggregate wages-fund,' the share of each labourer in which is supposed to become greater as the number sharing becomes smaller.* But the bargain of wages is a transaction between the individual employer and his men; what that employer can give depends on his own means or profits, and not on the sum of the funds in his own and other people's possession; nor are his means augmented by the scarcity of labour. Were only one labourer left in the country, would he earn as much as all the former labourers put together? Clearly not, unless he did as much work, and worked for all employers at once; for how else could the money be forthcoming to pay him? So far are wages from being equal through Ireland, as the doctrine of an aggregate wages-fund, shared by a smaller number of labourers, implies, that they vary from five shillings a-week to twelve shillings, and are highest where good labourers are most numerous, and on the side nearest England, instead of America. It is the English market for Irish commodities, not the American market for Irish labour, that raises wages in Ireland; to say that it is the latter, is as much as to say that the rich enable the poor to pay high prices for things by paying high prices themselves.

To the funds coming to Irish labourers from an English source must also be added the sums which the number who come over for the harvest bring back for the winter. And, speaking of this, one cannot but

---

* Mr. Mill has employed the phrase 'aggregate wages-fund' merely as a short term to comprise all the funds employed in the payment of labour, whether derived from capital or income. He never meant that the funds in all employers' possession are put together and divided, as gratuities to waiters in a coffee-room are sometimes thrown into a box, and afterwards distributed.

express abhorrence of that spurious patriotism which seeks to avenge the misfortunes of Ireland by the destruction of England. What have English labourers done, whose bread Irish labourers have divided for centuries, and never divided more largely than last year, that Irishmen should seek to ruin the country on which both subsist? What, on the other hand, have the multitude of poor Irish workmen done, who earn their living in England, that they should be marked out as the natural objects of suspicion and hatred, and exposed to violence, expulsion, and destitution? There was never a better year than the one that has just closed for the Irish labourers of the west in England and Scotland, and many who came for the season found it to their advantage to remain. If among these there are any who are parties to the crimes which Fenianism contemplates, they are guilty both of atrocious treachery to the people who have received and supported them, and of a most cruel offence against those of their countrymen who are their fellows in labour, but not their fellows in treason. If there are any among them who brood over the sad history of Ireland, and behold in it the cause of that torpor, too common among its inhabitants, which Bentham has catalogued as the third order of evil following long insecurity and oppression, let them look along the eastern shore of the island, and they will behold how the contact and commerce of England are enabling Irishmen to shake off that torpor of ages. Belfast itself, as a great manufacturing town, is but one generation old; its mechanical powers are of English invention, the advantage of its commercial position consists mainly in vicinity to England, and many inhabitants, of pure Irish as well as English descent, are sharing the fortunes of the town; from which long arms, moreover, are now being stretched in the spirit of English enterprise up and down through the island to explore and develop its resources. Of the success of several of these enterprises it may be too early to speak (Fenianism is one of their chief impediments), but the nascent spirit they show is more important than their results, however successful. It is a spirit which, with tranquillity and wise legislation, would soon stir the western half of the island, over which it is too true that desolation and decline have been more commonly spreading of late years than giving place to advancement; where the one great enterprise carried on upon a great scale is the emigration of the flower of the population from a deteriorating soil; and where cultivation has receded, and a retrogression has taken place from agriculture to the rudest system of pasture. The proverb is far from generally true in Ireland that the benefactor of his country is the man who makes two blades of grass grow where one grew before. And although it may not be denied that many of the former holdings were too small for even secure subsistence, the sweeping conversion of small farmers into labourers is, whether they go or stay, a revolution full of danger to both England and Ireland, as one may see in their darkening looks. M. de Lavergne wrote fifteen years ago: 'Notwithstanding its detestable rural system, Ireland seems to have preserved one excellent feature, namely, the almost entire absence of day labourers properly so called.' It does not possess that feature now. The change has taken place, too, at a peculiarly ill-timed epoch, when increased intelligence, communication with America, and ideas spreading over Europe, tended of necessity to make the Irishman less content than ever to descend to the rank of a servant. Instead of the conservative rural class of small farmers, with a fair security to improve, mixed with small proprietors, improving their own lands (which ought to have been the transformation effected after the famine), the real transformation is that a revolutionary and dangerous class has been established. Fenianism, in its worst form, is the direct result of the suspension of leases, the consolidation of farms, and that emigration to which so many proprietors have looked for the regeneration of Ireland.

The predominance of a current of economic decline, with its political consequences, on the western side of Ireland, will no doubt be ascribed by not a few to an inferior climate and soil, and an inferior and less mingled race. The theory of the faultiness of the Irish soil and climate is a late invention. The invaders held a different notion, and in saying so no impeachment of their descendants' title is intended, for the Milesians themselves had no other original title to their lands; their own legends and traditions tell that they took them by the sword. But of the natural character of those lands —the point here in question—Spenser thus wrote:—
' And sure Ireland is a most sweet and beautiful country as any is under heaven, besides the soil itself most fertile, and fit to yield all kind of fruit that shall be

committed thereunto. Lastly, the heavens most mild and temperate, though somewhat more moist than in the parts towards the east.' Quoting this passage some twenty years ago, an experienced English observer wrote : 'I have been over every part of Great Britain ; I have had occasion to direct my attention to the natural capabilities, to the mode of cultivation, and to the produce of many parts of it : this very year I have traversed the country from the Land's End in Cornwall to John o' Groat's in Caithness ; but in no part of it have I seen the natural capabilities of the soil and climate surpass those of Ireland, and in no part of it have I seen those natural capabilities more neglected, more uncultivated, more wasted than in Ireland.'* The inference Mr. Campbell Foster drew was one not favourable to the industrial powers and virtues of the natives of an island so favoured in its natural gifts ; and there are many to agree with him in Ireland itself as well as out of it. ' Mettez y des Flamands, ils transformeront l'Irlande, je pense,' said a Belgian economist and agriculturist lately to the present writer. But how are we to reconcile with the explanation of an inert race the fact that landlords in Ireland, not being of Irish race, were

* 'Letters on the Condition of Ireland,' by T. Campbell Foster, 1846. The eminent and accurate Professor of Agriculture, Dr. Hodges, at a later period says : 'The productive powers of the soil of this country are most remarkable, and enable it, even with its present imperfect culture, to produce crops which excite the astonishment of the most skilful farmers of England and Scotland. The island also possesses, it its geological structure and genial climate, such advantages as render it equal to any country in the world for the growth of plants and animals. May we not, therefore, conclude that it will yet be made to yield an amount of food far more than sufficient for rewarding the industry of any population it is ever likely to contain ? '—*Lessons in Chemistry in its Application to Agriculture*, 1860.

formerly quite as bad farmers, and otherwise as improvident in their way, all over Ireland, as the pure Irish tenants are still in the west, and are now very often (otherwise at least than in the matter of leases) both good farmers and prudent men? And again, that on the eastern side the Celtic tenant is found in many places now improving in his farming, encouraged by good markets, and instructed by good example? We may ask, too, what was the condition of farming generally over the most advanced parts of Europe fifty years ago,—Prussia, and the Lowlands of Scotland, for example? The race has not changed; what then has changed the agriculture? Is the race a different one, in each locality of England where you find the farming good, from that in the localities where you find it bad?

The true causes, in addition to the state of the law, of the stagnation, and even decline, of many parts of western Ireland are various, but among them one is chief; that there are the people who have suffered the most through history, who were thrust farthest from civilisation and commerce, who are still farthest from England and its markets, and whose chief landlords are far more commonly than in the east of the island absentees. One fact mentioned in the 'Evidence relating to Railways in Ireland, 1865,' illustrates sufficiently the nature of some of the disadvantages which the western farmer suffers from remoteness from England. The county of Donegal is one, generally speaking, of the most backward counties in the island, and in a corner of it one of the witnesses stated that he found fine chickens of good size selling in 1864 at $1\frac{1}{2}d.$ a piece.* It is not money only or profit which is excluded by such disadvantages, but also the ideas, the progress, the spirit, the methods, that are sure to flow in with commercial facilities of ingress. And, in fact, there are some indications of progress even in the west, and wherever they are they wear, as already said, the visible garb of their English origin. There are some English and Scotch settlers whose farming is excelled nowhere in Europe; the chief resident proprietors farm like English ones; and even the smallest holders here and there grow turnips (the crop of all others for Ireland), and begin to see the advantage of winter keep for their cattle, to mow their corn, to discard the old Irish log for the English spade, and to display the intelligence awakened through the national education established by England.

There is no source from which improvement can come to the stagnant and retrogressive quarters of Ireland save from English connexion and English legislation. A great and benevolent statesman is reported indeed to have said that Ireland ought to be governed according to Irish ideas. But what are Irish ideas? Are they the ideas of the Catholic clergy, an eminently virtuous class beyond question, but surely not the one to govern a nation in our time? Are they the ideas of the best educated Catholic laity, a quiet class, who keep their ideas too much to themselves?

* Provisions are now (January 1868) very dear in the county of Donegal, and the labourers and small farmers are suffering greatly in consequence; but this dearness comes of a failure of crops, not of a profitable market.

Are they the ideas of the large Anglo-Scotch and Protestant population of the island, whose ideas are English, with a little provincialism. Or are they ideas which are not Irish in any sense, but the ideas of the Pontiff and Cardinals of Rome? Whenever what are called Irish ideas are closely examined, they will turn out, if Irish at all, to be the ideas not of a nation, but of a class or a section: and Ireland has had only too much of class legislation and sectional government. It is English ideas—the ideas of the nearest part of civilised and progressive Europe—that are wanted for the control and guidance of Ireland; but when I say English ideas, I mean the ideas of the present English nation, not of the Anglo-Norman barons of the feudal age.

What then is the English nation to do for Ireland? No single measure, it may at once be affirmed, will make Ireland generally prosperous or appease the discontent existing among a large portion of its inhabitants. A combination of measures is necessary to arrest the progress of sedition, to encourage improvement in farming, to facilitate the rise of a class of yeoman and peasant proprietors, to remove legal impediments to the development of the natural resources of the island and natural impediments which individuals cannot remove, to make its real condition and resources known in England, to diffuse agricultural skill, to check the enormous evil of absenteeism, and to bring all Ireland closer to England, and to the markets and progress of the European world. In the few pages at the writer's disposal, it is evident that so extensive a programme cannot be discussed in detail, but some remarks are due to the readers who have followed him thus far.

Of Fenianism first : that is to say, Fenianism as an organised conspiracy for the ruin of England ; which ought to be suppressed if it were only in mercy to not a few reluctant accomplices on its roll, for there are always not a few reluctant accomplices of an Irish conspiracy. Fenianism knows too well its own utter imbecility as a belligerent power not to perish of sheer despair but for its hope in America, and the spoil it promises to the mercenary part of its adherents in an American war against England, or at least an American sanction to privateering against English trade. And in American hostility it has too much reason to believe— a hostility very unjust as against the whole English people, and their common country, but not unprovoked by a considerable section of Englishmen, blockade-runners, and newspaper scolds—if one must not add the laches or duplicity of some English officials during the late Civil War. The people of England owe it now to their own safety and strength to make generous compensation for the wrongs and insults of which the latter complain. If it be true, as the writer has some reason to believe, that the concession of British Columbia, really an American colony, would be accepted as a full compensation, that concession might perhaps be made. For while, by making it, England would get rid of a formidable embarrassment and danger, she would leave the resources of great regions to be developed to her own future advantage by the only people in a condition to develop them. America, too, ought to be thankful to be thereby released from the incubus of a claim, the attempt to enforce which, even if successful (a very doubtful matter), would do cruel injury to the very class of Englishmen who, for the sake of American freedom, were unmurmuring sufferers by the war which upheld it. The working-classes must be the chief victims of every war, the wealthier classes enduring, by comparison, no real privation; but a war between America and England, or against the commerce of England, would be one for the starvation of that very magnanimous working-class of Englishmen to whom America owes so much sympathy and admiration—not to say also gratitude, though they really could have added an English war to her late troubles, had they joined their voices to the disgraceful clamour of others for that end.

The next point in importance is the tenure of land, the difficulties of which cannot be surmounted by legislation relating to tenure alone. A parliamentary lease or settlement might necessitate a selection of tenants, which would by no means meet the views of all the present ones. On the other hand, England cannot leave the treatment of tenure to the landlords, who strangely tell us in one breath it is a settled axiom of political economy that a landlord's interest in his own property, just because it is his own, must lead him to improve it, and yet that Irish tenants will not improve if the holdings become their own for a time under a lease—or, in short, that insecurity, not security, is the great incentive to improvement on the part of a tenant. It is added, on the landlord's part, that many tenants do not wish for leases: when this is the case, as it sometimes is, from entire confidence in the landlord, it only shows that there is a supposed security in those cases; but even under excellent and trustworthy landlords, tenants are often shy of asking for a lease when they would be glad of one of sufficient length, were it not for its expense, and the fear at once of its legal technicalities and of offending the landlord by asking to be put out of his power.

The subject of the tenure of land is, in connection with the legal technicalities referred to, bound up with the whole law of real property, and to have a prosperous and contented agricultural population in Ireland there is needed not only a legal right to compensation for tenant's improvements, in the absence of a lease for thirty-one years at least, but also a complete liberation of the transfer of land from legal restrictions and difficulties, so that farmers might buy land as well as hold it securely. For this end primogeniture and entail must cease, and a simple system of the transfer of land by registration must be introduced. It is in this sense only that Ireland, to repeat an expression used before, ought to be de-Anglicised, though in truth the English law of real property is neither English in origin nor approved of by the English people, and contains nothing injurious to Ireland which is not so to England too; and it is only in respect of legal fetters which England ought to strike off from herself that she ought to follow the exhortation of an eminent

Irish lawyer in respect of Ireland, 'Loose her, and let her go.' *

The writer's limit prevents a demonstration here of the invalidity of current arguments against the possibility of yeomen and peasants prospering in either island as proprietors, or even becoming proprietors at all, under even rational land laws; but an illustration must be given of the obstructions which the land laws under which Ireland has been placed have opposed to the enterprise and prosperity of its people in other ways. 'About fifteen years ago,' Dr. Hancock relates, in his treatise on the 'Impediments to the Prosperity of Ireland,' 'an enterprising capitalist was anxious to build a flax-mill in the north of Ireland, as a change had become necessary in the linen trade from hand-spinning to mill-spinning. He selected as the site for his mill a place in a poor but populous district, situated on a navigable river, and in the immediate vicinity of extensive turf bogs. The capitalist applied to the landlord for a lease of fifty acres for a mill site, labourer's village, and his own residence, and of fifty-acres of bog, as it was proposed to use turf as the fuel for the steam-engines of the mill. The landlord was most anxious to encourage an enterprise so well calculated to improve his estate. An agreement was con-

---

* In November, 1852, Mr. Napier introduced a series of measures into the House of Commons for the adjustment of the relations of landlords and tenants in Ireland, saying, at the close of his speech: 'Enough for him, if he had provided a freer career for industry and raised up an obstacle to injustice. The voice of mercy had resuscitated Ireland, the flush and flow of returning life reanimated her frame; but she was still in the grave-clothes in which severe policy and sore affliction had bound her. Loose her, and let her go.'—*Hansard's Parliamentary Debates.*

cluded, but when the flax-spinner consulted his legal adviser, he discovered that the law prevented the landlord from carrying out the very liberal terms he had agreed to. He was bound by settlement to let at the best rent only; the longest lease he could grant was for three lives, or thirty-one years. Such a lease, however, at the full rent of the land, was quite too short a term to secure the flax-spinner in laying out his capital in building; the statute enabling tenants to lease for mill sites only allowing leases of three acres. The mill was not built, and mark the consequence. Some twenty miles from the spot alluded to, the flax-spinner found land in which he could get a perpetual interest; there he laid out his thousands; there he has for the last fifteen years given employment to hundreds of labourers, and has earned money. The poor but populous district continues as populous, but, if anything, poorer than it was. During the past seasons of distress, the people of that district suffered much from want of employment, the landlord's rents were worse paid out of it than from any other part of his estate. Could there be a stronger case to prove how much the present state of Ireland arises from the state of the law?'

The present writer knows of several similar cases; and when Lord Dufferin says of the industrial resources of Ireland, ' A hundred fountains remain to be unsealed,' he might have added that it is the seal of the law which closes them up, and that the law furnishes an answer to Bishop Berkeley's last question in the ' Querist,' a hundred and thirty years ago, 'Whose fault is it if poor Ireland still continues poor?' A part of the impoverishment which Ireland suffers, not only pecuniarily, but socially and morally, from entails, insecure tenures, incumbrances, and other consequences of the present state of the law, is absenteeism ; the evil of which is the one point about which all parties in Ireland are agreed, and in removing which the legislature would be really legislating according to Irish ideas.

The excellent results which in several counties have followed the Government grant for instructors in the best methods of growing and saving flax, exemplify another direction in which the interference of the State is urgently required, namely, for general agricultural instruction throughout Ireland. The suppression of the Chairs of Agriculture in the Queen's Colleges was an act of sheer fatuity, as the suppression of the Professorships of Irish was an act of sheer barbarism on the part of the Treasury. There ought to be a model-farm attached to a national school in every parish, and there is no sort of reason why the Irish peasant should not learn the all-important lesson of a rotation of crops, and of the proper house-feeding of cattle, as well as to read, write, and count. The intervention of the State is also indispensable for the deepening of rivers and providing outfalls for arterial drainage. The state of the Suck, for example, is a scandal to a civilised Government, and an insuperable obstacle to the improvement by private enterprise of a vast district which it floods. Lastly, remains the extension and cheapening of railway communication. The completion of a commercial union between the two islands is almost as vital a point as the maintenance of their political union, and a Government can look to indirect and distant results in promoting it, which are not economically within the contemplation of private enterprise. The English buyer, for example, who pays but a small sum to a company for his fare, may be worth more than a thousand times the amount to the trade of both islands; and a not unimportant economy in the workings of the Irish lines could be effected by a centralisation of management.*

Other things there are, doubtless, which ought to be done for Ireland, and among them are some which Parliament has not at present the requisite information to do; therefore, among the things which ought at once to be done is, to make inquiry into the actual condition and resources of the island, not for the purpose for which such inquiries have too often been made, of postponing legislation, but to prepare for it. But if even the measures sketched out in these pages were carried at once into effect, in the next generation but one economic current of progress

* It is to be feared that the purchase of the Irish railways by the State will meet with great difficulty from the exorbitant demands of Companies; and, perhaps, also from a demand on the part of the Government for a guarantee on the part of Ireland alone against loss, which the shareholders are very ready to offer on behalf of the people of Ireland, but which the latter ought not to be expected to give. A railway which carries the produce of the west of Ireland cheaper to England, benefits producers in the former and consumers in the latter; and why should the consumer in Ireland, who does not benefit as a producer—the fundholder, for example—pay part of the carriage of provisions away from himself? If the cost of carriage were annihilated between the islands, meat and other provisions would become cheaper in London, and dearer in Limerick and Galway. Why should consumers in Limerick and Galway, but not in London, guarantee the State against loss by a measure tending to that result?

would be found flowing through Ireland, and the answer to Bishop Berkeley's question would be that 'poor Ireland' does *not* still continue poor. The ballad might then ask with truth in 1898, the centenary of the last Rebellion,—

> 'Who fears to speak of '98?
> Who blushes at the name?'

THE IRISH LAND QUESTION, 1870.

MANY CAUSES have tended to concentrate almost exclusive attention on that side of the Irish Land System which relates to agricultural tenure. In so far as those causes are historical, they have been to some extent indicated in preceding pages. The exclusion of the Irish from the maritime ports of their own island, the confiscation of their lands, the denial of landed property to Catholics, restrictions on Irish manufactures and trade, have necessarily left their traces in the industrial economy of Ireland at this day. These historical causes, however, being now beyond control, are worth taking into practical account only as disposing of insolent theories of race on the one hand, and adding urgency on the other to the necessity for a thorough reformation of a land system, which, by making agriculture the only employment accessible to a great mass of the people, and tenancy the highest position to which they could aspire in connexion with agriculture, has made agricultural tenure appear almost the only land question. The real problem which the legislature has to solve relates to the Irish Land System as a whole, to the distribution of landed property, and the conditions of ownership as well as to tenure; to commerce, manufactures, and mines as well as to agriculture; to the towns, in short, as well as to the country. The system of agricultural tenure is admitted on all sides to be an intolerable evil, both politically and economically regarded; but it has become so, not through its own inherent impolicy and injustice alone, but by reason also of the entire structure of the land system, which gives the occupation of the tenant-farmer an undue predominance in the economy of the island as in the mind of the public. The position of the tenant-farmer cannot indeed be fully understood without reference to the unhealthy and unnatural economy produced by the land system as a whole.

A complete investigation of the condition of Ireland would show that its prosperity has been cramped in every direction, and with respect to all its resources and natural uses for its inhabitants. It would show that much as its cultivators have suffered from the insecurity of their own position, they have suffered more by its being generally the only career open to them above that of hired labour, by the excessive competition to which they have been exposed in it, and by the loss of the numerous local markets which a community flourishing in all the departments of industry would create. It would show, too, that much as the country has suffered under the present land system, the town—using the term for brevity, to denote non-agricultural employments in general—suffers still more, for it suffers extinction.

No more than an indication can be attempted in these pages of the manner in which both town and country are affected. The interests of both are closely interwoven, and it is a misfortune in this as in many other cases that a description in words cannot place things in their true relative position at once under the eye. As they can be presented only in succession, it is natural to glance first at the state of the country, which comes first in the natural order of development, and goes far to determine the state of the town; although it must be subsequently shown that it is by no means only by its effects on the rural population and on agriculture that the land system militates against the prosperity of other employments and classes. Not only is the town dependent on its rural neighbourhood for a local market, and for cheap supplies of materials and food, and is straitened accordingly if the population and cultivation around it decline, but security and freedom of action are even more necessary to its prosperity and its very existence. Town industry is a more delicate plant and of slower growth than the industry of the country. It is the creation of man—nature does nothing for it directly. The country cannot disappear under any land system, and will produce something, at least in these islands under any. Crops will rise and ripen even under a notice to quit; grass will grow over a soil so fertile as Ireland's without even an effort on the part of the husbandman. But the town draws no nutriment from the ground on which it stands, nor from the air around; rains do not refresh it, suns do not bring it to maturity, its harvests need much costlier sowing and labour, and much longer abstinence. Whatever evils then follow in the case of the country from insecurity and restraints on industrial energy must be tenfold greater in the case of the town. The effects of the Irish Land System on agriculture deserve attention accordingly, not only for their own sake, or for their immediate bearing on other industries, but also as examples of influences operating with far greater force on the latter; although for that very reason their effects may be to a great extent indiscernible. Towns and villages that are falling to decay may be seen, those which have altogether disappeared, and those which have been prevented from coming into existence, are invisible.

And looking even at the agricultural side of the island, one may see such evidence of the effects of a land system essentially anti-industrial (if the expression may be allowed) in its structure and principles, because essentially feudal, that the chief mark of its influence on the life and business of towns might almost be expected to be an entire absence of towns. It is not indeed a feudal land system in the sense of securing the defence of the State; but it is so in aiming at the concentration of territory and power in a few families and in the feudal line, by regulations and restrictions absolutely hostile to all commercial policy and industrial progress.

One observation relating to both country and town should be borne in mind throughout; namely, that there ought to have been in the case of both continuous and rapid improvement in the last twenty years; the period selected on all sides as a test of the working of the system under which the island is placed. That period includes the sudden removal of an enormous mass of pauperism; the effects of national education; an extensive system of drainage effected by public works and loans; a general advance throughout the world in the industrial arts; and an immense improvement in the commercial position of the island by means of roads, railways, and steam navigation, with a consequent augmentation of the value of Irish commodities which official statistics by no means sufficiently indicate. An illustration of the impetus which the combination of new methods of locomotion ought naturally to have given to agriculture is afforded in the instance of roads alone; with an excellent system of which the undervalued public works, executed during the famine, furnished the island. Describing in 1845 the importance of means of internal transportation for the development of the industrial resources of Ireland, Sir Robert Kane observed:—'The consequence of not having roads is illustrated by the evidence of Mr. Fetherstone, who, describing some of his important improvements to a Committee of the House of Commons, says, "The oats these lands grow is so very fine, and of such a rich gold colour, that if we can possibly get it down to the lowlands, we sell it for seed oats; but the roads being so bad, we put it to the purpose of illicit distillation. It is a great deal cheaper to distil it than bring it to market, for we could only bring a sack at a time. . . . There are no roads. The oats are beautiful, and an enormous crop; *but what is the good of it? you cannot send it to market."*' Add to roads railways, such as they ought to be, or even such as they are; to both add rapid conveyance to the chief English ports, and the consequent leap in the prices of Irish produce, and what ought not to have been the gains of Irish producers and the improvement in the methods of production? The following table of comparative prices was given in evidence before a Committee of the House of Lords in 1867:

	Butter per cwt.		Beef per cwt.		Mutton per cwt.		Pork per cwt.	
	s.	d.	s.	d.	s.	d.	s.	d.
1826	69	0	33	0	34	0	25	5
1866	109	3	59	1	66	6	51	10

Even this comparison (probably furnished from some principal town on the eastern coast) falls considerably short of showing the real rise in the prices of many Irish commodities throughout the greater part of the island in the last twenty years; for in numerous inland and western localities the prices of meat and butter were doubled—those of poultry much more than doubled—immediately by railways.* 'Markets,' says M. de Lavergne, in his work on the Rural Economy of England and Ireland, referring, it is well to observe, to the aptitude of some countries for small farms, 'this is the greatest and most pressing requirement of agriculture. There is only one law which admits of no exception, and which everywhere produces the same results—*the law of markets.*' But

* The following prices are given in 'Reports from Poor-Law Inspectors on Wages of Agricultural Labourers in Ireland, 1870,' p. 26:

	1849	1869
	s. d.	s. d.
Meat	0 2	0 5
Milk	0 5	0 8
Oatmeal, per cwt.	9 6	15 0

M. de Lavergne had first laid it down that the natural consequences of markets is the introduction of leases; just as Adam Smith traces the origin of long leases on the decline of feudalism to the new markets opened by commerce for the produce of agriculture and the necessity of increased security for its improvement. Rising prices in themselves and unaccompanied by security, only imperil the position of the tenant-farmer, by tempting the proprietor to sudden changes in the terms of the tenure, or in the tenancy itself. And in Ireland the actual accompaniment of markets was additional insecurity. Mere tenure-at-will became commoner than before the Devon Commission condemned it as 'a pressing grievance to all classes of tenants, paralysing all exertions, and placing a fatal impediment in the way of improvement.' The natural consequence has been that system of husbandry which so experienced a judge as Mr. Caird lately described as everywhere meeting his eye, save in Ulster and the eastern seaboard of the country : ' What the ground will yield from year to year at the least cost of time, labour, and money is taken from it.' The description might stand for an economic definition of tenure from year to year. On the very border of commerce with England, under better conditions of tenure than elsewhere prevalent, and under landowners more generally resident, a considerable change for the better in Irish husbandry has taken place on the whole; although there are indications that the progress even of that favoured side of the island has come to a stand-still, and that the Ulster farmer has been made to feel that, without legal security, improvement is dangerous. But taking Ireland as a whole, a glance at official statistics shows the general direction in which agriculture has been moving. One-half of the island in what is called grass or pasture, nearly one-fourth bog or waste, little more than one-fourth in cultivation, and but one and a-half per cent of the whole area wood or plantation, is the picture agricultural statistics present. But for the absence of wood, of which an explanation will be found in a subsequent page of this volume, one might suppose oneself looking at the statistics of a new country just occupied by a colony, in place of an old country which the inhabitants have been deserting in millions to seek subsistence elsewhere. Cultivation moreover has been receding much faster than statistics show at first sight. The entire area under crops was 5,970,139 acres in 1861, and but 5,575,843 in 1869; but these general figures are far from exhibiting the real retrogression, because the increase of cultivation which commenced after 1847 reached its maximum in different years in different counties, and then steadily declined in each. Comparing the entire number of acres under crops in 1869 with the number attained in all the counties together at their maximum of cultivation, it would be found that 1,398,881 acres in place of only 394,296 have gone out of cultivation.

It is not meant that in every case the substitution of pasture for tillage is a change for the worse, for a good tillage farm should have a portion, if possible, in permanent grass properly supplied with manure; but that the total extent of cultivation, in place of decreasing ought to have largely increased, is not only agreed by the highest authorities on agriculture in the island, but shows itself in an actual diminution in cattle as well as of crops, through the want of winter keep, and, what is worse, through a positive deterioration of the depastured soil. The following table, considering the rise in the price of cattle, and the decrease of crops, is startling :—

	Number of Horses	Cattle	Pigs
1859	629,075	3,815,598	1,265,751
1869	527,248	3,727,079	1,079,793

There has been, it is true, between 1859 and 1870 a considerable increase of sheep, but of that something hereafter.

Looking first at the effect of the grazing system on the number of cattle, it may be observed that a Scotch Member of Parliament, versed in the agriculture of his own country, yet apparently not opposed to a very different method of cattle-feeding in Ireland, himself states that on estates in the county of Mayo which he lately visited, where Italian ray grass for stall-feeding was substituted for natural pasturage, ' four cows were kept on the same extent of land as was barely sufficient for one cow under the old system.' * To this difference in summer food must be added the loss of winter food by ' the old system.' And to both we should add the loss of human food. 'In eleven years,' says a high scientific authority, 'Ireland has lost the power of feeding more than 1,800,000 of her population, while Scotland has gained the power of feeding about

* 'Land Culture, &c. in Ireland.' By P. Maclagan, M.P., 1869.

300,000 more people.'* Take further the difference of profit to the farmer and wages to the labourer. The lecturer at the Glasnevin Model Farm, who adds to high scientific attainments practical experience in agriculture in every province, has lately shown that on ordinary Irish soil, clay loam on a limestone formation, tillage properly conducted, gives an excess over pasture of 260l. in profit, though at lower than current prices of corn, and with an outlay in wages of 194l. instead of but 30l. to a single herd. This calculation, however, assumes a five-course rotation—an assumption involving a tenure sufficient not only for five years of cropping, but also for subsoiling, draining, and building, which in Ireland must be done by the tenant, if done at all.

For the effects of the Irish system of pasture on the soil, we may refer to the evidence of 'an Ulster landlord and tenant,' who, while writing energetically on the side of the landlords, incidentally states with respect to some land of his own, that 'used for several years as a grazing farm, and paying a good return, at length a portion showed symptoms of returning to coarse grass and heather, and twenty acres were broken up, limed, and cropped with oats.'†

Mr. Longfield draws a distinction between two kinds of Irish soil, one being rich stiff clay, and improving every year under pasture, another and lighter soil, on the contrary, if kept in pasture, having a tendency to run into unprofitable moss.‡ Without questioning this

* 'Of the Declining Production of Food in Ireland.' By Dr. Lyon Playfair, C.B., M.P. 'Recess Studies,' p. 249.
† Letters to the 'Standard,' January, 1870.
‡ Cobden Club Volume, p. 35.

distinction, it may be confidently maintained that a great part of the land actually in pasture in Ireland has tendencies of the latter character ; that the soils are few and rare in the island which, even if well adapted for pasture, could not yield at once more profit to the farmer, more wages to the labourer, and more food to both man and beast under a good system of tillage ; and that in the end the soils best adapted for grazing must be exhausted by the exportation of cattle without the restoration of the element of fertility withdrawn. It does not rain bones and flesh even in Ireland.

Mr. Brodrick, in one of the essays which the Irish land question has elicited from distinguished Englishmen, mentions with something of surprise, as a fact of which his inquiries in the island have convinced him, that fifteen and ten acre farmers in Ireland pay a higher rent than larger farmers, with at least equal punctuality.* The truth is that they generally produce more ; and that the consolidation of farms means the diminution of crops, the extension of grazing, and sooner or later, the exhaustion of the soil. The table in the note, taken from the last volume of Irish agricultural statistics, affords conclusive evidence that cultivation decreases, and 'grass, bog, and waste' increase in exact proportion to the size of farms.† It may be true that not a few of the small holdings which have disappeared in recent years were, soil and situation considered, too diminutive ; but they

---

* 'Irish Land Question.' By the Honourable George Charles Brodrick. 'Recess Studies.'

† 'The number of holdings; the quantity of land held by each class of landholders ; the area and proportion under crops, grass, fallow, woods

were so because the best land has been generally given to large grazing farms; and because the same error which has made landowners look with disfavour on small farms, has led them to drive them to the worst ground and the worst situations, and to limit unduly both the duration of their tenure and the amount of land left to them.*

and plantations, and bog and waste, and also the average extent of the holdings, are given in the following tables:

'*The Number of Holdings by Classes in* 1868; *the entire extent of Land under each Class; also the Area under Crops, Grass, Fallow, Plantations, and Bog and Waste, unoccupied, in the several Classes.*

Classification of Holdings	No. of Holdings in each class	Extent of Land held by each class of Landholders	Division of Land			
			Under Crops	Grazing Land	Fallow	Woods and Plantations	Bog and Waste
		Acres	Acres	Acres	Acres	Acres	Acres
Holdings not exceeding 1 Acre	49,709	25,014	21,062	1,489	38	235	2,190
do. above 1 5 Acres	77,108	273,930	171,438	77,056	323	2,785	22,328
do. above 5 15 ,,	172,040	1,799,683	841,224	782,442	1,590	10,303	164,124
do. above 15 30 ,,	136,580	3,050,954	2,216,862	1,473,431	3,179	16,472	341,010
do. above 30 50 ,,	72,205	2,913,712	1,019,919	1,483,887	3,849	20,875	385,182
do. above 50 100 ,,	54,840	4,028,455	1,156,204	2,182,055	6,002	44,470	639,724
do. above 100 200 ,,	22,106	3,321,675	697,698	1,865,315	4,205	68,639	685,818
do. above 200 500 ,,	8,181	2,807,038	352,548	1,465,000	2,647	90,672	897,171
do. above 500 Acres	1,572	2,099,463	71,016	668,718	277	67,807	1,291,645
Total	594,341	20,319,924	5,547,971	9,999,393	22,110	322,258	4,428,192

The foregoing Table reduced to Proportions per Cent.

Classification of Holdings	Proportion per cent. of Holdings in each Class	Under Crops	Grass	Fallow	Woods and Plantations	Bog and Waste	Total	Average Extent of the Holdings in each Class
								A. R. P.
Holdings not exceeding 1 Acre	8.4	84.2	6.0	0.2	0.9	8.7	100	0 2 1
do. above 1 5 ,,	13.0	62.6	28.1	0.1	1.0	8.2	100	3 2 13
do. above 5 15 ,,	28.9	46.7	43.5	0.1	0.6	9.1	100	10 1 34
do. above 15 30 ,,	23.0	39.9	48.3	0.1	0.5	11.2	100	22 1 14
do. above 30 50 ,,	12.1	35.0	51.0	0.1	0.7	13.2	100	40 1 17
do. above 50 100 ,,	9.2	28.7	54.2	0.1	1.1	15.9	100	73 1 33
do. above 100 200 ,,	3.7	21.0	56.2	0.1	2.1	20.6	100	150 1 2
do. above 200 500 ,,	1.4	12.6	52.2	0.1	3.2	31.9	100	343 0 19
do. above 500 acres	0.3	3.4	31.9	0.0	3.2	61.5	100	1,335 2 6
Total	100.0	27.3	49.2	0.1	1.6	21.8	100	—

* On this subject, as on many others which cannot be discussed with the same advantage in these pages, the reader is referred to the letters of Mr. Morris, Times Commissioner, on the 'Irish Land Question.'

The consolidation of farms, in place of being an advance, has involved a palpable retrogression in Irish husbandry and in its productiveness. But the mischief does not end in the country, it goes on to the town. The disappearance of the agricultural holding has involved the disappearance of the town holding; the decline of agriculture has been followed by the decline of neighbouring trade and manufactures; just as in the sixteenth century, 'the decay of husbandmen' in England was followed by the decay of the country town and the village. It has been stated that against the decrease of both crops and cattle there is to be set a large increase of sheep; and the effect on both town and country is well exemplified by a statement cited, for a different purpose, by Lord Dufferin from the evidence given before the Devon Commission : ' Upon the plains of Roscommon one man has 4,000 sheep and only two herds attending the flock.' * At that time the number of sheep in the county Roscommon was under 100,000; it had increased to 213,134 in 1868; and the following figures sufficiently indicate the differences in respect of both town and country between the counties in which sheep are many and those in which they are few :—

	Number of sheep in 1868		Number of sheep in 1868
Antrim	19,255	Galway	710,279
Armagh	16,500	Mayo	372,231
Down	76,996	Roscommon	213,134

* 'Irish Emigration and Tenure.' By Lord Dufferin, p. 153.

If the picture of a fertile island, half under grass and nearly one-fourth waste, is one of stagnation and desolation, it is nevertheless life and activity compared with the scene which statistics of towns, manufactures, and trade, as complete as those of agriculture, would present. It is no small defect in administrative art that no such statistics are forthcoming. Mr. Thom's 'Almanack' affords on this, as on other subjects, a prodigious amount of information for a private work; but a private work cannot perform the office of a statistical department. Attention has often been drawn of late years to the diminished proportion in Ireland of houses of the lowest class which statistics exhibit; but there are no statistics of the dwellings of all classes which have fallen to ruin in the towns, nor of the multitude of villages whose place knows them no more. Draw a line from Dublin to the nearest point of Lough Swilly in the north, and another to Bantry Bay in the south, and the angle contained by those lines between the capital and the Atlantic—covering about three-fourths of an island which ought to be studded with cities, fine country towns, and smiling villages—does not include one large or flourishing city, and includes hardly a town or village whose trade and population have not decreased in the last twenty years. It includes, indeed, but few which are not in a state of complete decay, in spite of all the auxiliaries to town industry, mechanical, chemical, and intellectual, which those twenty years have created. Referring to the town of Longford in his statistics of boroughs and municipal towns, Mr.

Thom states: 'This place is by far the most thriving and important town between Dublin and Sligo. Population in 1861, 4,872.' Of Sligo itself he states that it is 'the most important seaport on the north-west coast;' and its population was but 13,361 in 1861—having been 14,318 at the previous census. Limerick is the only large town in the angle above described, and Mr. Monsell portrays its condition as follows: 'I have taken some pains to ascertain the condition of the population in the city of Limerick, the centre of a rich grazing district. In the old town the poor live generally in large, decaying houses, a single family rarely occupying more than one room, and sometimes three or four families living together in the same room. There is seldom more than one bed for a family, and this bed consists frequently of straw with an old quilt or blanket, to which are added at night the day garments of the family. The furniture is made up of an iron pot, a few old saucepans, a rickety table, and one or two old chairs—very often there is neither table nor chair. These rooms are exposed day and night to cold wind and rain. It is quite common to meet in these rooms grown persons who are unable to go out for days and weeks on account of want of clothes.'* Mr. Monsell instances Limerick in connection with his statement that 'the most miserable portion of the agricultural population is to be found in the grazing districts.' Adam Smith pointed out that the town follows the country in 'the natural order of

* 'Address to the Statistical Society of Ireland.' By the Right Honourable William Monsell, M.P., 1869.

opulence;' and Limerick shows that the town likewise follows the country in the natural order of indigence. A Scotch member, already cited, says of the towns of Ireland: 'In Cork, Waterford, Belfast, and Derry, we have all the bustle of mercantile and manufacturing towns; in the interior of the country we have neat pretty towns such as Parsonstown; and in the towns situated in an agricultural district we have far more bustle and stir than in similar towns in Scotland, showing a larger population in Ireland and the larger trade done between town and country.' The concluding sentence of this statement illustrates the connection between a large country population and the business and life of towns. But Mr. Maclagan does not specify the 'agricultural districts' to which he refers. The four great 'mercantile and manufacturing towns' are on the eastern side of the island, and outside of the angle described above. Parsonstown is a flourishing country town, which will be referred to again; but how many such towns did Mr. Maclagan see in all the western and midland counties together? He speaks himself of other towns 'which show strong traces of decay;' instancing Galway, where 'tottering walls of uninhabited houses threaten to fall on us; or the frequent gaps in the streets tell us that buildings once stood there which it would not pay to rebuild.'*
Galway may be taken as a type of the town throughout the west of the island; as Trim, again, the capital of the chief grazing county, may be taken as a type of the town in the midland counties. 'Trim,' says

---

* 'Land Culture, &c. in Ireland.' By P. Maclagan, M.P., p. 3.

Mr. Morris, 'is the capital of the county of Meath; but it is little more than a declining village, and it has a dreary and decaying aspect.'* One more example is afforded in the capital town of the county in whose plains we have seen that two herds fill so prominent a position. Mr. Thom's account of its population and wealth is as follows:—'Population in 1861, 2,619; town rates in 1869, 90*l.* 13*s.* 11*d.*; town revenue, 123*l.* 4*s.* 5*d.*'

Mr. Smiles, describing the industrial progress of England, remarks that its early industry was almost exclusively pastoral, its principal staple being wool. He might add that Ireland has in the last twenty years been rapidly returning to that primitive condition of industry.

The losses which both country and towns in Ireland sustain from the absenteeism of great landowners, drawing immense revenues from the island, have been recently described with great force by a very eminent writer. Not only does the peasant lose a large custom close at hand for his poultry, eggs, and butter, but also in the neighbouring village, 'the shops are few and ill supplied; goods are sold at a high price; and yet for want of sufficient custom the profit of the shopkeeper is very small.'† Great, however, as is the loss to a country town, such as Lisburn (to take an actual instance) of remitting from its immediate neighbourhood fifty or sixty thousand a-year to an English Marquis in Paris,

---

* 'The Irish Land Question.' By W. O. Morris, Times Commissioner.
† 'The Tenure of Land in Ireland.' By the Right Honourable M. Longfield, 'Cobden Club Volume,' pp. 10, 11.

it is small compared with the loss sustained by the country towns throughout Ireland from the absence (arising from the same causes which have created great absentees) of a large and prosperous peasantry and yeomanry round them. Travelling among the half-clad peasantry of France, before the Revolution, Arthur Young indignantly denounced the blindness of a Government which could not see how much more important to the trade and manufactures of a kingdom is a prosperous rural population than a wealthy nobility. Divide the lands which yield to a Marquis 60,000*l.* in rent among a thousand peasants, and how much greater and more constant will be their custom with the market-town than it could derive from the expenditure of the Marquis, even if frequently on the spot? 'The peasant proprietor,' as Sismondi said, ' is of all cultivators the one who gets most from the soil. Of all cultivators the peasant proprietor is the one who gives most encouragement to commerce and manufactures, because he is the richest.' *

The island of Jersey is owned and for the most part farmed by small proprietors, and with less than 28,000 acres, has a population of 55,613, and 55,000 tons of local shipping, carrying on trade with every quarter of the world. The Isle of Wight has not one peasant proprietor, and with 86,810 acres of land has a population of 55,362, and scarcely any commerce or shipping.† But the trade which a prosperous rural

* See Mr. Mill's Chapters and Speeches on the 'Irish Land Question,' p. 5.

† For much useful information, respecting the Channel Islands and

population creates, is not only much larger than that which springs from the demand of a wealthy few; it is also much less precarious. And there is a similar difference between the industries which rest on a local market, and have, as it were, an agricultural basis, and those which depend on a foreign demand. The principal manufactures of Ireland are branches of one great staple, mainly dependent on an external market. But since the close of the American war, these manufactures have been by no means in a flourishing state; and the linen factories of Ulster have been working short time, or only a part of their machinery, while its artificial manure factories have been doing as large a business as ever with the tenant-right farmers of the province. The clothing merchant's trade in Belfast, in like manner, is slack with all the manufacturing population, and also with the farmers dependent on the prosperity of flax; while it continues to be brisk with the rest of the rural population. In the villages round Belfast, the same principle finds examples. There are three not many miles distant, all beginning with the Irish name for a town; two of which were dependent on weaving, and these are dwindling into mere hamlets; while the third (the trade of which springs from the agricultural population of its neighbourhood) has grown in a few years into a small town of 1,300 inhabitants with a flourishing business.

It is true that the decline of the trade of some of

their laws, see 'Observations on the Law of Descent in the United Kingdom.' By Henry Tupper, of the Royal Court of Guernsey.

the towns of Ireland has been in part natural and unavoidable—resulting from a change in the lines of communication and traffic, with railways and steamers. Such changes, however, only alter the sites of traffic, and do not destroy it; they afford, moreover, an additional illustration of the importance to towns of a local demand which does not shift with every variation in the course of external commerce.

But it is by no means only through its effects on the country that the Irish land system cramps the growth of the town, or suppresses it altogether. The accumulation of the greater part of the national territory in unproductive hands, settlements with the difficulties of title and transfer they cause, the obstacles to industrial progress arising from the feudal principles of English law, the intricacy of the most technical and tortuous jurisprudence the world has ever known, the uncertainty and enormous cost of litigation, the insecurity of town as well as of agricultural holdings, compose a network of restrictions to the development of the manufacturing, mining, and commercial resources of the island which have been more fatal to the prosperity of the town than even to that of the country. The first sentence of Mr. Furlong's treatise on the 'Law of Landlord and Tenant in Ireland,' is 'The common law regulating the enjoyment of real property, both in England and Ireland, is founded upon and governed by the principles of the feudal system.' But the feudal system contemplated agriculture, although in a servile form; it never contemplated manufactures, mines, or commerce. Belfast, the only great manufacturing city in Ireland, owes, as has been mentioned in a previous page, its greatness to a fortunate accident which converted the ground on which it stands from feudal into commercial territory, by transferring it from a great noble to its own citizens. But the growth of Belfast itself, on one side has been strictly circumscribed by the rival claims of two noble proprietors, who were in litigation respecting them for more than a generation; and in a step the inhabitant passes from new streets to a filthy and decaying suburb, into which the most enterprising capitalist in the neighbourhood has been prevented from extending his improvements.* On the other side of the town is some ground which the capitalist just referred to bought three years ago for the purpose of building; but which remains unbuilt on, in consequence of difficulties in the legal title; although in equity the title is indisputable, and is not disputed. Some years ago the same capitalist contracted for the purchase of another plot of ground in the neighbourhood. It proved, however, that the vendor was precluded by his marriage settlement from completing the contract, although it reserved to him the unusual power to grant leases for 999 years. That, however, did not answer the same purpose; in the first place, because (a consequence of the land system, with its distinction between real and personal property) the succession duties are heavier on leasehold than on freehold estates. What is more important, a tenant for years has not the rights of ownership, as was afterwards experienced in the very

---

* See also on this subject the next article.

case before us. The capitalist accepted a lease for 999 years; although diverted from his original design with respect to the ground. In putting it to a different purpose, he proceeded to level an eminence, and to carry away the gravel for use elsewhere. But the Law of Landlord and Tenant says: 'If a tenant open pits for the purpose of raising stone or waste, it will be waste.' And this being the law, the landlord actually obtained an injunction to restrain the tenant's proceedings and mulcted him in damages.

Once more; in another county the very same capitalist opened an iron mine by arrangement with the lord of the soil, and commenced works on an extensive scale. The landlord then demanded terms to which he was not entitled by his contract; but the price of Irish iron has not been high enough of late years to defray the cost of a Chancery suit in addition to the cost of production; and delay, worry, and anxiety are not inducements to industrial enterprise, so the iron works were suspended.

Here are five cases within the author's knowledge, all happening in recent years, in which a single individual has been arrested in the course of town enterprise and improvement by the state of the law. Add centuries to the last few years, and multiply this one individual by all the others whose industrial efforts have been cramped and restrained directly by the state of the law, and even then the full tale of the mischief is not told. For whenever one individual starts a new and successful business, it leads to other advances and improvements great and small; and the smothering of a single enterprise may entail indirectly the loss of the growth of a town. Look, then, with this consideration in mind, at the loss Ulster has sustained by the conduct of the twelve London companies who hold a great part of the county of Londonderry in mortmain, and who have added to the injury of absenteeism the crime of refusing leases. 'It is well known that there are no manufacturing establishments on the companies' estates, because these London guilds persistently refuse to give perpetuity lease for such purposes; while on the borders of the county Cookstown, Ballymena, Ballymoney, and Coleraine, where such leases are granted, manufactures have increased and prospered, and even in the county, where freehold sites can be procured, manufactures have taken root.' *

In a passage quoted above Mr. Maclagan speaks of smart country towns in the interior of Ireland, naming, however, Parsonstown only, the prosperity of which is mainly due to its exceptional good fortune in obtaining long leases. But Mr. Maclagan himself discovered 'whole villages and towns which have been built by the tenants, and from which the landlord can evict them at a six-months' notice.' A notion was formerly carefully diffused by way of apology for the land system of Ireland, that it had no natural capability for manufactures, that agriculture was therefore at once its only trade, and an unremunerative one for want of home markets. The truth is, the industrial resources of the island are considerable. The outcrop of iron is

* 'The Irish Land Question, and the Twelve London Companies in the County of Londonderry,' p. 24.

large, and an instance has been given of the fate of an attempt to turn it to account. There is no lack of material for fuel, if invention once got fairly to work at it; coal, too, can be carried to Dublin cheaper than to London; and with a proper railway system, the cost of English coal would create no obstacle to manufactures in the West. Holland without mines is becoming again a manufacturing country, by means of low railway freights for coal and iron from the Ruhr Basin and Belgium. Ireland moreover is rich in marble, stone, and clays available for many industrial purposes, and rich also both in materials for textile and leather manufactures, and in the genius of the people for manufacturing them; as is proved not only by the ancient success of some which legislation, followed by heavy duties on coal, extinguished, but also by existing fabrics in all parts of the island, lace, tabinets, sewed muslins, damasks, linen and frieze, leather works, all of indigenous growth; besides rising cottons and woollens after the English model in a few favoured situations.

The truth is that the law and the land system built on the law have cramped the manufactures even more than the agriculture of Ireland, because the former stand even more in need of security and liberty for their prosperity, and are not the first necessaries of life. The saying of Swift that in the arithmetic of the customs, two and two instead of making four, sometimes made only one, is yet truer of the political arithmetic of the Irish territorial system, with its contrivances for adding acres indivisibly together in unproductive hands. Substitute the land system for 'slavery' and tenants-at-will for 'slaves' in the following passage, in which Mr. Cairnes a few years ago described ' the kind of economic success which slavery had achieved in the Southern States of America,' and the passage will read as true as before. ' It consists in the rapid extraction from the soil of the most easily obtained portion of its wealth, by a process which exhausts the soil, and consigns to waste all the other resources of the country where it is practised. By proscribing manufactures and commerce and confining agriculture within narrow bounds, by rendering impossible the rise of a free peasantry, by checking the growth of population, in a word by blasting every germ from which national well-being may spring; at this cost, with the further condition of encroaching through a reckless system of culture on the stores designed by Providence for future generations, slavery may undoubtedly for a time be made conducive to the interests of the man who keeps slaves.' Mr. Caird fell naturally almost into Mr. Cairnes' first words when he said of the results of the Irish land system : ' What the ground will yield from year to year at the least cost of time, labour and money, is taken from it.'

One large business indeed, a system which ' exhausts the soil, proscribes manufactures and commerce, and confines agriculture within narrow bounds,' does nevertheless create. It necessitates the existence of a large army of policemen and soldiers. In the tenant-right and agricultural county of Down (outside of Belfast) 1 in 1,112 of the population is a policeman; in the great grazing county of Meath the proportion is 1 in 379.

In the last eleven years the cost of the army and navy of the United Kingdom has amounted to three hundred millions—no small part of that cost being in reality caused by the disaffection of Ireland—yet there are economists who argue that the Treasury cannot afford to advance a few millions to enable Irish tenants to purchase their holdings, although the Treasury actually has for a number of years been lending money to landlords in both England and Ireland. But even three hundred millions is a small sum compared with the waste of productive power in both country and town which the Irish land system has caused in the eleven last years.

A perception that other interests besides those of tenant-farmers are concerned in the land system has sometimes led opponents of the tenants to reply, truly enough, that they are not the only class in the nation; but the proper inference is that the entire land system of every country in any age ought to be, and, in a democratic age, must be constructed with no other object than to make the national territory minister to the general welfare and happiness of the nation, and that for the sake of at once strengthening the foundations of property and diffusing the sources of prosperity, it must aim both at a wide distribution of landed property, and at opening all the industrial resources which land comprehends to productive use and investment. The problem accordingly which the legislature has before it will not be solved by legislation relating solely to agriculture and agricultural holdings. The prohibition of entail, reform of the law of intestate succession, the transfer of land by simple registration at the least possible cost,* security of tenure, the sale of absentee estates to the tenants, or in towns to trustees for the citizens, are measures even more necessary for manufactures and commerce than for agriculture in a country in such a condition as Ireland's; measures, too, in favour of the town, are measures in favour of the country. 'If you wish to encourage agriculture, develope manufactures and commerce which multiply consumers; improve the means of communication which bring consumers and producers nearer to each other. The agricultural question is nothing else than one of general prosperity.' †

Mere reformation, however, of the laws relating to land, trusting to the gradual operation of wise and just institutions in the future, is by no means sufficient now, either for the general prosperity of Ireland or for that of its agriculture in particular. The legislature has not only noxious and barbarous laws, but also their effects, both economical and political, to remove. On a population cut off from manufactures and commerce, a land system has been imposed, carefully contrived to exclude

* As an example of the close connection of the reforms needed in the Irish land system, it is worth observing that to give the force of law to the Ulster custom of tenant-right will be a positive injury to many tenants, without a simple law of transfer and succession; since the interest of the tenants will otherwise become subject at once to the costs and risks on account of which they have invested their capital in the purchase of a customary right instead of in the purchase of land. The Landed Estates Court, it may be added, is not a poor man's court, and is a very costly and tedious court even for a rich man.

† 'Rural Economy of England, Scotland, and Ireland.' By M. de Lavergne.

them from property in the soil, and even from the secure cultivation of the small farms to which they were driven for subsistence. In France, Germany, and Belgium, landed property is a national institution, and a national benefit, and the nation is *for* it ; in Ireland it has been, both in origin and in effect, a hostile institution, and the nation is against it. Yet the very causes which have produced this unnatural situation have concealed themselves in the violence of their own effects ; and the system of tenure has appeared the only great evil, because it has been almost the only career open to the nation ; proprietorship having been altogether denied to it. The system of property, an oligarchic and feudal system of property, is the radical evil, of which the system of tenure is only a single branch. The great aim of Parliament ought to be to diffuse property in land widely throughout the nation ; treating all immediate cost incurred for that end in compensating existing proprietors as incurred, not only for the improvement of Ireland, but also for the security of the Empire. The provisions of the Irish Land Bill now before Parliament need much amendment for the protection of tenants. But the success of any law of tenure, however well framed in itself, will mainly depend on the number of proprietors the conditions of purchase and reforms in the law of property shall call into being.

POLITICAL ECONOMY AND EMIGRATION.*

THANKS to four or five great writers in a century, a few statesmen, and the particular interests and accidents which led to a comparatively early adoption of free trade, England is looked up to on the Continent as *par excellence* the country of political economy. In few other countries nevertheless is this branch of political philosophy less carefully or commonly studied, however commonly its terms are in use; and it becomes daily more evident that the air ought to be cleared of clouds of confusion enveloping those very terms. For instead of facilitating thought, as the terms of a science should do, they have come to supersede it; they are taken to settle several problems about which economic inquiry is almost in its infancy; and, what is yet more misleading, they have caused different and even opposite things to be confounded under one name—as has been the case not only with several economic terms commonly made use of in discussing emigration, but with emigration itself.

In no other branch of philosophy indeed, unless metaphysics itself, does the ancient mist of realism continue so to ' darken counsel by words without

* Reprinted from 'Fraser's Magazine,' May 1868.

knowledge.' A resemblance has been seen by a philosopher in a number of different things viewed in one particular light, and a common name has been given to them with reference only to that point of resemblance; often indeed the general term introduced in this way was not originally meant to denote a complete induction, but simply to put a conspicuous part for the whole, leaving something to human intelligence; presently, however, the entire class comes to assume a perfect identity in the minds of some of the philosopher's most intelligent followers. In like manner, a phrase used at first to signify merely a tendency of things under particular conditions comes to stand for a universal law or principle of nature, and a generalisation, which originally threw a new light upon phenomena, finally involves them in almost impenetrable obscurity. Emigration, for example, though really a name for several different kinds of emigration, and, in particular, for two opposite kinds on which we shall have particularly to dwell, has been spoken of as a thing, the beneficial effects of which, in every case, have an *à priori* certainty that leaves no room for discussion. It is all supply and demand, one person will tell you; labour, whether it be English labour or Irish labour, is a commodity which finds its way to the best market. Another, arriving by a somewhat less mechanical process at the same positive conclusion, tells you that it must be beneficial, since it takes place through the operation of the private interest of all the parties concerned—the term 'private interest,' it will be observed, being in all such reasoning confounded with another deceitful abstraction, 'the desire of wealth.' A third argues that it must of necessity raise the rate of wages, by distributing the 'aggregate wages fund' among a smaller number of labourers.

That the rate of wages is not determined by any single law or set of conditions, we hope to demonstrate in a subsequent article.* At present it is enough to remark, in the first place, that there are no funds necessarily destined to employment as wages; and coincidently with a vast emigration there may be, as its very result or as the result of a common cause, a substitution of pasture for tillage, and a withdrawal of capital from farming, with a diminished demand for labour in consequence. Moreover, the aggregate amount of the funds expendible as wages does not, given the number of labourers, determine the rate of wages at all. If a single employer, or a few who could combine, had the entire amount, all the labour in the country which could not emigrate might be hired for its bare subsistence, whatever the rate in the power of the employer to give. Again, if the whole amount were, as it really is, very unequally shared among employers, the price of labour might be immeasurably lower than if it were equally shared; just as at an auction, the prices paid for things will probably be immensely higher if the purchasers have equal means, than if most of the money is in the hands of a few. If two bidders, for example, have each 50*l.*, one of them may have to spend his whole fifty to get half what he wants; but if one of them has but 5*l.*

* See Appendix. 'Political Economy and the Rate of Wages.'

and the other has 95*l.*, the latter may get all he wants for 5*l.* 5*s.*

There may be a convenience in having a collective term for all the sources of wages, all the funds, whether capital, income, or the revenue of the State, expendible upon labour ; but the misfortune is that the collective term employed for this purpose has created an imaginary collective fund destined to the payment of labour; and the payment is inferred to be higher or lower in proportion to the number of labourers. In like manner the phrase ' private interest,' though really a collective term for a number of individual interests, by no means all for the public interest, has assumed, in the minds of a number of economists, the form of a single beneficent principle, animating and regulating the whole economic world. ' The desire for wealth,' in the same way (which is by no means, as already observed, the same thing with private interest, for wealth is not the predominant interest of the most powerful classes*),

---

* 'There is a firm oasis in the desert upon which we may safely rest, and that is afforded us by the principles of political economy. I entertain a prejudice adopted by Adam Smith, that a man is at liberty to do what he likes with his own, and that, having land, it is not unreasonable that he should be free to let his land to a person upon the terms upon which they shall mutually agree. That I believe to be good political economy.' [Speech of Mr. Lowe in the House of Commons, March 14.]

Now what has Adam Smith really said ? ' It seldom happens that a great proprietor is a great improver. But if great improvements are seldom to be expected from great proprietors, they are least of all to be expected when they employ slaves for their workmen. The experience of all ages demonstrates that the work done by slaves is in the end the dearest of any.' 'The pride of man,' nevertheless, he continues, ' makes him love to domineer. Wherever the law allows it therefore, he will generally prefer the service of slaves to that of freemen.'—*Wealth of Nations,* book 3, chap. ii. And in the only sentence in which Adam Smith speaks of allowing the landlord to pursue his own interest in his is really a name for a multiplicity of wants, passions, and ideas, widely differing from each other, both in their nature and in their effects on production—as the accumulation of land differs from the hunger for bread —yet it stands for one identical and industrious principle with many considerable speakers and writers. And in virtue of these terms, and a few others of like generality, a school of economists of no small pretensions, strongly represented in Parliament, supposes itself to be furnished with a complete apparatus of formulas, within which all economic knowledge is comprised;— which clearly and satisfactorily expounds all the phenomena of wealth, and renders all further investigation of the causes and effects of the existing economy of society needless, and even mischievous as tending to introduce doubt and heresy into a scientific world of certainty and truth, and discontent and disturbance into a social world of order and prosperity. Political writers and speakers of this school have long enjoyed the double satisfaction of beholding in themselves the masters of a difficult study, and of pleasing the powers that be, by lending the sanction of 'science' to all established institutions and customs, unless, indeed, customs of the poor. Instead of a science of wealth, they give us a science *for* wealth. And so blind has been the faith reposed, even by acute and logical minds, in the infallibility of the formulas, that Arch-

own way, he insists upon the State giving to the tenants 'the most perfect security that they shall enjoy the full recompense of their own industry.' Adam Smith, moreover, has pronounced, without reserve, against the system of proprietorship and management of land created by primogeniture and entails.

bishop Whately could point to the play of demand and supply, as the most striking proof natural theology can adduce of omniscient and benevolent design, instancing, in particular, in his argument the beneficent results of private interest in the dealings of the London retailers of food. For ourselves, we are convinced both that no branch of philosophy has suffered more than political economy from the intellectual weakness which M. de Tocqueville contrasts with omniscience in the following passage, and that evidence of that weakness is what is most striking in such arguments as the Archbishop's; a weakness which leads men to imagine an unreal uniformity and order in the world, corresponding with their own classifications, and which arises mainly from the inaccuracy and inadequacy of the general terms in which they place such unlimited confidence :—

'Dieu ne songe point au genre humain en général. Il voit d'un seul coup d'œil et séparément tous les êtres dont l'humanité se compose, et il aperçoit chacun d'eux avec les ressemblances qui le rapprochent de tous et les différences qui l'en isolent. Dieu n'a donc pas besoin d'idées générales ; c'est-à-dire qu'il ne sent jamais la nécessité de renfermer un très-grand nombre d'objets analogues sous une même forme afin d'y penser plus commodément. Il n'en est point ainsi de l'homme. Si l'esprit humain entreprenait d'examiner et de juger individuellement tous les cas particuliers qui le frappent, il se perdrait bientôt au milieu de l'immensité des détails et ne verrait plus rien ; dans cette extrémité, il a recours à un procédé imparfait mais nécessaire, qui aide sa faiblesse et qui la prouve. Après avoir considéré superficiellement un certain nombre d'objets, et remarqué qu'ils se ressemblent, il leur donne à tous un même nom, et poursuit sa route. Les idées générales n'attestent point la force de l'intelligence humaine, mais plutôt son insuffisance, car il n'y a point d'êtres exactement semblables dans la nature ; point de faits identiques ; point de règles applicables indistinctement et de la même manière à plusieurs objets à la fois. Les idées générales ont cela d'admirable qu'elles permettent à l'esprit humain de porter des jugements rapides sur un grand nombre d'objets à la fois ; mais d'une autre part, elles ne lui fournissent jamais que des notions incomplètes, et elles lui font toujours perdre en exactitude ce qu'elles lui donnent en étendue.' *

Emigration is, for example, one word, and it has become accordingly to many economists one thing. Yet the history of mankind might be called the history of emigration, and does any one see in that great historical movement a single phenomenon ? Emigrants founded, and emigrants overthrew, the empire of Rome ; emigrants raised all the modern States of Europe, and planted the new worlds ; and, as Tocqueville's observation suggests, omniscience would see in those movements the individual actions of every member of the Aryan family, not to speak of other races. Or, confining the view to a much smaller field, looking, that is to say, only to the emigration of fifteen recent years from the United Kingdom, as given in the last statistical abstract, omniscience would see in it the separate departures of more than three million persons to various

* 'De la Démocratie en Amérique.'

places, for various individual reasons, and with various individual results.

Number of Emigrants from the United Kingdom to various Destinations.

Years	To the North American Colonies	To the United States	To the Australian Colonies and New Zealand	To Other Places	Total
1852	32,873	244,261	87,881	3,749	368,764
1853	34,522	230,885	61,401	3,129	329,937
1854	43,761	193,065	83,237	3,366	323,429
1855	17,966	103,414	52,309	3,118	176,807
1856	16,378	111,837	44,584	3,755	176,554
1857	21,001	126,905	61,248	3,721	212,875
1858	9,704	59,716	39,295	5,257	113,972
1859	6,689	70,303	31,013	12,427	120,432
1860	9,786	87,500	24,302	6,881	128,469
1861	12,707	49,764	23,738	5,561	91,770
1862	15,522	58,706	41,843	5,143	121,214
1863	18,083	146,813	53,054	5,808	223,758
1864	12,721	147,042	40,942	8,195	208,900
1865	17,211	146,258	37,283	8,049	209,801
1866	13,255	161,000	24,097	6,530	204,882
					3,009,463

The science of the human economist must fall infinitely short of affording him such complete knowledge, as he contemplates such a table; but it ought at least to help him to see in its figures something more than the 'total' column, or one general movement of the British population: it ought to suggest some economic difference in the different streams of emigration 'to the North American Colonies, to the United States, to the Australian Colonies and New Zealand, and to other places.' We need not here, however, dwell upon more than one main distinction, that is to say, between the nature and effects of the movements to Australia, New Zealand, and Canada on the one hand, and of that to the United States upon the other. It is not difficult on a moment's reflection to perceive that emigration is here a name for at least two great movements as widely different in the main, both in respect of their causes and their results, as colonization is from depopulation, as improvement is from waste, and as enterprise and hope are from ruin and despair. It is a name, on the one hand, for the intelligence, energy, and facility with which the labour and capital of old countries now flow to distant regions; for a healthy tendency of the age to develop the resources of the whole world, especially in places hitherto neglected and backward; and, on the other hand, for insuperable obstacles to the prosperity and improvement of old countries themselves, and of a consequent flight of industrious enterprise and productive power from places whose natural resources are made, in a great measure, inaccessible to industry and development. Even in the emigration from Ireland, there has been this double movement: there has been a healthy emigration (though comparatively on a very small scale) springing from increased intelligence and knowledge, from the accumulation of small capitals, and from new outlets for energy, strength, and skill, as well as an emigration springing from misery, discontent, and the absence of all other prospect of a career: and there has been a reflux of emigrants whose fortunes have been made, and of their industrial spirit, as well as of Fenians and Fenianism.

'At this moment,' says Lord Dufferin, speaking of Ulster, 'some of the most prosperous farmers on my estate are men who went in their youth to Australia and America, and have returned in the prime of life with an ample supply of capital.' Even in the south of the island some similar cases are known to the writer. But there would have been much more of this healthy and natural emigration—Australia, New Zealand, and Canada would have received and made the fortunes of many more Irishmen, and sent more back with full hands to their native land—had there not been also a different emigration, on an immensely greater scale, with an opposite reflux. Lord Mayo said truly enough of the different feelings toward Great Britain of Irish emigrants in America and Australia : 'In Australia, though their numbers are not reckoned by millions, the Irishmen who have settled there do not exhibit towards Great Britain any of those hostile feelings which unhappily are found in America;' but it seems not to have occurred to the noble earl that they brought out different feelings, that they emigrated for the most part for different reasons, and that to suffer the emigration to the United States to take such a direction, is a proof of the same want of statesmanship which has failed to remove, or even, as it should seem, to discover its causes. For if it were true, as we hope to show it was not, that most of those who went to America could not have been supported in comfort at home, it would nevertheless be true that half of the four hundred millions expended in the last fourteen years on a wooden fleet, on useless fortifications, on an 'army of deserters' (as a large portion of the British army has with harsh truth been called),* on military and naval mismanagement of every kind, might have planted New Zealand, Australia, and Canada with loyal subjects, instead of the United States with enemies to Great Britain.

There have been however, as already said, two opposite streams of emigration even from Ireland, and how are we to measure their relative breadth? Something of a measure is afforded, as already observed, by the direction of the streams, but it is possible also, as we hope to show, to discover another. We must first allude to an alleged criterion in the rate of wages, the rise in which, according to some writers, proves that the whole emigration from Ireland has been beneficial, and gives the exact measure of the benefit. Even Lord Dufferin, apparently regarding Irish emigration in the main rather as a necessary evil than as a good, sees in it a curative process, and refers to the rise in wages as evidence. We undertake to show that, on the contrary, the bulk of the emigration from Ireland has been the result of a perpetuation of the evils of Ireland instead of a cure for them; that it is a waste of industrial power arising from obstacles to industrial enterprises of every kind in Ireland itself; and with regard to wages, that the rise is not only due principally to

* Of the recruits obtained in the seven years, 1859-65, upwards of 47,000 deserted.—See Report of the Commissioners to Inquire into the Recruiting for the Army, 1867. Appendix 12, 8.

other causes than emigration, but would have been considerably greater if there had been no such emigration,—that is to say, if the enormous emigration ascribable to the cause just adverted to had not taken place; if the natural resources of Ireland had been all freely accessible; if the most vigorous part of the population and much capital had not been removed by it from a great part of the island; if a decline in the fertility of the soil, with a retrograde movement of husbandry, had not been its accompaniment; and if Fenianism and popular discontent and disquiet were not among its results.

The writers who attribute the rise in wages to emigration are oblivious alike of the accompanying rise in the price of commodities and of the principal monetary phenomena of the twenty years of new gold mines, steam, and free trade—of an equalisation of prices, and a consequent rise in the price of both labour and commodities in all parts of the world, where means of communication with the best markets have been greatly improved. Dr. Johnson in the last century, talking of turnpike roads in England, said: 'Every place communicating with every other. Before there were cheap places and dear places; now all refuges for poverty are destroyed.' Add steam-navigation and railways to roads; add the treasure of California, Australia, New Zealand, and British Columbia, to the money circulated by them in 'cheap places,' and it is not difficult to discover why they have become 'dear places;' or why the prices of both labour and commodities have risen in Ireland as they have risen in India, in Egypt, and in every provincial town in France, in the same period, though emigration cannot be assigned as the cause. It ought to be sufficiently clear to every professed economist that, although emigration may force employers either to pay more for labour or to forego it, it cannot enable them to pay more for it as higher prices of produce will do; and that it may, on the contrary, compel or determine them to diminish their outlay upon it, may force or induce them to relinquish enterprises already on foot, to forsake tillage for pasture, to emigrate themselves, and in various other ways to withdraw funds from the labour market. It may actually disable them from paying the same rate of wages as formerly, by withdrawing the strongest and most skilful hands from their employment; and again, in place of being the cause of a rise in the rate of wages, it may be the consequence of a fall. These are not merely possible cases (though even as such they are enough to dispose of the argument that emigration must have raised wages by diminishing the number of labourers competing for employment); they are, as we shall presently see, cases of actual occurrence in Ireland. But let us glance first at the true causes of the rise in the price of labour in Ireland, and the corresponding rise in the price of commodities which has in a great measure neutralised its purchasing power to the labourer.

In the town of Wexford, between thirty and forty years ago, the price of meat was $2\frac{1}{2}d.$ a pound; it rose with steam-communication to $4d.$; and with improvements in steam it had risen, ten years ago, to between

98 LAND SYSTEMS AND INDUSTRIAL ECONOMY.

7d. and 8d. In Athlone down to 1852, meat continued to sell at from 3d. to 4d. a pound, and then rose at once with railway communication to between 7d. and 8d. What, then, has raised prices generally throughout Ireland? The answer is evident. Roads, railways, steamers, proximity to the English markets, increased demand in those markets, the influx of gold, the equalisation of prices, and the immigration of money, not the emigration of labour. What conclusively proves that emigration is not the chief cause of the rise is, that for nine years the money rate of wages has remained stationary throughout the greater part of the island in spite of enormous emigrations in the interval. The writer has for many years been collecting statistics of prices in connection with a different question, and can affirm that wages have remained at 1s. a day throughout the greater part of Ireland, since 1859. Earl Russell has recently cited ' on official authority,' some figures which illustrate the real movement since 1831, and show how small is its connection with emigration—beginning before emigration and not continuing with it:

County	1831	1841	1851	1861	1866
	$s.$	$s.$	$s.$	$s.$	$s.$
Kildare .	little money wages	4 to 5	7	8	8
Tipperary .	5	6	7	8	8
Wexford .	5 to 6	5 to 6	6	6 to 7	6 to 7
Kilkenny .	5 to 6	5 to 6	6	6 to 7	6 to 7

Nor in estimating the effects of emigration upon the real condition of the Irish labourers can we leave out of the account the loss of their little farms by some 400,000 small occupiers who, with their sons, were formerly the chief agricultural labourers of the island. It is a great mistake to take the money-rate of wages in 1845 and 1848 as a criterion of the comparative condition of the labourer at the two periods, not only on account of the rise in the price of provisions, but also because the agricultural labourer has generally a little farm of his own as every agricultural labourer should have, and rarely possesses one now. 'Notwithstanding its detestable rural system,' said M. de Lavergne, some fifteen years ago, 'Ireland seems to have preserved one excellent feature, namely, the almost entire absence of day labourers, properly so called.' It has no such feature now.

So much with respect to the alleged rise in the price of labour arising from emigration. We have now to show that, instead of causing a rise of wages, emigration has been, in many cases, the consequence of a fall—in most cases of their continuing wretchedly low because of obstacles to the combination of the three instruments of production, labour, capital, and natural agents; and that every source of national income, wages, profit, and rent would have been more abundant had there been much less emigration—that is to say, had none of that emigration taken place which has been caused by legal impediments to the prosperity of the island, to the development of its industrial resources, and to the use of the great aids to their development, from roads, railways, steam-navigation, English markets, education, and the ingress of that spirit of enterprise shown even in emigration itself. The true inference from the rise of prices in Ireland, is not that emigration has been beneficial, but that a great market ought to have been found for Irish labour at home, and that the enormous loss of industrial power is the more lamentable, apart from its political consequences and the economic evils resulting, in that it has taken place at a period when there ought to have been an immense burst of prosperity.*

* From an essay, published some years ago, on the movements of prices in different parts of the world, the writer takes leave to quote the following sentences in illustration both of the causes of the rise in Ireland and of the inference above. 'The chief monetary phenomenon of the period is the rise of prices in remote places, put suddenly more nearly on a level with the neighbourhood of the great centres of consumption as regards the market for their produce. The ruder and remoter regions are at length, if commerce be allowed its natural course, brought into neighbourhood with the regions more advanced, and endowed with the same advantages, especially with that advantage to which the latter mainly owed their earlier progress—the advantage of a good commercial situation, which steam-navigation, railways, and roads, are giving to many districts rich in food and the materials of industry, but until lately unable to dispose of their wealth, unless upon beggarly terms.'—*Macmillan's Magazine*, August, 1864. See also ' North British Review,' June, 1865, Art. ' Gold Mines and Prices.'

Compare with this the following, from Sir Richard Temple's recent 'Letter to the Government of India on British and Native Systems of Government':—

'In the north-west provinces a great increase of cultivation could be statistically proved. Similar proof could be obtained for the Punjaub generally. Oude will so readily suggest itself that I need not allude to it further. In Bengal Proper there has certainly been a great increase. In Madras and Bombay the revenue survey records will show specifically great increase of cultivation. In Berar the astonishing rise of cultivation during the few years of British administration, is shown by the figures of our annual reports. The rapid growth of British Burmah is attested by facts recently published. . . .

' Under British rule the prices of everything, necessaries and luxuries,

Of Irish emigration being in many cases the consequence of a fall instead of the cause of a rise in wages, one example deserves particular attention, from the light it throws on another phase of the subject. Not long ago one of the most successful capitalists in the island undertook a mining enterprise in a backward county of lakes and bogs, having obtained a license for the purpose from several adjoining proprietors. Wages were at 5s. a week in the locality when he began his operations, and before they stopped, a few months ago, the same men were earning weekly sums varying from 8s. to 18s. One of the landed proprietors unfortunately conceived that an enterprise so lucrative to others ought to be more so to himself; and having entered only into an 'equitable,' as distinguished from a 'legal' agreement—a distinction to the cause and effects of which no small part of the poverty of Ireland and the

have advanced steadily—of late years, with a progressive ratio of speed. In many, if not in all parts of the country, wages have risen, not always proportionately, but still very much. In many districts full evidence could be obtained that the people are better set up than in former days, better furnished, too, with all domestic utensils, so much so, that it is a common saying that the earthen vessels have been converted into brass vessels.'

The defect of Sir R. Temple's account is, that it does not refer to the great influx of money, and the improvement in means of both internal communication and foreign trade, as the main causes of the rise of prices and the prosperity he describes. Writing on the 14th of March last, the 'Times' correspondent says of Bombay: 'From 80 to 100 millions sterling, in addition to the normal price of cotton, were poured into this place, and where is it? Much, there is happily good reason to believe, is with the peasant. All testimony bears out that he has freed himself from centuries of hereditary debt, from the grip of the usurer, from the peculations of the petty bazaar dealers. He now sells his own cotton direct in many cases, and is a shrewd and cautious seller. He lives more comfortably, and there is evidence that he is seeking education for his children.'

consequent emigration may directly or indirectly be traced—he demanded conditions which the capitalist could not fulfil without incurring a loss. The consequence is that the works have been stopped, wages have receded to their old rate, emigration has been stimulated, and Fenianism alone will henceforward derive any advantage from the mine, until a Chancery suit shall determine whether law or equity is to prevail. Take again the emigration of navvies from Ireland. Has it caused a rise in the price of that kind of labour? On the contrary, it is the result of there being no employment or wages for navvies in the island, although the works wanted are legion. In like manner skilled labourers have disappeared altogether from many places, and Lord Dufferin's book on emigration itself contains evidence that new hands are not being brought up in their place, because, instead of an increasing demand, there has been a cessation of it, from the decay of country towns. In Belfast, to take one more illustration, wages doubled while the population quadrupled, in little more than a single generation; but lately, owing to the slackness of trade, a fall in the rate of wages took place, and it is said that immigration was at once checked, and that an emigration began which would have been considerable but for the slackness of trade also in America—where likewise we find that the real sequence of antecedence and consequence is not emigration and high wages, but high wages and immigration, low wages and emigration.

A writer in the 'Economist' recently argued that 'the idea that wages cannot be increased in agriculture is fallacious. Every business worth carrying on at all can and must pay the market rate, and invariably either does adjust itself until it can do it, or *transfers itself to some other country.*' Those who argue that emigration must raise agricultural wages in Ireland, forget that agriculture has that alternative, and we shall see that it has been adopted. In 1847, the cereal crops produced 16,248,934 quarters; in 1866, they produced 8,840,277 quarters; in 1847, the green crops gave 8,785,144 tons; in 1866, they gave 7,387,741. In 1860, there were nearly 6,000,000 acres under crops, there are now half a million less. M. de Lavergne indeed exclaims, ' that to complain of the extension of pasture is to reproach Heaven for its gifts.' But we may accept M. de Lavergne as the highest authority on the rural economy of France—and he tells us that peasant properties there are twice as productive as large properties—without accepting him as an authority for Ireland. A generation ago, Sir Robert Kane, reviewing the industrial resources of Ireland too sanguinely, predicted that pasture was about to give way before civilisation and industry in the island :—' Mere industry has been in Ireland connected with the idea of a vulgar and depressed caste. The possession of a farm constituted in itself the criterion of respectability. The working of a cottage farm, even though more profitable, was thus fatal to the social position of the occupier ; whilst, if he only kept a herd to mind some cattle, and spent his time and money in hunting and drinking, he looked down with scorn on all that savoured of occupations vile, of industry and intelligence.

'These ideas have been already very considerably disturbed. Prior to the introduction of turnip husbandry, and to the cultivation of the artificial grasses, it might be a question as to the relative profit of grazing, and of a very imperfect tillage which gradually reduced the land to a condition of almost perfect barrenness. But a crop which produces three times as much food will feed three times as many cattle; and it is hence unavoidable that, as agriculture progresses, the ordinary grass crops will be replaced by the more nutritious carrots, turnips, clover, &c.; the animals, in place of roving over extensive grounds which recall the idea of the prairie existence of a half civilised hunting population, will be suitably confined, that their food may not be wasted in muscular efforts inconsistent with their ultimate perfection as food for man. The rearing of cattle will thus in itself become a branch, as it really is one of the most important, of tillage husbandry. It is in this form that agriculture ought to be carried on in Ireland.' *

The extension of pasture, which has baffled this prediction, is thus a sign of retrogression, not of advancement; as it is also at once a cause and an effect of emigration. In a recent report to the Chemico-Agricultural Society of Ulster, Professor Hodges, after pointing out that the extraordinary richness of ancient Irish pastures had been in a great measure exhausted by the grazing and importation of cattle, observed:—
'Ireland may be made to yield food for a far larger population than it is ever likely to contain; but it is

* 'Industrial Resources of Ireland.'

not by abandoning the cultivation of the turnip and artificial grasses for the pasture system which some would extend that the wealth of the country is to be increased. It has been correctly observed that you may judge of the condition of the agriculture of a country by the attention which is devoted to the turnip husbandry. Yet in many parts of Ireland we find that the produce of the soil has been seriously diminished by the injudicious substitution of miserable pasture for the cultivation of the turnip and other suitable crops. Hence, from recent returns we find that in Ireland only 23 per cent. of the green crops are turnips, while in England the percentage is 60, and in Scotland it is 72·6. In Ireland, again, the proportion of mangolds, which can be so successfully grown in every province, and which are so valuable as food for stock, especially in a country where pasture has begun to fail, is only 1·3 per cent., while in England it is 9·4.'

In the Irish Registrar-General's Agricultural Statistics of 1867 we read that ' there was a decrease of 61,623 acres in the land under crops in 1867 compared with 1866; grass increased by 52,828 acres; fallow by 772 acres; bog and waste by 13,176 acres; woods and plantations show a decrease of 5,153 acres.' And whoever looks at such statistics with any knowledge of the island and of husbandry must perceive that the continued substitution of grazing for tillage which proceeded since 1860 is a fact of the same class with the increase " of fallow, bog, and waste unoccupied," and the decrease of woods and plantations. It was irreverently said of a late amiable Lord-Lieutenant, who was wont to descant on the increase of cattle in the island, 'that he babbled of green fields.' There are now, out of 20,319,924 acres, only 5,458,945 under crops, or little more than a quarter of the island, though two thirds of its area are better adapted for root crops than for natural grass.

The decrease in woods and plantations just noticed is a fact which deserves the reader's particular attention. In the work already referred to upon the industrial resources of the island, Sir Robert Kane observed that the island was once covered with forests, yet that we may practically exclude wood from our consideration as one of its actual resources: 'The timber grown is not sufficient for those uses for which it is specially adapted, and, as a fact, we may consider it never to be employed.' Twenty years ago Dr. Hancock applied himself to discover the cause of this absence of trees (and whoever compares Dr. Hancock's 'Impediments to the Prosperity of Ireland' with any such book as Sir R. Kane's 'Industrial Resources' will perceive that, twenty years ago, the legislature had abundant information before it how to remove the chief causes of the emigration which has taken place since); and the cause he discovered is admirably illustrated by a communication to Lord Devon's Commission, which we beg our readers to study, not for its direct application to trees only, but for all the analogous impediments to improvement and cultivation it suggests: 'Under the encouragement [says the writer] which I conceived the laws in force afforded to me, I planted trees extensively on lands which I held by a terminable lease. They are mine, I said, to all intents and purposes. I took the best care of them; fenced and protected them; and, of course, paid rent, &c., for the land they grew on for a number of years, and I considered them not only as a shelter and ornament to my place, but as a crop which I was raising on my farm for the benefit of myself and my family. But *legibus aliter visum est*. On taking out a renewal of my lease, it appeared that my crop of timber, most of which had been growing for nearly forty years, while I paid the rent, could not be mine by law. Let me do the landlord no injustice. He had no disposition to possess himself of my trees. He felt that they ought to be mine. But the only lease he could give me was one by which I not only can never call one branch of the trees I planted, protected, and paid for, mine, but by which I am liable to very severe penalties if I cut a switch off any of them .... My lord, 'tis monstrous! Will the face of the country improve under such a law? Shall I be mad enough now to begin planting again, and leave a copy of this statement for my son, with *da capo* written at the end of it, against the expiration of my present lease? No; I may grow furze, or heath, or brambles, but I won't grow timber.'

A legislature of landlords, devising a code of laws for Ireland, has thought only of the landlord; and the ground has been cursed for his sake. Does any one need further illustration of the fundamental policy of that code? He will find it in a passage of the standard treatise on 'The Law of Landlord and Tenant in Ireland,' defining what *waste* is in the eye of the law: ' A tenant has no right to alter the nature of land demised, by converting ancient pasture into arable land, or arable land into wood land, or by enclosing and cultivating waste land included in the demise. If a tenant burn the surface of the land for the purpose of manure, or open pits for the purpose of raising stone or gravel, or carry away gravel or brick earth, or do any act calculated to alter the evidence of the landlord's title, it will be *waste*. If a lessee raise stone in a quarry, or ore in a mine, and the quarry or the mine were not open at the time of the demise, it will be *waste*.'

Is it not rightly named a law of waste? To keep the land of the island unchanged, unchangeable, and unimproved alike in its own condition and its ownership; to keep the world standing still from age to age, and therefore tumbling to decay; to make the interest of the lord of the soil (as it was conceived to be in a time of barbarism) the supreme concern of the law and of the courts of justice; to force the occupier of the ground to bury his talent, regarding his absent lord as a hard man, reaping where he hath not sown, and gathering where he hath not strewed;—such is the policy no fault of which, according to Mr. Lowe, drives either capital or labour from Ireland. The right honourable member adds that all the Parliamentary inquiries into the results of the law have not made out a single case of grievance or ill-treatment of a tenant; and another member, speaking also as a political economist as well as a senator, cited the evidence collected by Lord Clanricarde's Committee last year in support of his conclusion that the legislature ought to leave things as they are, or leave them to the care of the lords of the soil. From the evidence referred to by the honourable member we cite the following example of the nature and causes of Irish emigration: Mr. Mackay, a landowner and also tenant farmer of 610 acres, states:—

'The late Marquis of Thomond died, and the property was sold, and I witnessed at that sale as cruel a scene as a man could witness. The tenantry had no leases; they thought no evil could befall them, having such a good man for their landlord. I saw at the sale a man with his friends around him, who had a small farm that he had improved upon the coast, hoping to purchase the little spot. After taking with him all the money that he could possibly manage to raise, he failed in effecting what he desired, *and he went away to America.*'

It will be observed that this poor man's farm would have sold for a lower price, and he would have had more money to buy it with, had he never spent a sixpence on improvement; and, again, that he would have been better off with a bad landlord, in whom he could place or misplace no confidence, than with the good or good-natured landlord he had.

Another witness before the same Commission, in reply to a question whether any neighbours of his had, to his knowledge, been turned out of their holdings, or had their rents raised after they had made improvements without a lease, stated:—

'I know there are a great many. I saw people who

did as much improvement as I did myself who were turned out without any remuneration. There were twenty-six families turned out on the 25th of March.

'They were turned out after improving the land?— Yes.

'What sort of tenants were they, large or small?— They were large tenants.

'They were your neighbours, so that you are sure of the facts?—I could tell you who they were. But I understood that the landlord was not aware of it; that it was the agent who did it; and that the landlord was sorry afterwards when he came to know that they were turned out.

'Did it make a great disturbance in the country?— It did, indeed.'

It should be borne in mind that Irish land-agents are paid by a commission, and have a strong personal interest in raising rents; nor can it in any way tend to compensate tenants who have been turned out for that purpose that the landlord may be sorry afterwards, 'when he comes to know it.' The evidence of a third witness before the committee, a solicitor, showed moreover that the landlord himself may not always be reluctant to raise the rent if he sees any signs of improvement or comfort about a farm :—

'A considerable part of my practice consists in the loan of money on mortgage, and I have been constantly asked by farmers to invest money for them on mortgage. They have told me as a matter of great secrecy that they had saved certain sums of money, and they were afraid to invest these moneys on their farms, inasmuch as they had no hold, as they expressed it, of the land; and they requested me to try and find some place where it would be safe. They also assured me that they were afraid to let the landlord or the agent know that they had it. They were afraid not only to invest it, as it ought to be invested, on their farms, but actually to let it be known that they had it, or to assume other appearances of comfort. Moreover, we know from bank returns that Irish farmers have actually 17,000,000*l*. lying idle in banks.

'Do you really think there was the slightest foundation for such a fear?—I do, most sincerely; and I am quite certain that in many cases it would be highly imprudent for a tenant, holding his land at will, to let the agent for the property know that he was worth a thousand pounds, and had saved it from the proceeds of his agriculture. His rent may be raised, or some fine required.

'You really think so?—I am cognisant of an instance in the county of Cork within the last few months.'

Lord Dufferin has cited as an argument in favour of emigration, a passage in which Mr. Fawcett remarks that 'the world was made for the occupation of the human race, and it never could have been intended that fertile soils should grow nothing but rank and useless vegetation; it never could have been intended that rivers which might stimulate the production of untold wealth should continue to flow through solitudes.' But the principal cause of emigration from Ireland is, that fertile soils *do* grow nothing but rank and useless vegetation, and that rivers, lakes, and seas which might stimulate the production of untold wealth *do* wash solitudes, while the labour which might fill those solitudes with wealth is sent abroad to develop the resources of other lands, with laws less inhospitable to industry and less hostile to improvement. Mr. Lowe, designating his own reasoning with perfect propriety, says : ' Thus we get into this vicious circle,—Ireland is miserable, because capital cannot be brought into it to take the people from the cultivation of the land— to which employment their energies are too much restricted—and capital cannot be brought into it because Irishmen will assert that the condition of the country is worse than it is. What is required to bring about a happier time? Why, capital ought to be thrown into it, with which manufactures could be established.'

We have shown why the cultivation of the land affords such poor and scanty employment, but it is the same with manufactures. ' It is vain,' says Dr. Hancock, citing a striking example of manufacturing enterprise excluded by the operation of settlements, to which we know many parallels, ' to tell the people that it is their fault if they have not employment at millspinning like their neighbours, when the law stops the erection of mills.' * Lord Dufferin himself has expressed a conviction that ' were it not for the agitation which now scares capital from its shores, and prevents the development of her industrial resources, Ireland might be rendered capable of sustaining a population

---

* See 'Impediments to the Prosperity of Ireland,' chap. xix., and 'Fortnightly Review,' February 1868, p. 142.

far larger than it has ever borne.' But the same noble lord, referring to certain ancient restrictions on commerce and manufactures, says, 'Would you see what Ireland might have been, go to Belfast. Would you ascertain how the numerical strength of a nation may be multiplied, go to Belfast: where, within a single generation, the population has quadrupled, and the wages of labour have more than doubled.'

We have gone to Belfast, and traversing its quarters have many times passed through a long, dismal, decaying suburban street, bordered by waste ground, which reminded us, by its contrast with the life and riches of the rest of the town, of an historian's remark upon the valley of the Nile: 'Even in the valley itself, the separation of the fruitful land from the solitary waste is distinctly seen: the empire of life borders on the empire of death.' On investigating the causes of this contrast we were not remitted to ancient and nonexisting restrictions upon trade. During the very generation in which the population of the rest of Belfast has quadrupled, while individual wealth has more than doubled (which it never would have done but for an Act of Parliament that made the ground they occupy an instrument of production for a commercial community instead of the instrument of political power for a single proprietor, as it had previously been), the unbuilt part of the suburb referred to has been the subject of a protracted law-suit between that same proprietor and another noble; while the part which is occupied by decaying and ruinous houses belongs at present to a third great proprietor (with reversion to one of the two others), who cannot give a lease of sufficient length to tempt builders. A part of this very suburb, in which perpetual interests could be purchased, has been renovated like the rest of the town, and is the site of one of its principal enterprises.

We may thus dismiss to the final receptacle of what have been called *sophismes économiques* the theory that the rise in the price of labour proves and measures the benefit of emigration to Ireland. A much more rational criterion has been suggested by a judicious writer who distinguishes between the first flight of the famine-stricken victims of the potato disease, and the emigration in steamers of later years. Admitting the soundness of the distinction, we, however, include in one economic category of wasteful depopulation the whole exodus caused by obstacles to the development of the industrial resources of the island. The whole stream of emigration which flows from that source—from imprisoned natural wealth, from the legal insecurity of industrial enterprise and improvement—is a current of decline, not of progress; and it is among the grave mischiefs of the doctrines so sedulously diffused respecting the advantage of emigration, that it misleads the mind of the public and of the Irish proprietors to look for a cure of the evils of Ireland in one of the results of their perpetuation. If the natural resources of Ireland had been made as accessible as those of America, in a cosmopolitan sense (though not necessarily in reference to the interests of Ireland or the United Kingdom even in that case), whatever emigration might have taken place, might be pronounced natural and beneficial. But so long as Ireland has natural resources undeveloped, and capital unemployed, through the state of the law, the departure of the flower of the population must be laid to the charge of the legislature as a calamity resulting from its neglect. 'The law is the same in England,' a legislator answers. The law of tenure is not the same, as a legislator ought to know; still less are the customs the same upon which the law in both islands is based. And it is upon a country with the calamitous history of Ireland that a legal system has been imposed, of which the results even in England are to be seen in the faces of its crowded city population, and of its degraded agricultural labourers. At the beginning of this article reference was made to the frequent confusion under a common name of different and even opposite phenomena, of industrial energy with the love of idle power under the name of private interest, or the desire of wealth, of the most unequal means of payment and unequal wages, under the denomination of an aggregate wages fund, of demands which are not supplied along with demands which are, under the formula of demand and supply. We believe that candid readers of these pages will pronounce not only that the history of Ireland has been one long profligate waste of national resources of every kind, but that one of the most monstrous episodes in that history is the waste of industrial power, and of national strength which takes the name of emigration, along with that widely different movement of industrial enterprise and colonising vigour which peoples and reclaims the waste places of the earth. On April 1, 1845 the population of Ireland was not far short of eight millions and a half; on April 1, 1868 it was little above five millions and a half; on April 1, 1871, there is reason to believe it will scarcely exceed the population of Belgium on little more than a third of the space. So much the better, we have heard it said; Ireland ought to be a sheep-farm for England. And why not England a sheep-farm for France? as it perhaps might have become before now but for its over populated cities, and the mines in which its people can be packed under ground.

What must be the feeling of the exiled peasantry of Ireland at the other side of the Atlantic, when a grave American professor, in a treatise on the principles of political economy, speaks as follows of Irish emigration?—'The policy of English landlords is to depopulate their estates, to make the peasantry give place to flocks and herds as in the north of Scotland, or to compel them to emigrate to foreign lands as in Ireland. Thus they imitate the system which has been practised for centuries in the Roman Campagna, which reduced the fields of Italy in the age of Pliny to a desert, and subsequently surrendered them to the northern barbarians because there were not men enough to defend them.' The political instinct must be absent from the present generation, if it does not see the wrong which is being done to the next one—a wrong in the strictest economic sense as regards the loss of security as well as of industrial power.

> Audiet pugnas vitio parentum
> Rara juventus.

POLITICAL ECONOMY AND THE TENURE OF LAND.*

THE proposal of the Government to give the tenantry of Ireland some legal security for improvements has been encountered by an objection, claiming to possess the authority of an economic maxim, and seeking to stifle *in limine* all legislation in favour of tenants, on the ground that it is a settled principle of political economy that the management of private property should be left to private interest; and that the relation of landlord and tenant being one of contract, the sole duty of the State is to enforce the performance of contracts. At first sight, this might appear to derive strong confirmation from the general tendency of the jurisprudence of societies, as they advance in civilisation to extend the sphere of free contract, and to curtail that of control on the part of the State. Mr. Maine, in his philosophical comparison of modern with ancient law, observes, ' The society of our day is mainly distinguished from that of preceding generations by the largeness of the sphere which is occupied in it by contract. . . . The science of political economy would fail to correspond with the facts of life, if it were not true that imperative law had abandoned the largest

* Reprinted from the 'Fortnightly Review,' June 1, 1866.

part of the field which it once occupied. The bias, indeed, of most persons trained in political economy, is to consider the general truth as entitled to become universal; and when they apply this science as an art, their efforts are ordinarily directed to enlarging the province of contract, and to curtailing that of imperative law, except so far as law is necessary to enforce the performance of contracts.'* But it is very remarkable that as regards the relation of landlord and tenant, the tendency, both of the jurisprudence of our Courts and of the direct legislation of Parliament, has been steadily in the opposite direction to that described by Mr. Maine; step after step has been taken to give tenants by law a security and encouragement for improvements which their own contracts fail to afford. The question arises whether these interpositions of the law are really violations of the policy of non-interference, except to secure the protection of property and the performance of contracts? I shall endeavour to show that such interferences not only are based on the very principle of economical policy on account of which the State does interfere to protect property and enforce contracts, but fall far short of affording the degree of security which the position of tenants and the interests of the public, especially in Ireland, require.

It was not until the last century that the Courts, exercising, as they have often beneficially done, their power of indirect legislation in opposition to the old common law, decided that buildings and other fixtures

* 'Ancient Law,' chap. ix.

for the purposes of trade or manufacture should, without any special agreement, become the property of the tenant, if erected by him. 'The reason which induced the Courts to relax the strictness of the old rules of law, and to admit an innovation in this particular instance, was that the commercial interests of the country might be advanced by the encouragement given to tenants to employ their capital in making improvements for carrying on their trade, with the certainty of having the benefit of their expenditure secured to them at the end of their terms.'* The principle of this change in the law was extended by subsequent decisions to fixtures connected with mining, and some other improvements. In the case of agricultural fixtures, the legislature directly interfered to give tenants similar protection. In 1848, a Parliamentary Committee on Agricultural Customs recommended the application of the principle established by the Courts in the case of trade-fixtures, to fixtures for agricultural purposes; and, in 1851, an Act was passed, making farm-buildings erected by tenants, with the landlord's consent, the property of the tenant. In 1860, this provision was extended by Mr. Cardwell's Act. Almost the only benefit of these enactments, however, lies in the principle they establish of the tenant's right to benefit by his own improvements; for they afford little substantial protection, and would afford little, even if they covered in terms, cases such as drainage, and the reclamation of waste land, to which they do not apply. To permit the Irish tenant to take

* Amos and Ferard on the 'Law of Fixtures.

down the materials of his buildings and take up those of his drains, and remove them, it may be to America, is to permit him to add to the loss he has already sustained by their construction. Yet to give him any other form of compensation is supposed by many landlords to be both revolutionary legislation and heretical political economy. I shall attempt to show that it is neither. The majority of landholders seem to misapprehend altogether both their legal and economical situation. They seem to imagine both that the law has conferred on them the same absolute dominion over the land in which they have estates, as traders have over their goods; and that the public can place the same reliance on the private interest of the landlord as on that of the trader, to insure good management and improvement. Those who entertain such opinions need to be reminded in the first place, that the law of the country has maintained from the Conquest that fundamental distinction between property in land, and all other kinds of property, for which Mr. Mill has contended on the ground of theoretical justice.

No Act of Parliament is required to establish the subordination of private property in land to the interests of the State; the land itself belongs by law to the State;* the highest interest in it which any subject can possess is a tenure in fee under the Crown; nor can the Crown either create a higher estate or absolve the existing landholders of the condition of

* ' The first thing the student has to do, is to get rid of the idea of absolute ownership. Such an idea is quite unknown to the English law. No man is in law the absolute owner of lands. He can only hold an estate in them.'—*Williams on the Law of Real Property.*

tenure. The nature and obligations of this tenure deserve some slight notice. From the Conquest to the Restoration the greater part of the land of the realm in private hands was held under a military, and the remainder under a civil tenure. When military tenure was extinguished on the Restoration, the legislature, instead of abolishing the condition of tenure altogether, converted it into the civil tenure of socage,— a name which has unfortunately become nearly obsolete along with the class of socage tenants who once fulfilled its obligations. Anciently the king's socage tenants held, as Lord Bacon says, ' by continual service of ploughing his land, repairing his houses, parks, pales, and the like.' The ancient socage tenant was thus a very different character from the modern one. He was the farmer himself; and it was on account of the importance of security of tenure for the encouragement of farming, that he could not be ousted so long as he performed the services appertaining to his tenure, and that he was exempted from military duties. All the highest ancient legal authorities, including Bracton, Britton, Littleton, Coke and Lord Bacon, derive the name of socage tenure from a plough. Another derivation from *soc*, a privilege, seems to have been suggested by the privileges, especially that of security of tenure, which, for the encouragement of agriculture, the soc-man enjoyed. The value of this class of independent cultivators did not indeed consist solely in their services to the country as farmers. Mr. Hallam speaks of the original soc-men as ' the root of a noble plant, the free socage tenants, or English yeomanry, whose independence has stamped with peculiar features both our constitution and our national character.' That noble plant has been almost extirpated from the soil; socage tenure, by becoming in most cases, in fact, naked proprietorship, has become so as a right in the estimation of the socage tenants themselves.

But although they can hardly be called upon now to fulfil in its integrity the literal condition of their tenure, it is at least the duty of the State to provide that they shall not refuse to the farmers, whom they put in their place, the essential conditions of good farming. They remain the socage tenants of the Crown; and this negative obligation is a very light one to fasten on their tenure, and a very lenient interpretation of the maxim, that landed property has its duties as well as its rights. To enforce such an obligation is the more properly the express duty of the State, since the existence of a non-cultivating class of proprietors, and the whole structure of landed property in this country, with its large estates and few owners, are traceable, not to the natural course of commerce and succession, but to the interference of the law, which substituted primogeniture and entails for the ancient custom of equal partition. And while, through this interference of the law, the number of the owners of land has steadily diminished in most parts of the country, and its monopoly become stricter, the demand for land for a variety of purposes is yearly increasing with the increase of wealth, trade, and population, and the portion applied to other purposes constantly diminishes the extent left to supply the first requisites of existence to the people. Parks, gardens, villas, factories, railways, and urban improvements are yearly encroaching upon the demesne both of national agriculture and national habitation. Mr. Mill finds a natural claim on the part of the State for the public to the absolute ownership of land, in the fact that man did not make it : ' It is the original inheritance of the whole species.' It must be confessed that the original common, or patrimony of the tribe, was in these islands, and still more so in Holland and Belgium, a very poor property, and that to take land out of a state of nature has been the great problem of agriculture. That problem requires for its solution the permission of private possession ; yet the State cannot abandon its paramount proprietorship, not only because land may be directed altogether to unproductive uses by private proprietors, but because it is the sphere, not of agriculture alone, but of every form of human industry, and even human existence,— a consideration of constantly growing importance, now that the difficulty of finding house accommodation for the people, and room to live and move and have their being, has already become urgently felt. No principle of political economy is better settled than that the maxim of *laisser faire* is inapplicable to a monopoly of the necessaries of life, and the law of the country has not only created such a monopoly, but armed its possessors with powers of enforcing the terms it enables them to grant, such as it has not conferred upon the owners of any other commodity.

It has, however, been urged, even by economists of the eminence of Mr. Lowe, that the best security the public can obtain for the good management of land is the personal interest of its private holders. The desire of wealth, it is urged, must impel the possessors of land, like the owners of capital in trade, to make the best commercial and productive use they can of their possessions. Political economy, I must affirm, countenances no such assumption. The desire of wealth is far from being a productive impulse under all circumstances; it is, on the contrary, sometimes a predatory one. And the fundamental assumption of political economy with respect to it is, that men desire to get wealth with the least possible trouble, exertion, and sacrifice; that besides wealth they desire ease, pleasure, social position, and political power; and that they will combine all the gratification they can of their other desires with the acquisition of wealth. The situation of the inheritor of a large landed estate is entirely different from that of the trader, of whom (trained to habits of business, exposed to competition, and influenced not only by the desire of gain, but by the fear of being driven from the market altogether by better producers) it is true that the best security the public can have for the good management of his capital is his own private interest. It is as contrary to political economy as to common sense to assume that a rich sinecure tends to make its possessor industrious and improving; and the landholders of this country are the holders, not only of rich sinecures, but of sinecures the value of which tends steadily, and often rapidly, to increase without any exertion on their part. Even 'producers and dealers,' Mr. Mill has observed, ' when relieved from the immediate stimulus of competition, grow indifferent to the dictates of their ultimate pecuniary interest, preferring to the most hopeful prospects the present ease of adhering to routine. A person who is already thriving seldom puts himself out of the way to commence even a lucrative improvement, unless urged by the additional motive of fear lest some rival should supplant him.' And, economically speaking, landlords are not producers but consumers—*fruges consumere nati*; nor is it in human nature that they should, as a class, devote themselves to production, like persons engaged in a competitive trade. It would, indeed, be their pecuniary interest to do so, but that is not their sole interest. 'A man's interest,' says Mr. Mill, ' consists of whatever he takes interest *in*.' And the interest of the proprietors of land is, according to the assumption their own conduct compels us to make, to get as much, not only of money, but of amusement, social consideration, and political influence as they can, making as little sacrifice as they can in return for any of those advantages, in the shape of leases to their tenants, the improvement of their estates, or even residence upon them when other places are more agreeable. That they are frequently guided solely by their interest in this sense is borne out by notorious facts; by absenteeism, by the frequent absence of all improvement on the part of the landlord and the refusal of any security to the tenant, by the mischievous extent of the preservation of game and the extension of deer forests over what once was cultivated land. The single circumstance that tenancy from year to year, a tenure incompatible with good agriculture, is the commonest tenure in both England and Ireland, affords positive proof that the interest of the landlord is no security to the public for the good management of the land in the absence of all interference of law.

Let us look next at the interest of the tenant. *His* interest it certainly is, upon economical principles, to cultivate and improve the land to the best of his power, provided he is secure of reaping the fruits of his labour and outlay. He is a farmer by profession, with the habits of one, and exposed to much competition; he has his livelihood to make, and he would of course be glad to make his fortune, too, by his farming. The public can therefore count upon the tenant doing his best by the land, if he is sure of deriving the benefit. But if he has no prospect of doing so, it becomes, on the contrary, his interest to labour only for the present, and to employ his savings and leisure anywhere rather than upon the permanent improvement of his farm. And that he cannot obtain the requisite security from contract alone, is evident both from what has been said of the interest and conduct of landlords in the matter, and from the fact previously mentioned that the courts and the legislature have found it necessary to interpose law after law to secure the property in their own improvements to the tenants. There is, indeed, only one kind of contract which would give adequate security for every kind of agricultural improvement, and it is one which landlords almost universally refuse—namely, a lease of sufficient length to compensate for all possible improvements. Even if landlords were willing, which they are not, to covenant beforehand in every short lease to compensate for all improvements there specified by the tenant, the contract would be inadequate, since the tenant cannot foresee what improvements he may be able to make. What capital he may save, succeed to, or borrow, he cannot foretell; and experience of his farm, the progress of science and art, and the course of commerce and prices, may alter his plans altogether. But since tenants cannot obtain under contract the security they require, the State, upon the narrowest view of its province and duties, should interfere to afford them such security. There is one thing which private enterprise cannot produce, that is, security; and to afford it is universally acknowledged to be the proper business of the State. When, therefore, contracts do not by themselves give such security, or exclude it, the State should interfere for the same reason that in ordinary cases it interferes to secure the performance of contracts. For why does the State interfere to enforce contracts, save to promote confidence, and to encourage industry, invention, thrift, and improvement? Its interference for the security of farmers is in perfect accordance with the true meaning of the maxim of *laisser faire*, which originated in the answer of a merchant to Colbert, the Minister of Louis XIV. The Minister asked what the King could do for trade, and the merchant replied that his Majesty should *laisser faire et passer*; * that is to say, that people engaged in

---

* This aphorism has also been attributed to M. de Gournay, a friend of Quesnay, and one of the physiocrats; but the above appears to be the true account.

production and trade should be enabled by the State to manage their business as they think best, and that a non-trading class should not control them, or deprive them of the liberty and security the business requires.

These considerations would justify the interference of the State to afford agricultural tenants in England greater security than they at present enjoy. But the claim of the tenant in Ireland on the protection of the State is infinitely stronger. The landholders of Ireland are not only, in the same sense as those of England, the creatures, the tenants of the State, but they are the creatures of a violent interference with pre-existing rights of property. Moreover, by further violent interference in the shape of penal laws, directed expressly against industry and accumulation on the part of the bulk of the people, and precluding the acquisition of property and capital and the rise of other industries, the State forced the great mass of the population to become competitors for the occupation of land as a means of subsistence. They were thus placed even more at the mercy of the landlord than the Egyptians were at the mercy of Pharaoh in the famine, for their lands as well as their cattle and money were gone, and nothing remained to exchange for bread but their bodies and their labour. Rent under these circumstances became, not what political economists define it, the surplus above average wages and profit, but the surplus above minimum wages, without any profit at all. Instead of the conditions to which the maxim of non-interference applies, is a system of interference which has made the landlord independent of all exercise of frugality and improvement, and deprived the tenant of all security for it. And the natural consequence is that neither landlords nor tenants, as a rule, make any improvements, and there are parts of the island in which the soil has actually deteriorated.

The provisions of the Government Bill * relating to tenants' improvements in Ireland have met with the obvious objection, that the valuation is proposed at the determination of the tenure, when no just estimate may be possible of the increased value fairly attributable to the outlay and labour of the tenant. And it is has been suggested that a valuation of the tenant's outlay at the time it is made would insure just compensation. But even this would not suffice. A progressive fall in the value of money, from the increased production of the precious metals, would lead to the repayment of the tenant's expenditure in a depreciated currency, and would not even restore his pecuniary outlay by an equivalent sum. Again, there are many important improvements, such as the reclamation of waste land, which in Ireland are effected mainly by the labour of the tenant, spread over a number of years, and the value of which can only be judged by the result, and cannot be measured while being made by any official valuation. But, thirdly, the main object of legislation should be to induce, and if necessary to compel, landlords to grant sufficient leases to afford compensation by mere length of possession. Leases of sufficient length have the double advantage of disposing the tenant to improve his farm as a whole by all the means

* The Bill of 1866, when this article was written.

in his power (instead of confining his aim to the particular improvements it may be easiest to recover compensation for), and of recompensing him without the intervention of any external authority, or the risk of dispute with his landlord.

The merit of the Government Bill is that, but for one fatal and contradictory clause, its provisions would make it the interest of landlords to grant leases of considerable length, in order to avoid all claims for specific improvements at the end of the tenure. This merit is lost by a clause enabling the landlord to avoid all claims by a written prohibition of all improvements, as well as by a lease. It has, indeed, been urged as an objection to leases in Ireland, that the holdings are already too small, and that long leases have been found to lead to subdivision. The answer to this, in the first place, is, that without better security than is afforded at present, neither large nor small holdings can be even tolerably farmed, not to say highly; and the prevailing tenancy at will is the very worst system upon which land can be held, next to that of cultivation by slaves. Moreover, the comparative productiveness of the two systems of husbandry has been by no means decisively settled against small farms. 'The larger farms in Flanders,' says M. de Laveleye, 'tend constantly towards subdivision, for the very simple reason that when subdivided they yield a much larger rent. This subdivision, too, increases the gross, not less than the net, produce. It is an accredited opinion that large farming alone can give to the soil the proper crops, and devote to it the requisite capital to call all its productive forces into action. In Flanders it is the reverse which is true. In general, the smaller the farm the greater the produce of the soil. Cultivators and proprietors alike rejoice in the subdivision—the former because it places more land within their reach, the latter because it doubles their rents. It is in East Flanders, the country of small farms *par excellence*, that statistics most clearly attest the perfection of husbandry, and the amount of production to which land so subdivided gives birth. There each cultivator, having for the exercise of his industry little more than a single hectare (about $2\frac{1}{2}$ acres), feeds as many individuals as an English cultivator feeds with the produce of three hectares.' *

It is true that the small farmers of Flanders derive but scanty incomes for their own support; but this is so partly from the higher proportionate rents which they pay, partly through the immense competition for land which the excess of population and the love of agriculture create, and partly because the customary term of a Flemish lease is altogether too short, although coupled with a tenant-right in unexhausted improvements.

The objection that long leases were found formerly to lead to subdivision in Ireland, deserves little attention on several accounts. In many cases the subdivision was more nominal than real, the land comprised in the

---

* 'Essai sur l'Économie rurale de la Belgique.' Deuxième édition. 1863. This admirable essay formed the subject of a special report to the Academy of France, by M. de Lavergne. Its author is not only distinguished as an Economist, but intimately acquainted with practical agriculture in Belgium.

original demise having been chiefly waste land which was thus brought into cultivation; and although a division took place, there was no real subdivision of the amount of land in cultivation. Moreover, the subdivision, where it was real, was created partly by penal laws, which prevented parents from providing otherwise for their children: and partly by the expenses attending the sale of interests in land, which made it easier to sub-let than to sell, especially with the aid of the law of distress. An improved system of transfer of all interests in land is an essential part of legislation in favour of tenants and agriculture. Lastly, if it be true that the tendency of husbandry is necessarily towards large farms, it is clear that the small holders will be compelled to part with their farms, and subdivision will be impossible.

The chief practical objections to legislation on the subject are really, on the one hand, the objections of landholders to abandon any part of the absolute control over the soil which, as I have attempted to show, they have no claim to, either upon legal or economical grounds; and, on the other hand, the objection of legislators to grapple with a difficult question. For the Legislature to leave Ireland as it is, would be, in Bacon's phrase, 'to enact a law of neglect,' not to act upon the economical maxim of *laisser faire*.

LORD DUFFERIN ON THE TENURE OF LAND.*

At the opening of his work upon Democracy, M. de Tocqueville sketches in a few sentences the political history of Europe for seven hundred years, from a time 'at which the right of governing descended with family inheritances, force was the only means by which man could act upon man, and landed property was the sole source of power.' Hardly a single event of importance in history, he proceeds, not one step in human progress since then, not one acquisition material or immaterial to the domain of civilization, but has raised rivals to the great landed proprietors, placed sources of social and political power at the disposal of new classes, and tended to the furtherance of equality. ' Poetry, eloquence, memory, the charms of wit, the glow of imagination, profoundness of thought, all the gifts which Heaven imparts indiscriminately, have turned to the advantage of democracy; and even when they have been found in the possession of its opponents, they have still done service to its cause by bringing into relief man's natural greatness; its conquests have spread therefore with those of civilization

* Reprinted from 'Macmillan's Magazine,' July 1867.

and knowledge, and literature has become an arsenal open to all, in which the weak and the poor have found arms every day.' Whoever uses M. de Tocqueville's eyes to read the signs of the time, will accordingly see in the part taken by Lord Dufferin—at once a noble, a landowner, and a man of letters and genius—in the controversy relating to land, not a vindication of its proprietors which will exempt their conduct henceforward from scrutiny, but a mark of the irresistible force of a movement which is setting up rivals in every direction to inherited distinctions and territorial power; rendering public opinion the sovereign authority, and the public good the sole foundation on which institutions, however ancient, can base their continuance;—above all, making landed property, once the sole source of legislation, now its recognised subject and creature, possessed of no title which is not derived from the public advantage, and amenable in all its relations to the control of the State. A great step has been made towards making the use of landed property reasonable, when its proprietors themselves begin to reason about it; not only is it a sign that they are ceasing to rely solely on power, but it exposes whatever is indefensible in their pretensions to immediate detection. A fool is said to be wiser in his own conceit than seven men that can render a reason, but sometimes he is wise beyond his conceit, for it may be ten times harder to answer folly than reason. The old vague and intractable assertions of 'the rights of property,' for example, however little to the intellectual credit of those who employed them, were not without an impenetrable power of resistance to argument, which enabled them to hold ground; just as the stupidest animals are the most obstinate in an encounter, because they cannot see when they are beaten, and hold on to the death.

If, however, such characteristics as the foregoing of the great movement delineated in M. de Tocqueville's pages may awaken pleasure and hope in the minds of his disciples, others, unfortunately, are not wanting which cannot be viewed without both regret and alarm, even by those whose confidence is strongest that it is upon the whole a movement for good. Not the least portentous among these is that growing severance of the peasantry from the soil, and that increasingly selfish and exclusive use of dominion over it by its proprietors, of which M. de Tocqueville speaks as follows:—' An aristocracy does not die like a man in a day. Long before open war has broken out against it, the bond which had united the higher classes with the lower is seen to loosen by degrees; the relations between the poor and the rich become fewer and less kindly; rents rise. This is not actually the result of democratic revolution, but it is its certain indication. For an aristocracy which has definitively let the heart of the people slip from its hands is like a tree which is dead at its roots, and which the winds overturn the more easily the higher it is. I have often heard great English proprietors congratulate themselves that they derive much more money from their estates than their fathers did. They may be in the right to rejoice, but assuredly they do not know at what they rejoice.

They imagine they are making a net profit when they are only making an exchange. What they gain in money they are on the point of losing in power. . . . There is yet another sign that a great democratic movement is being accomplished or is in preparation. In the middle age almost all landed property was let in perpetuity, or at least for a very long term. When one studies the economy of that period, one finds that leases for ninety years were commoner than leases for twelve years are now.' In his celebrated Essay on M. de Tocqueville's book, Mr. Mill has with similar prescience remarked that without a large agricultural class, with an attachment to the soil, a permanent connection with it, and the tranquillity and simplicity of rural habits and tastes, there can be no check to the total predominance of an unsettled, uneasy, gain-seeking, commercial democracy. 'Our town population,' it has long been remarked, 'is becoming almost as mobile and uneasy as the American. It ought not to be so with our agriculturists; they ought to be the counterbalancing element in the national character; they should represent the type opposite to the commercial—that of moderate wishes, tranquil tastes, and cultivation of the enjoyments compatible with their existing position. To attain this object, how much alteration may be requisite in the system of rack-renting and tenancy-at-will we cannot undertake to show in this place.' *

So, in a late debate upon Irish tenures, in Parliament, it was argued with unanswerable force by Mr. Gregory, in reference to the tenure now generally pre-

* 'Dissertations and Discussions,' ii. 75.

valent in the island: 'There could be no attachment to the institutions of a country in which the whole of a peasantry existed merely on sufferance; certainly there was nothing conservative in tenancies at will: indeed he believed such tenancies to be the most revolutionary in the world.' The conclusion is irresistible that the true revolutionary party in Ireland are unconsciously and unwillingly, but not the less certainly, the owners of land. When therefore it is alleged that the chronic absence of tranquillity and the periodical recurrence of sedition prevent the rise of other occupations than agriculture, thereby placing almost the whole population at the mercy of the landlords, who can in consequence impose unreasonable terms, the answer is obvious,—first, that prosperous agriculture and continued political tranquillity are equally incompatible with such a tenure; secondly, that a prosperous agriculture is itself the true natural source and support of all other industries; and thirdly, that the allegation itself involves an admission that the power of the landlords is excessive. So far, moreover, is the competition for land from being the cause—it could in no case be the excuse—of the insecurity of tenure in Ireland, that the immense reduction in the population and the number of the competitors for the occupation of land has been attended with increased insecurity. Before the failure of the potato, the Devon Commission urged the interference of Parliament, because the industry of the cultivators of the soil was paralysed by insecurity. 'The most general and indeed universal complaint,' they reported, 'brought before us in every part of Ireland was, " the want of tenure," to use the expression most commonly employed by the witnesses. The uncertainty of tenure is constantly referred to as a pressing grievance by all classes of tenants. It is said to paralyse all exertion, and to place a fatal impediment in the way of improvement. We have no doubt that this is so in many instances.' Since that Report, famine and emigration have reduced the population by nearly three millions in twenty-one years, and statesmen of both parties have repeatedly adopted the conclusion of the Devon Commission, both as regards the effects of the insecurity of tenure and the necessity of interference. Yet the actual condition of things is that the radical evil has increased—that leases have become fewer and evictions more frequent. So lost to the Irish proprietor's mind is indeed the very conception of a true rural population and of the best uses of land, that even so enlightened a landlord as Lord Dufferin regards the love of the soil, and of a little farm of his own on the part of the peasant, not as a healthy affection and natural blending of associations, not as the true spirit of agriculture and the germ of many social and civil virtues, not as the best ally of industrious enterprise in other pursuits, but as a morbid and mischievous propensity to be condemned and discouraged. His lordship's ideal of a happy and prosperous peasant seems to be the English agricultural labourer with no root in the soil, no interest in it, and no love for it; and he proposes to the small farmer as a means of improving his condition, a descent to the rank of a labourer for hire. Speaking in the House of Lords last year, the noble lord said: 'From an inherent desire to possess land, and in a most unhappy fancy that he loses caste if he passes from the condition of an embarrassed tenant to that of an independent labourer, the tenant is ready to run any risk rather than abandon his favourite pursuit.' The same leading idea presents itself again and again both in his lordship's letters to the *Times* and in his recent volume.* For example: —'In proportion as the peasant becomes aware of a more hopeful theatre for his industry, whether at home or abroad, that morbid hunger for a bit of land which has been the bane of Ireland will subside.' . . . 'The labourer's dream is to become a tenant, the tenant's greatest ambition is to enjoy the dignity of a landlord. What he cannot be brought to realize is that an independent labourer is a more respectable person than a struggling farmer.' . . . 'The alternative of adequate wages is open to him; the reckless acquisition of land to which he cannot do justice is the result of a passion to be discouraged rather than stimulated.'

If the actual use of land throughout Great Britain had not given rise to a singular set of conceptions with regard to its true use, it would be superfluous to urge that political economy has always recognized in the pleasures of rural life and occupations—in the love of a farm and the sense of independence it should be so held as to bestow—in the desire of the labourer to become a tenant-farmer and of the tenant-farmer to possess land of his own—not only legitimate sources of

* 'Irish Emigration and the Tenure of Land in Ireland.' By Lord Dufferin.

happiness, but motives to agricultural industry, beyond its pecuniary returns, which both the laws and the customs of a country ought to foster. 'The beauty of the country,' says Adam Smith, 'the pleasures of country life, the tranquillity of mind which it promises, and wherever the injustice of human laws does not disturb, the independence which it really affords, have charms that more or less attract everybody; and as to cultivate the ground was the original destination of man, so in every age he seems to retain a predilection for the primitive employment.' The productive value of the affectionate interest in the land which the Continental peasant feels, after what Mr. Mill has done to make it known to insular minds, ought to need no allusion. Moreover, the social distinctions between labourer and tenant-farmer, and between the tenant-farmer and the farmer of his own land, are natural distinctions, and political economy has always recognized the desire of men to rise in the social scale as an incentive to industry, frugality, and enterprise. The Irish labourer's dream of becoming a tenant is a just and laudable ambition, capable of being turned to the most productive account; and so again is the dream of the tenant to possess land of his own. The existence of peasant proprietors, the facility and frequency of the purchase of small estates, are among the principal causes of the prodigies performed by the peasants of Flanders on almost the worst soil in the world—because constituting both objects of industry and thrift and models of good farming.

'In Belgium,' Lord Dufferin states, 'leases for three,

six, and nine years are the accepted terms.' They are the accepted terms, because better terms are not offered. But M. de Laveleye writes :—' Three, six, and nine years cannot be properly called the approved terms in Belgium. They are approved only by the landlords. All the independent agricultural associations, all the economists are for long leases, and that is my own opinion. Tenancies at will would be considered here as an odious abuse. In Flanders, too, the farmer gets a good house, and his right to be reimbursed for unexhausted manure is a privilege which descends from the middle age, the good effects of which are always acknowledged. The number of peasant proprietors is besides very great. If Ireland had but half as many, it would, I imagine, be well for her.' *

If, however, to talk of peasant proprietors in these islands sounds like talking sedition, the peasant's love of the land and ambition to rise in agricultural rank might be turned to productive account, without permitting a poor man to possess a farm as proprietor. That upward movement which ought to be possible in all occupations, may be made possible in agriculture, even in the British isles, under a rational system of tenure, and with a judicious diversity in the sizes of farms. ' I cannot,'—writes Dr. Mackenzie of Eileanach, after long and extensive experience of estates, and of Celtic tenants, who are supposed to possess in a peculiar degree a morbid hunger for land,—' imagine greater folly than discouraging the planting of a number of cotters on every estate, from the class with, say a

* Letter to the writer.

quarter of an acre, who will supply the labour needed by the large farmer, up to the five-acre holder, whose strength is needed to crop his own land and manage his own estate. Next should come the two-horse farm, a fair object of ambition to which the five-acre cotter might expect to rise; after that, farms of several pairs of horses, or even steam-engines perhaps. An estate or country thus planted, would offer a reasonable variety of objects of ambition to the intelligent labourer who had to begin at the bottom of the ladder; so that he might wish to remain in Great Britain, instead of emigrating, and leaving behind him the mere refuse of his class " as hewers and drawers," without a prospect of anything in life but hard labour (harder than in our jails) and the workhouse when they are used up.' *

Instead of such an upward movement as Dr. Mackenzie describes, from the rank of the labourer to that of the small farmer, and again from the small to the large farm, the movement which Lord Dufferin commends to the peasant's acceptance is a downward one—' from the condition of an embarrassed tenant to that of an independent labourer.' What kind of ' independence ' does the labourer really enjoy? a choice of masters, from a shilling to one and sixpence a day, or even more, while he is active and strong, and the workhouse in his old age. The tenant of a farm, however small, with the security of a lease of sufficient duration, is surely much more independent. He is not subject to orders or to immediate dismissal, his time is at his own disposal, he works for himself when he is

* Letter to the writer, March 11, 1867.

well, he need not work if he is ill, and he earns both wages and profit. It is indeed only to the 'embarrassed' tenant that Lord Dufferin offers the position of labourer on another man's farm; but the general cause of the tenant's embarrassment in Ireland (to which ought to be added the supineness of landlords in regard to instruction in agriculture) is that, virtually, he *is* a mere labourer on another man's farm, for which he is expected to furnish the capital without the security requisite either to borrow it or to expend it if he possesses it, or—what landlords cannot imagine—to *make* it by labour and thrift. 'To refuse a lease to a solvent industrious tenant,' Lord Dufferin justly pronounces, ' is little short of a crime. The prosperity of agriculture depends on security of tenure, and the only proper tenure is a liberal lease.' But if the prosperity of agriculture does depend on security of tenure, and if the only proper tenure is a liberal lease, how can the Irish tenant-at-will be expected to be solvent, or industrious to any good purpose? Must it not be also 'little short of a crime' first to refuse him the conditions of solvency and of prosperous agriculture, and then to make his embarrassment and unprosperous farming a reason for turning him out of his farm? 'Every variation of his conception of property in land,' it has been very well said by Mr. Newman, 'every limitation or extension of proprietary right, develops a new type of human character. If the proprietor, the lessee, the tenant-at-will, differ in extent of proprietary interest, they differ also in moral feature.'* The moral feature

* 'Questions for a Reformed Parliament,' p. 79.

of the tenant-at-will can hardly be that of 'a solvent industrious tenant.' What sort of houses, factories, and shops would be seen in our towns, and what sort of tenants and traders would occupy them, on a tenure at will?

The small farmer in Ireland has little or no capital, it is indeed urged, and good farming is hopeless without it. Yet this difficulty is more serious in Flanders, from the exigent nature of the soil, and M. de Laveleye describes how it is overcome: 'The labourer gets a corner of uncleared land at a low rent, which his wife assists him to clear. They reduce their consumption to the barest necessaries, they economise all they can; the husband goes to a distance, often to France, to reap the harvest, and thus to bring back some fifty francs at the end of three weeks of incredible toils. When they have collected the materials for the cottage, husband and wife go to work, and at length sleep under a roof of their own. The next thing is to have cattle, that foundation of all cultivation. First they feed a goat and some rabbits, and then a calf on the herbs that spring about. When at last they possess a cow, the family is safe; there is now milk, butter, and manure. Little by little a capital is made; at the end of some years, the labourer has become a farmer. As the population increases, new cottages spring up, the old ones are enlarged. In half a century the whole district is made a complete conquest to cultivation, thanks to incessant labours which the capitalist could not have paid for at the average rate of wages without incurring a loss. The petty cultivator, who is assured of enjoying for at least thirty years the fruits of his efforts, spares neither his time nor his trouble. Working with more zeal and intelligence than he could exert for another, he gives value to a soil which *la grande culture* would have no interest in attempting to cultivate.' * The Fleming, however, it may be supposed is an exceptional being. But almost exactly the same thing takes place in the Highlands of Scotland, where the Celtic cotter is given a chance—though a poor one—as Dr. Mackenzie describes it. 'In this country a man comes to me, and offers to rent some acres of waste land, to trench, clear, drain, and cultivate it on a nineteen years' lease for a small rent ; he putting up the cottage, the new land supplying the stones, and I giving him the necessary wood. And generally, with not 10*l.* of his own at starting, we see this man put up his buildings, mostly with his own hands, improve his land, and rise to a considerable degree of prosperity, so as, at least, to have food, good clothing, and decent furniture, and, at the same time, pay his rent with regularity during his lease; at the end of which his land is all in decent crop, ready for a new lease at an improved rent, although all that the landlord has done towards this has been to grant rough standing wood for the buildings. A *theorist* would say, the cotter without capital could never improve his moor. But the fact is, the country *is* improved exactly as I have described. The improver finds work in his vicinity for a time, runs home with his wages, and till they are done, tears up his land, gets some seed borrowed and sown, and off again to

---

* 'Économie rurale des Flandres,' second edition, p. 82.

another job at daily wages, of which less than our southern friends would credit is spent upon food. Had landlords to put up smart cottages for such land improvers, improvement would soon come to an end in this country. In my memory, all hereabout, most of our large farms, extending over thousands and thousands of acres, on which I have shot grouse and deer, have been brought to their present shape on the above plan. For generally,' to the shame of those whom it concerns, Dr. Mackenzie adds, ' soon after a contiguous batch of such crofts as I have described have been put into crop, the improvers are all ejected, without payment for what they have done, unless from some thin-skinned, laughed at, *rara avis* of a philanthropist landlord, and one large farm is made of them.' *

If there are any readers who are doubtful of the disposition of cotters in Ireland to improve, they would do well to consult the evidence of Mr. Curling, an English agent, of great experience, before the Commission on the Tenure and Improvement of Land in 1865, from which the following answers are taken:—

'You have been the manager of the Devon estate for seventeen years, you say?—Yes.

'Do you think there is anything deficient in the character of the people which would prevent improvements from being made, provided a just law were given to them?—I do not; I think they are as energetic, as industrious, as moral, and as well-behaved a people as I have ever met with, and more grateful than any other people I know.

* Letter to the writer, March 11, 1867.

'Grateful for what?—For even fair play: not favours only, but even fair play.

'What has been their character as to peace and order for seventeen years?—I do not remember that a single crime, even to stealing a chicken, has been committed on the Devon estate for seventeen years.

'Are they frugal in their habits?—Very much so: too much so.

'Do you think that security, whether by a lease, or by an extended period of compensation, is necessary as a stimulus to the tenants to make improvements?—I think a tenant is a fool to expend his money without a security of that description.

'Have large improvements been made on the estate which you manage?—They have.

'By whom has the mountain land been reclaimed?— Exclusively by the tenants.

'I believe that you hold different opinions on certain points from witnesses who have been previously examined?—First of all, I do not concur with those who conceive that no additional legislation is required to stimulate Irish tenants to invest their capital in improvements.'

Lord Dufferin is no adversary to additional legislation to stimulate Irish tenants to invest their capital in improvements; on the contrary, he contributes towards it an excellent suggestion.* But he bids us expect little from such legislation, and certainly ' no comprehensive remedy for the perennial discontent of Ireland, or to unprecedented emigration from her shores.' His

* 'Irish Emigration and the Tenure of Land,' pp. 271, 272.

first and last lesson is that 'no nation can be made industrious, provident, skilful, by Act of Parliament. It is to time, to education, and above all to the development of our manufacturing resources, that we must look for the reinvigoration of our economic constitution.' It might, we do not hesitate to assert, be said with more justice, that every people is industrious, provident, and skilful just in proportion to the security given by its Government, laws, and customs as powerful as laws, that he who sows shall also reap. What has time, to which Lord Dufferin looks, done hitherto for Ireland, but maintain a system which, in the words used by the Devon Commissioners, paralyses all exertion, and places fatal impediments in the way of improvement? What practical lesson does education, again, teach the Irish peasant more plainly than this, that an intelligent man can always get on in America, and can seldom do so in Ireland? Lord Dufferin's readers will easily believe that so generous a mind 'cannot contemplate the expatriation of so many brave hearts and strong right arms with equanimity.' But when he adds, 'The true remedy is to be found in the development of our commercial enterprise, of our mineral resources, of our manufacturing industry,' we are driven to ask, why not in the development of our agricultural industry, the prime industry of all, the healthiest, and the natural base of all other industries? According to the natural course of things, Adam Smith has striven to impress upon mankind, the greater part of every growing society is first directed to agriculture, afterwards to manufacture.*

* 'Wealth of Nations,' book iii. chap. i.

To the same purpose Mr. Mill observes that 'in every country without exception in which peasant properties prevail, the towns, from the larger surplus which remains after feeding the agricultural classes, are increasing both in population and in the well-being of their inhabitants.' The present landowners of Ireland may therefore assure themselves that the conviction will at length force itself upon the public, that for the prosperity, not of agriculture alone, but of all the other industries of which the island is capable, either tenancies at will must cease to exist, or peasant properties must at any cost be created. M. de Tocqueville's reflection has already been quoted, that it is a sign of the imminent subversion of aristocratic institutions when the relation between landlord and tenant has become one of the briefest duration; but he adds the significant remark that if democratic tendencies shorten the duration of tenures, democratic institutions 'tend powerfully to increase the number of properties, and to diminish the number of tenant-farmers.' The land system of Ireland is one without the advantages either of feudalism or of democracy. 'As long as a numerous population,' says Lord Dufferin, ' is cursed with a morbid craving to possess land, so long will the owner be able to drive hard bargains.' The conclusion which these 'hard bargains' are likely to force before long on the public mind is, that the morbid craving for land with which the people of Ireland have been cursed, is that which moralists in every age have denounced, and against which the prophet cried, 'Woe unto them that join house to house, that lay field to field, till there be no place, that they may be placed alone in the earth.' The landlords of England may likewise rest assured that their own interests are involved in the Irish land question in a different manner from what they suppose. They are afraid of a precedent of interference with established territorial institutions; they have more to fear their self-condemnation.

Mr. SENIOR ON IRELAND.*

AFTER centuries of alternate rebellion and famine, and finally the loss of a third of the Irish nation in twenty-two years, the Irish question—'for,' as Mr. Senior said a generation ago, 'there is but one'—has become the English question too, the main question on which a general election is about to turn. Some of the chief guides of public opinion in England nevertheless profess themselves still in perplexity as to what the Irish question is. For their information, and to find the key to its solution, let us state the question in Mr. Senior's words: 'The detestation by the mass of the people of Ireland of her institutions,' being he said the fundamental evil, 'the first step towards the cure of this detestation must be to remove its causes; the first step towards making the institutions of Ireland popular must be to make them deserve to be so. If, indeed, they were deserving of popularity, the remedy would be hopeless. But this is an impossible supposition. No population hates the mass of its existing laws without sufficient reason. The tendency is to cling to whatever is established, merely because it is established.'

This statement of the question seems to us com-

* Reprinted from the 'Fortnightly Review,' November 1868..

plete. We cannot, however, say as much for either Mr. Senior's solution, or his explanation of the long delay of any solution. 'The object of every statesman,' we fully admit, ought now, as in 1844, when Mr. Senior said so, 'to be that the Irish Catholics should feel themselves, to use O'Connell's words, "subjects out and out as the Protestants are."' But when it is added that 'this feeling will be produced by a provision for the Irish Catholic clergy from the Imperial revenue, and can be produced by nothing else,' we must assert a conviction that such a provision twenty-five years ago (if accepted, which is very doubtful) would not only have left the original Irish question remaining, but have added another. Had the Irish Catholic Church been endowed by the State a generation ago, its disendowment would be one of the questions before the generation to come. In like manner we must reject the explanation Mr. Senior has given of the non-solution of the original question. 'The prejudices and passions of England and Scotland,' he says, 'rendered it useless to suggest, because they rendered it impossible to apply, the means by which the misery of Ireland might be relieved.' Unless in the sense in which under one name a nation is confounded with its government—a confusion which, as was pointed out in a former article, lies at the root of a number of national evils and international feuds*—it is most unjust to

---

* 'Nations and International Law.' 'Fortnightly Review,' July 1, 1868, p. 90. For 'Baron von *Ompleton,*' p. 92 in that article, read 'Baron von *Ompteda.*' For 'investing the appeal to force in this regulated form *to* the,' p. 100, line 15, read 'investing, &c., *with* the.' For 'the later Roman law of *nations,*' p. 100, line 22, read 'the later Roman law of *actions.*'

hold England and Scotland responsible for the long misery of Ireland. On the contrary, no sooner does national, that is to say popular, feeling in England and Scotland obtain some considerable influence over political questions, than the first question is 'the Irish question'—the question how to give Ireland good and popular laws, and to remove the institutions she detests. The plain reason is, that equality in the constitution, popular government, leads to equality in the laws, popular institutions; and the Irish question is but the most urgent side of the general question of equal and popular legislation for the whole kingdom, because inequality in legislation takes in Ireland the grossest and most intolerable forms. The reason, on the other hand, of the long continuance of the Irish question is equally plain. 'The history of this country,' said Mr. Lowe, in the most famous of his speeches against the admission of the people to a share in political power, 'the glorious and happy history of this country has been a conflict between two aristocratic parties.' Whose glory, we ask, and whose happiness? In the brief history of legislation for the English labouring classes, from 1349 to 1834, given in Mr. Senior's volumes on Ireland,* the reader will find a chapter in that 'glorious and happy history,' and a continuation of it may be found in the state of the agricultural labourers of England, and the proceedings in Parliament respecting them from that day to this. It is, however, to Ireland especially we must look for the kind of glory and happiness produced by a perpetual

* 'Journals,' &c., i. pp. 143–147.

'conflict between two aristocratic parties.' There was their favourite battle-field. There lay the richest booty for the conquerors. There once had lain extensive and fertile lands; there still lay salaries, titles, and promotion; there was the road to viceregal state and revenue, to earldoms, marquisates, and dukedoms, to bishoprics and archbishoprics, to secretaryships and seats in the Cabinet—it might be from the misgovernment of five millions and a half to the government of a hundred and fifty millions of men. Fixed on high thoughts like these, how could 'two aristocratic parties' stoop to heed the squalor, rage, and detestation of the wretched crowd beneath? Tocqueville affirmed that nothing that had passed in the English Parliament for one hundred and fifty years had produced much echo abroad, even its first orators commanding small sympathy or attention in neighbouring countries. 'The reason is,' he said, 'that in an aristocratic senate the orator's most eloquent appeals are confined to the sentiments and sympathies, the rights and privileges, of the dominant class he addresses; whereas in a popular legislature the orator speaks to a whole nation and on behalf of one, and though addressing only his fellow-citizens, often speaks to mankind.' Who can forget a signal example of this in the scorn and indignation which transported two 'aristocratic parties' when one of the chief orators among them spoke of a part of their fellow-citizens, whom he desired to admit to a voice in the laws, as of the same blood with themselves? The same exclusiveness of feeling, the same narrowness of political ideas, the same jealous regard to dominion and rank which have controlled the debate, have dictated the statute ; and hence it is that the Irish question, the question of giving equal and popular laws to the Irish people, awaits the solution of a popular Parliament, capable of entertaining the idea of equality, and of putting it into the laws.

Let it not then be dreamt that the question of the Irish Church is the whole Irish question. The inequality in that respect, although perhaps the one most extensively felt, is not the one felt most deeply. The Established Church is not the institution the majority of Irishmen detest most; Irish Catholics (we speak of the laity only) are more tolerant than most Protestants suppose ; and in so far as they do detest the Protestant Church, it is in general not for her doctrines (to which they pay little attention), nor yet for her endowments (with respect to which they will not be the party most opposed to a liberal settlement), but for her inequality —as a Church which 'exalts her mitred front in Courts and Parliaments '—Courts where they have been studiously shunned, and Parliaments which enacted the laws that have goaded them to rebellion and murder. 'Ireland,' to use Mr. Senior's language once more, 'is still governed by two codes: one deriving its validity from Acts of Parliament, and maintained by the magistrate ; the other laid down by the tenants, and enforced by assassination.' Until these two codes are brought into harmony, until the code regulating the ownership, tenure, transfer, and inheritance of land becomes an equal one, regarding the poor as much as the rich, the tenant as much as the landlord, the Irish question will never be solved. It will never be solved, therefore, so long as Parliament is occupied with 'a conflict between two aristocratic parties.' As, moreover, it is a question relating above all things to land, on which the very existence of the mass of the Irish people depends, it will never be solved in a Parliament which listens only to great landed proprietors, and to the political economy congenial to them.

A generation ago, Mr. Senior, no revolutionary economist, and writing in no revolutionary organ, pronounced that the chief material evil of Ireland, because the one which occasioned the other ('the want of capital'), was 'the want of small proprietors.' A people, he said, consisting chiefly of small proprietors, 'though without a middle class, and without the diffusion of moral and intellectual cultivation which a middle class produces, may be happy. If it have a good Government, it will have intelligence and self-respect. It will so regulate its numbers as not to subdivide its holdings into portions minuter than those which will maintain a family in the comforts which the habits of the people require. Each family, secure of its estate, will improve it with the industry, and endeavour to add to it by the frugality, which the feeling of property inspires. In time it will acquire capital, and with capital will come towns, manufactures, and the complicated social relations which belong to a rich, civilised community.' Under a system of large proprietors, what do we find Mr. Senior affirming of the tendency of things? 'The duty,' he declares with emphasis, in respect to both Ireland and England, 'which I hold to be the specific duty of a landlord, is *the keeping down population.* If there were no one whose interest it was to limit the number of the occupants of the land, it would be tenanted by all whom it could maintain. Competition would force them to use the food that was most abundant; they would have no division of labour, no manufactures, no separation of ranks, no literature; in short, no civilisation.'* Mr. Senior, however, omitted to consider another great Irish want besides that of small proprietors; one, created by large proprietors; one, too, which caused the very improvidence and consequent over-population he considers it their prime duty to prevent. 'The most general, and indeed universal, complaint,' the Devon Commission reported, ' brought before us in every part of Ireland, was "the want of tenure," to use the expression most commonly employed by the witnesses. It is said to paralyse all exertion, and to place a fatal impediment in the way of improvement.' It was this want—one persistently maintained to this day by large proprietors—combined with the want of all public relief of destitution, which produced the violence on the part of trade-unions and combinations, from which Ireland formerly suffered so much. When no Poor Law existed in Ireland— when the refuge of emigration was yet inaccessible— when evictions were frequent and sweeping—when the operatives in towns were in hourly danger of invasion

* 'Journals,' &c., i. 294, 295.

by a crowd of starving competitors from the country—when, too, no system of national education was established, it is not surprising if ignorant men in such a position sought to defend themselves by a merciless code. They were fighting for their existence, and their code for that end had the same origin as the fierce code of the Irish tenants of which Mr. Senior speaks. In England, too, as in Ireland, the labour question is in a great measure a land question. M. Léonce de Lavergne relates, in his essays on 'Agriculture and Population,' that in 1848 a personage in England replied to some one who feared an invasion of revolutionary ideas among English labouring classes,—'No, there is no danger, they know too much political economy.' The danger would be greater if they knew more: if they knew the economic causes of the wretchedness of their dwellings in town on the one hand, and of their degraded and hopeless condition in the country on the other. Mr. Senior himself, in treating of the causes of Irish misery, was led to say of the operation of similar causes in England, 'We bitterly regret that our execrable system of tenures, by making the legal forms attending the sale and purchase of a small piece of ground cost more than the value of the thing which they convey, and our execrable law of settlement, have destroyed the small properties of England. We believe that if we could recall into existence the English yeoman, we should add to our social system a most valuable member. We believe that the remnants of that race are the best agricultural population in Great Britain.'

'The Irish Question' is, in short, in every sense, the English question too. It is a question of equal laws—above all, of laws relating to land; it is a question which 'two aristocratic parties' have created, and which only a great national party can solve.

THE LAND SYSTEM OF ENGLAND, 1867.*

It is becoming apprehended by all classes, and apprehended in the sense of dread by some, that the question of Reform is not only a great political, but also a great economical question, concerning, especially, legislation calculated to modify the structure of our territorial system. It may, perhaps, tend to reassure those to whose minds the presentiment takes the form that private property is in danger, to be reminded that a lawyer of the highest eminence, now a peer and an ex-Chancellor, and in the enjoyment of all the rights of property known to English law, assured the House of Commons, on the third reading of the Reform Bill of 1832, that 'he could conscientiously say, that looking to his own interests as a member of the community, and casting about to see how he might place any property he might possess in security, he was at a loss to find out a satisfactory way, and he believed that a large proportion of those who possessed property thought with him. He came down to this House night after night to discuss the Bill, but he felt—as he believed others did—depressed more and more on each occasion, with the fear of the results from it.' Sir Robert Peel, too, at various stages of the Bill, uttered several gloomy

* Reprinted from 'Fraser's Magazine,' February 1867.

presages, foreshadowing among them, as tending to shake the security of property, the very measures on which his own reputation rests,*—of which the one evil has been that they have so prodigiously added to property and wealth, that members of Parliament are disposed to think no evils remain requiring another reform of Parliament for their redress.† The object of this article is to show that evils of great magnitude do remain in our land system, urgently demanding measures of reform which Parliament, as at present constituted, would not even patiently consider, although they are measures in perfect harmony with, and the mere logical development of, successive improvements in our jurisprudence for many centuries, are essential to its symmetry and simplification, and are, moreover, measures which, so far from confiscating the present rights of property in land of its possessors, would very greatly enlarge them.

The prospect of a failure of the supply of coal before many generations pass has occasioned serious alarm, but a far greater peril is at our doors. The supply of

---

* 'With respect to property, he had no fear of its destruction by confiscation; but he was afraid that some popularity-seeking Chancellor of the Exchequer might be found by a democratic assembly to propose the repeal of taxes, and adopt steps the ultimate tendency of which would be to shake the confidence of the country in the security of property; and that confidence once shaken, there would be an end to the chief stimulus to productive industry, the foundation of all our wealth, power, and eminence.'—*Speech of Sir R. Peel, on the second reading of the Reform Bill,* March 22, 1832.

† 'I believe the problem of Reform may be thus stated: On the one hand we have a system which since the great Reform Bill of 1832 has worked admirably, which has carried out so many reforms that no practical grievances remain to be redressed.'—*Speech of Mr. Laing to his Constituents,* August 27, 1866.

land has already failed. This failure presents itself in the most palpable form in great cities, and most people are more or less distinctly aware that throughout the country also there is an insufficiency of land for the requirements of the population; but the connection of the failure of the supply in cities with its failure in the country, and with the entire structure of our territorial system—with the unseating of the rural population, and their decline in numbers and prosperity; with artificial restrictions of the business of towns to particular spots, and with a forced and unnatural aggregation of disproportionate multitudes in a few principal towns—especially the metropolis—seems hitherto to have escaped attention. It will be the first object of this article to exhibit, step by step, the connection of these facts.

Paradoxical as it may be, especially in contrast with the progress of England in trade and manufactures, and the progressive rise of the cultivators of the soil in all other civilised countries, from the Southern States of America to Russia, it is strictly true, that the condition of the English rural population in every grade below the landed gentry has retrograded; and, in fact, there is no longer a true rural population remaining for the ends, political, social, and economic, which such a population ought to fulfil. The grounds of this assertion are well known to students of our social history; but it is necessary to a sufficient presentment of the state of the land question to show what they are. The different grades which are still sometimes, in un-

THE LAND SYSTEM OF ENGLAND, 1867. 163

conscious irony, spoken of as the landed interest, once had a common interest in the land; an unbroken connection both with the soil and with each other subsisted between the landed gentry, the yeomanry who farmed their own estates, the tenant-farmers, and the agricultural labourers. From the yeomanry who owned land downwards, moreover, each of the lower rural grades had risen politically, economically, and socially; and there was for the members of each a prospect of a higher personal elevation and a larger interest in the soil. Now the landed yeomanry, insignificant in number and a nullity in political power, are steadily disappearing altogether; the tenant-farmers have lost the security of tenure, the political independence, and the prospect of one day farming their own estate, which they formerly enjoyed; and lastly, the inferior peasantry not only have lost ground in the literal sense, and have rarely any other connection with the soil than a pauper's claim, but have sunk deplorably in other economical aspects below their condition in former centuries. Thus a soil eminently adapted by natural gifts to sustain a numerous and flourishing rural population of every grade, has almost the thinnest and absolutely the most joyless peasantry in the civilised world, and its chief end as regards human beings seems only to be a nursery of over-population and misery in cities.

The landed yeomanry at the head of the triple agricultural class, once so numerous in England, were many of them the descendants of peasants who had held their land in villenage, or by a yet more servile tenure; and in the sixteenth century, after villenage had become extinct, we find their numbers, in spite of a succession of adverse circumstances, still recruited from a humbler rank, and themselves recruiting one above them. The graphic chronicler of that age, describing the yeomanry with small estates to the value of six pounds a year in the money of time, says; 'These commonly live wealthily, keep good houses, and travail to get riches. They are also for the most part farmers to gentlemen, or at the least artificers, and do come to great wealth, insomuch that many of them are able and do buy the lands of unthrifty gentlemen, and often setting of their sons to the schools, to the universities, and to the inns of court, or otherwise leaving them sufficient lands whereby they may live without labour, do make them by those means to become gentlemen. These,' he concludes—and the conclusion is important—' were they that in times past made all France afraid.' The important and independent part which such small landowners continued long to fill in both the social and the political world has attracted the notice of all historians. In the last quarter of the seventeenth century their number exceeded that of the tenant-farmers, amounting at the most moderate estimate 'to not less than 160,000 proprietors, who with their families must have made more than a seventh of the whole population.' * How great a change in the English polity is made by the gradual disappearance and political annihilation of this ancient order, and the absorption of their territorial influence and representation along with their estates by a higher

* Macaulay's 'History of England,' chap. iii.

class, must strike any reader of the passage in which Lord Macaulay briefly paints their former place in constitutional history :—' A large portion of the yeomanry had from the Reformation leaned towards Puritanism; had in the Civil War taken the side of the Parliament; had after the Reformation persisted in hearing Presbyterian and Independent preachers; had at the elections strenuously supported the Exclusionists; and had continued, even after the discovery of the Rye House Plot and the proscription of the Whig leaders, to regard Popery and arbitrary power with unmitigated hostility.'

In some few counties, descendants of these small proprietors may still be found in the possession of their estates, but they are each year becoming fewer; and instead of exceeding, as they did two centuries ago, the tenant-farmers in number, the latter, though far fewer than they might be, are now more than twenty times as many. Historical evidence has been adduced by several writers to prove that the total number of persons now in possession of land is less than it was at the Conquest; but the literal exactness of such evidence appears of small moment when it is carried in mind that the greater part of the island was then in forest or waste, and was actually to spare. The extent of land really engrossed by a few is now greater by all that has since been applied to private use; and again, of the actual number of landowners, a small proportion holds most of the land in the kingdom. The total number of landowners enumerated in the last census was 30,766, which is said to omit some returned under other denominations; but, on the other hand, it is well known to include many who, on very little ground, in the literal sense, assume the title of landowners as one of social distinction, often having above them, moreover, some lord of the soil, who is the real proprietor.* The exact number of hundreds or thousands of owners of land is, in fact, of no importance or relevance here. The question we are concerned with is one that relates, not to the hundreds or thousands, but to the millions— to the amount of room left for the nation at large, in town and country together. Of the disappearance of yeomen proprietors, however, it may be added that many enumerated as landowners in the census belong to a civic rather than to a rural class of proprietors, and, in place of adding to the latter, occupy the places of ancient yeomanry, whose estates they have bought at a price men of a yeoman class could not afford. It is sometimes alleged that this is the result of economic liberty and the natural play of commerce, and therefore beneficial; but it is easily shown to be the result of an artificial system, which makes the greater part of

* The Duke of Argyll, criticising, before the Statistical Society, a paper by Mr. Leone Levi on the Economic Situation of the Highlands, found fault with official statistics quoted in that paper for enormously exaggerating the number of landed proprietors in some counties in Scotland. Mr Levi, he said, upon those returns 'gave the number of proprietors in Sutherland as 272, but every one knew that Sutherland was in the hands of five or six.' Mr Levi really much understated his own case by assuming for the moment the correctness of the official return; and the duke's criticism only exemplifies in the case of one county what is true of Great Britain, that most of the land is really owned by fewer persons than any official enumeration is likely to show.

It may be added that in a speech on a bill before the House of Commons, relating to the succession to real estates, a noble lord asserted that a recent return showed the number of landed yeomen to be at least 300,000; but the noble lord must have confounded those who by technical title are freeholders with yeoman proprietors land unmarketable, and therefore makes the little that is sold a luxury for the rich, and an unprofitable investment for the poor. In the language of Adam Smith, it is the result of 'regulations which keep so much land out of the market, that there are always more capitals to buy than there is land to sell, so that what is sold sells at a monopoly price. The small quantity of land which is brought to market, and the high price of what is brought, moreover, prevents a great number of small capitals from being employed in its cultivation, which would otherwise have taken that direction.' By one and the same system, the old farming class of proprietors is extinguished, a new farming class is prevented from rising in their place, and a non-productive class is maintained and gains ground. A line of eldest sons has the odds against it, in the long run, in any line of business; and accumulating family charges and legal costs and difficulties swell the odds against the small proprietors with whom farming is a business. The unproductive owners of great estates, upon the other hand, though heavily encumbered for the most part, too, are seldom actually dislodged; and when they are, a rich man buys their estates. He does not buy them for immediate profit; and he can afford to buy legal advice in his subsequent dealings with them.

The disappearance of the yeoman landholders evidently renders it of great importance that the next agricultural order, that of the tenant-farmers, should possess such security for improvement and such political independence as should both enable them to fill to some extent the place in society and in the constitution of the disappearing grade above, and also furnish them with some substitute for their ancient prospect of acquiring land of their own. But here, too, we find a retrograde movement, and the course of ancient progress interrupted and reversed.

The tenant-farmers of this country were originally of two descriptions—copyholders, and tenants for terms of years—both of whom rose gradually from a servile status and dependence for their holding on the mere will of the landlord, to a position of great security and independence. The copyholders, who might once be ousted at the pleasure of their lords, gained by successive steps the point at which Sir Edward Coke could say: 'Now copyholders stand upon sure ground; now they weigh not their lords' displeasure; they shake not at every blast of wind; they eat and drink securely; only having an especial care of the main chance, namely, to perform carefully what services their tenure doth exact;—then let lord frown, the copyholder cares not, knowing himself safe.' The estates of this once numerous order of agricultural tenants have long been passing, like those of the yeomanry, to a different class; and as with the yeomanry, so with the copyholders, 'vestigia nulla retrorsum.' The other class of tenant-farmers, those who held for years, were originally in the eye of the law the mere husbandmen of the landlord; but their position in like manner was improved by successive steps, until they gained the remedy of ejectment against both lord and stranger; and a legal writer concludes the history of their gradual ascent: 'Thus were tenants for years at last placed on the same level with the freeholder as regards the security of their estates.' This gradual elevation of the English tenantry, and the growth of a custom of long leases, has been dwelt upon with especial emphasis by the author of the 'Wealth of Nations,' who, after remarking that a great part of them in his time held by a freehold tenure which gave them votes, and 'made the whole order respectable' by the political consideration it gave, concludes by attributing the grandeur which England had attained to in his time especially to the growth of laws and customs so favourable to its agricultural tenantry. At the same period, Dr. Johnson, notwithstanding the strength of his political bias on the side of rank, and his confession that if he were a landed gentlemen he would turn out every tenant he could who did not vote as he desired, expressed his opinion that none but bad men could refuse leases to their tenants, or desire 'to keep them in perpetual dependence, mere ephemeræ—mere beings of an hour.'

A writer of our own generation, not without something of Dr. Johnson's bias, comments, in various editions of the 'Wealth of Nations,' on Adam Smith's opinion of the value of the suffrage to the farming class, when safe from dispossession, as many were by the freehold tenure common at that time; and after remarking that the last Reform Act extended the franchise to all tenants at a certain value, adds: 'There is too much reason to fear that it will in the end subvert that system of giving leases for nineteen or twenty years certain, that has been the main cause of the wonderful improvement of Scotch agriculture. Tenants, as such, are the last description of persons on whom the franchise ought to be conferred. It would be easy to corroborate this by reference to the history of land both in England and in Ireland, in both of which the conferring of the franchise on tenants has been most injurious to agriculture and to the public interest. But the circumstances must be perfectly well known to all moderately well-informed readers.* Mr. M'Culloch's premiss that the actual consequence of the extension of the franchise—a consequence, as he says, 'most injurious to agriculture, and to the public interest'—has been a subversion of the ancient English custom of long leases, is beyond dispute. Where the legislature meant to enlarge the political representation of the farming class, the result has been that they have lost at once their old political representation and their old security of tenure; their votes have become part of the private property of their landlords, and they have ceased to have a voice in legislation for their own interests, or even to have a claim to the suffrage according to an old doctrine of constitutional writers that the ground of the freeholder's vote was his absolute independence of the will of his lord. But instead of the conclusion which Mr. M'Culloch draws, that tenants are the last description of persons on whom the franchise ought to be conferred, the true conclusion is evident, that the country needs another Reform Act to restore the independence and security of its tenant-farmers. At present, instead of balancing the power

* Adam Smith's 'Wealth of Nations,' by J. R. M'Culloch.

of the great territorial proprietors, they only swell the power of the latter to legislate adversely to their tenants, when matters which concern them, such as game laws and compensation for improvements, are before Parliament.

Passing next to the third agricultural order, the labourers, we find here again the ancient course of upward movement turned into a decline. Not to advance is to fall back in a progressive world; but the peasantry of England have in many important particulars positively as well as relatively retrograded. By the aid of Christianity and commerce, and of fundamental principles of the common law, derived from the civilised jurisprudence of Rome, and in perpetual conflict with the barbarous jurisprudence of feudalism, the serf became at length a free labourer for hire. The legislation respecting his wages and apparel in the fifteenth century, though intended to restrict them, proves that his condition had become one of affluence compared with what it is at present. The rules of the Church alone limited his consumption of animal food, and his clothing was abundant and even rich for the age.* Soon afterwards, indeed, his class began to lose in many instances the best of their possessions, their little plot of ground; and by the eviction of numbers of the peasantry of every grade was laid the foundation of English pauperism, and of that unnatural migration to great cities of which we have to speak. Nevertheless, the connection of the

* 'History of the English Peasantry: Over-population and it Remedy.' By W. T. Thornton.

lowest grade of the rural population with the soil, and their comparative real wealth at the close of the last century, was still such that Arthur Young could say, 'I know not a single cottage without a piece of ground belonging to it.' The eminent agriculturist who, in the middle of our own century, trod in the steps of Arthur Young, would have been nearer the truth in saying of several counties, 'I know scarcely a single cottage with a piece of ground belonging to it.' Mr. Caird's tour in 1850 and 1851 through the counties of England established, moreover, that while in the purely agricultural counties the rent of land and the rent of a labourer's cottage had risen since the tour of Arthur Young 100 per cent., the price of butter 100 per cent., and of meat 70 per cent., the rise in the labourer's wages was but 14 per cent. Mr. Caird adds, indeed, that the price of bread, 'the great staple of the English labourer,' was about the same in 1850 as in 1770; but bread was not always the labourer's staple.

In the year in which Mr. Caird began his tour, Mr. Kay's admirable book on the 'Social Condition of the People of Europe' was published, with the following description of the cottages of the people of England: 'The accounts we receive from all parts of the country show that their miserable cottages are crowded in the extreme, and that the crowding is progressively increasing. People of both sexes and all ages, both married and unmarried, parents, brothers, sisters, and strangers, sleep in the same room, and often in the same bed.' Thus by the middle of this century not only the plot of ground and the cottage had gone, but

a separate room, and even a separate bed, was going or gone. And following the chain of evidence to the present decade, we find the rural labourer still descending in the scale of material civilisation, and the room made for him in the land diminishing fast. Accounts published by Parliament last year showed that between 1851 and 1861 the number of houses had diminished in 821 agricultural parishes, while the population had increased; and it is known that in many other parishes a decrease in the rural population was accompanied by a still greater decrease in the number of houses in the same period. Nor does what has been said exhibit the whole change for the worse in the agricultural labourer's lot. 'A hundred and fifty years ago there was scarcely a parish without a considerable extent of common, on which every householder was at liberty to turn out a cow or a pig, or a few sheep or fowls. The poor man, therefore, even after the loss of the fields attached to his cottage, might nevertheless contrive to supply his family with plenty of milk and eggs and bacon at little or no expense to himself. He has since, in most cases, been deprived of this advantage too.' *
The process of enclosing common land began in the reign of Anne on a scarcely perceptible scale, increased steadily in the two following reigns, and afterwards with such rapidity, that between 1760 and 1834 nearly seven million acres had been taken from the patrimony of the poor and added to the private property of the rich. The legislature of the present reign has only put a limit to the process by almost completing it.

* Thornton's 'Over-Population and its Remedy.'

Thus every grade of the rural population has sunk; the landed yeomanry are almost gone; the tenant-farmers have lost their ancient independence and interest in the soil; the labourers have lost their separate cottages and plots of ground, and their share in a common fund of land; and whereas all these grades were once rising, the prospect of the landed yeomanry is now one of total extinction; that of the tenant-farmers, increasing insecurity;* that of the agricultural labourer, to find the distance between his own grade and the one above him wider and more impassable than ever, while the condition of his own grade is scarcely above that of the brutes. Once, from the meanest peasant to the greatest noble all had land, and he who had least might hope for more; now there is being taken away from him who has little, even that which he has—his cottage, nay, his separate room. Once there was an ascending movement from the lowest grade towards the highest; now there is a descending movement in every grade below the highest. Once the agricultural class had a political representation, and a voice in legislation which they dared to raise against the landed gentry and nobility; now the latter have the supreme command at once of the soil and of the suffrages of its cultivators. Sir James Kay Shuttleworth, in a recent interesting essay, argues, with respect to agricultural labourers, that 'time is a necessary element in the elevation of any class,' and that 'the extension of the suffrage to any class enfeebled by traditional dependence and servile habits results in its political subserviency.' But time is

* Caird's 'English Agriculture,' p. 505.

only a name for the operation of causes which may tend either to elevate or to depress, according to their nature. The very steps by which the villein rose, as Sir James Shuttleworth describes them, are now lost to the peasantry of England: 'Our ancient Saxon polity had a representative constitution in which the villein gradually rose to participate, and that just in proportion as he was admitted to the possession of property independently of the lord of the soil. The gradual transition from the occupation of land by villenage to the cultivation of loan land, and the freedom of the tenant to migrate, to carry with him his acquisitions, and to acquire land as a personal possession, are the chief steps of advance of the class of villeins to the class of small tenant-farmers, and to the establishment of the independent class of yeomen and "statesmen" who cultivated their own land.' Only one of these steps can now be said to remain—the freedom to migrate; and the consequence is a forced and unnatural migration from the country to a few great manufacturing towns and the metropolis, largely swollen by other circumstances (also connected with our territorial system), which limit to a few centres the space for manufactures and urban employments.

We are told that the movement of the rural population to cities is an effect and symptom of progress, resulting from the great increase of manufacturing employment and wages on the one hand, and the economy of labour by the natural tendency to the enlargement of farms on the other. With respect to the former of these allegations, it will presently be shown that the same causes which limit the employment, the wages, and the room for the labouring population in the country diminish all three for the labouring population in towns. But it ought first to be shown to be a wholly fallacious assertion that the natural tendency of agricultural improvement in England is towards the enlargement of farms and a smaller employment of labour. The chapter at the end of Mr. Caird's standard treatise on 'English Agriculture in 1850–1851,' contains a table of the rent of farms in different counties, and the following observations upon it: 'The great corn-growing counties of the east coast yield an average rent of 23s. 8d. an acre; the more mixed husbandry of the midland counties, and the grazing, green crop, and dairy districts of the west, 31s. 5d. Leases are the exception throughout England; and though more prevalent in the west, there has been no sufficient uniformity to account for the difference of rent. But the *size* of farms has an undoubted influence on the rent. In the dry climate of the counties on the east coast the operations of a corn farm can be carried on on an extensive scale. By this means the landlord's outlay in buildings and fences is economised. As we proceed westward the country becomes more wooded, and better adapted for pasturage; the enclosures are smaller, the farms less extensive. Still farther west the moistness of the climate materially affects the mode of cultivation—unfavourable to corn crops, and favourable to grass. The farms are of small extent, and held by a numerous class of tenants, who live frugally, and in many cases assist, with their families, in the labours of the farm. We have here all the elements necessary to make a difference in the rate of rent. The large eastern farmer looks principally to barley and wheat. The landlord of the western and midland counties possesses the two great advantages of his soil being used for the production of the most valuable of our agricultural commodities, *whilst his farms, from their size, are accessible to a larger body of competitors, in short, are in greater demand than the (large) farms of the east.*'

After these conclusions with respect to the past, Mr. Caird proceeds to some with reference to the future:

'As the country becomes more prosperous, the difference in the relative value of corn and stock will gradually be increased. The production of vegetables and fresh meat, hay for forage, and pasture for dairy cattle, which were formerly confined to the neighbourhood of towns, will necessarily extend as the towns become more numerous and populous. The facilities of communication must increase this tendency. Our insular position, with a limited territory and an increasingly dense manufacturing population, is yearly extending the circle within which the production of fresh food—animal, vegetable, and forage—will be needed for daily supply, and which cannot be brought from distant countries. They can be produced in no country as well as our own. Wool has likewise increased in value as much as any agricultural product, and there is a good prospect of flax becoming an article in extensive demand. The manufacture of sugar from beet-root may yet be found very profitable to the

English agriculturist. Now, all these products require the employment of considerable labour, very minute care, skill, and attention, and a larger acreable application of capital than is requisite for the production of corn. This will inevitably lead to the gradual diminution of the largest farms, and to the concentration of the capital and attention of the farmer on a smaller space.'

In a speech in the House of Commons little more than two years ago, we find Mr. Caird again saying: 'I differ with my honourable friend (Mr. Dunlop) with regard to the change which he asserts to be taking place in Scotland. My honourable friend says that the small-farm system is disappearing, or is likely to disappear. My own observation leads me to say that it is quite the contrary. The more minute and perfect the system of farming adopted in order to work them with profit, the more likely is the system of small farms to increase than to diminish. The arable farms in Scotland and the north of England sixteen or twenty years ago were much greater in extent than they are at present.'

It is thus clear that the natural tendency of this country was never, and is less now than ever, towards large farms; and that the causes of the tendency which formerly existed, and which still exists in many of the counties of England, towards the extinction of small farms, have been the following: first, and especially, the inability and indisposition of encumbered inheritors of great estates upon the one hand, and of tenants without leases on the other, to furnish small farms with the requisite buildings and fixtures; secondly, the artificial pauperism produced by causes already mentioned, and the anxiety of landlords, resulting therefrom and from the frame of the Poor-law, to clear their estates of the peasantry; thirdly, protectionist legislation in favour of corn. The chief of these causes are still in existence, and customs and opinions engendered by the rest also remain.

One of the ablest living advocates of the existing law of primogeniture has urged that it is favourable to agriculture, because large estates tend to make large farms.* They certainly do; but it is because they are encumbered, and because their owners prefer political power to good farming, such as leases alone can produce. It is beyond contradiction that the products which are best suited to the soil and climate of England are those which small farmers produce best; it is found that small farmers can and do pay higher rents than large farmers in England itself, as in Flanders; and it follows that the English peasantry have been dislodged from the soil and degraded in condition by laws and customs contrary to those of political economy and nature. There is no reason in political economy or in nature why there should not be in England a predominance, not only of small farms, but of farms such as foreigners call small. The petty farmer of a few acres outbids every other in Flanders on a soil far inferior to that of England.† 'The larger farms in Flanders,' says

---

* Speech of Sir H. Cairns on the Real Estates Intestacy Bill, 1859.

† On the natural quality of the soil of Flanders, see M. de Laveleye's 'Essai sur l'Économie rurale de la Belgique,' pp. 1, 2, and 37.

the highest authority on the subject,* 'tend constantly towards subdivision, for the simple reason that when subdivided they yield a higher rent. This subdivision, too, increases the gross no less than the net produce. In general, the smaller the farm the greater the produce of the soil. Cultivators and proprietors alike rejoice in the subdivision : the former, because it places more land within their reach; the latter, because it doubles their rents.' When to this we add the consideration that the farm produce for which England is best suited requires, as Mr. Caird states, an immensity of labour, and that, as Mr. Thornton expresses it, 'English agriculture would be exceedingly benefited by the application to it of at least double the actual quantity of labour,' we may pronounce that England is fitted by nature to support an immense rural population in comfort; that landlords, in clearing their estates of the labourers' little farms and cottages to diminish pauperism, have fallen into the common error of mistaking the preventive for the disease; that the immense migration from the country to the city has been a forced and unnatural movement; and that the misery and decline of the English rural population is the result of a system adverse to the interests of all classes, not excepting the proprietors of the soil. But the evils of the system do not end here. As it has cramped and misdirected the industry of the country, so has it the industry of the town; and the migration of the pea-

* M. de Laveleye may be called the highest authority on this subject, because he not only has made it a special study, but is both a distinguished professor of political economy and one of 'the landed interest.'

santry has been accompanied by another forced movement of the population to a few great cities, to which urban industry has been in a great measure unnaturally restricted. The result is, that enormously disproportionate numbers are huddled together in a space which yearly becomes less as those numbers increase; that the town population, like that of the country, has yearly less room for its growth; that the mass of the labouring population is degenerating both in country and in town; and that a land question has arisen in our cities, more imperiously demanding solution than even the land question in the country.

Adam Smith observes that, contrary to the course of nature (which makes agriculture the first, because the most necessary and the most attractive, of human occupations), the first growth of industry and opulence in mediæval Europe was in towns; and that this inversion of the natural order of progress was caused by the insecurity and oppression of the cultivators of the soil, while the inhabitants of towns enjoyed comparative liberty and safety. But the philosopher's reasoning, taken along with well-known facts of history, leads to a further conclusion which he does not expressly state, that urban industry was itself unnaturally confined to a few walled and chartered cities, within which the inhabitants might leave their substance to their children, and were tolerably secure from both legal and illegal pillage. Such of these towns as made remarkable progress were uniformly enabled by their situation to obtain supplies of food and materials of industry and trade from a distance; but it was not so much the superior facility as the superior security of water carriage which gave towns in such places their principal advantage, for the want of means of land carriage was more the consequence than the cause of the backwardness and misgovernment of the country. The villein need not have fled to remote fortified cities, had artificers been free to settle at his door; towns would have come to him, would have grown up around him by the gradual extension and improvement of village manufactures. But civic industry and traffic were confined by feudal laws and customs to certain privileged sites, and custom and prestige, and the facilities which time and labour bring, gave some of them a lasting superiority not ascribable to natural gifts alone. So far the past operation of our territorial system is in fault. The truth, however, is that it tends at this day to limit trade and manufactures to places with no economic superiority over a number of others from which they are excluded by the great monopoly of land; and that immense unapproachable estates, overgrown demesnes, restricted rights of proprietorship, defective titles, and all the other causes which keep land out of the market, keep out manufactures and trade from many natural homes for their settlement, and imprison them within bounds where space is at once insufficient and extravagantly dear. One of the most flourishing towns in the United Kingdom owes its extraordinary progress in the present generation chiefly to the fact that it stands upon ground which the sale of the estates of a ruined noble made the property of its citizens, and thus transferred to the many from the one. Those who are versed in the published and unpublished history of towns will readily call up several similar cases. But of many eligible sites for urban industry and opulence the history has not been suffered to begin. In the same county in which the town just spoken of is situated, a wealthy manufacturer deplored to the writer of this paper, some years ago, that he could not extend his manufacturing premises where he lived, and had been driven to invest a large capital in a factory many miles from his own eye, because he could not obtain the security of a sufficient lease from a proprietor of the soil who had only once visited his immense estate, and had not even a residence upon it. In such and many other ways the space for urban life and industry is artificially limited. 'Even in towns,' a member of Parliament complains, 'the great landed monopoly is often grievously felt. How many towns there are, favoured by natural position, whose growth is stunted, and the prosperity of the inhabitants cut short, because the great proprietor under whose shadow they lie would rather preserve the privacy of his demesne than add to its revenue. Nor is this the only way in which a town is liable to suffer from the contiguity of a great estate, and the abuse of the power that belongs to it. It is matter of notoriety that in many cases the course of a railway has been marked out, and the places of its stations have been selected, to suit the convenience of the landowner, in place of that of the small town.' *

* 'The History of the Law of Entail and Settlement.' By Charles Neate, Esq., M.P.

Thus it is that the paths and homes and bounds of trade are far from being what nature would have made them; nor can there be a reasonable doubt that although time and legislation never may restore the course of nature altogether, yet, if the restrictions which now surround them were once removed, the population and capital in our straitened cities could forthwith find an outlet and a relief, and much capital which leaves our shores would find new and profitable employment upon English ground. Nor is it capitalists and labourers alone who are pent unnaturally within a few great cities. There, behind counters, is the pale youth which might have recruited the ranks of a blooming tenantry; there the children and descendants of the fading yeomanry, of the rural clergy, and of country gentlemen themselves, are gathered; there are the many shops and trades that might have prospered well in country towns; there are the families of every middle grade whose incomes are no longer equal to the costly luxury of a country home. Thus the middle classes involuntarily occupy the space in our chief towns which the working-classes want; and the tide of immigration from all ranks throughout the country meets a town population yearly increasing from within in a space long since insufficient, and ever growing less. Already in 1861 it was found that while the country population of England little exceeded nine millions, nearly eleven millions were inhabitants of towns, and of these more than seven millions and a half had congregated into the larger towns.* Of the

* These towns contained in 1801 a population of only 2,221,753.

latter number, again, nearly three millions (more than a million of whom were born elsewhere) peopled the metropolis, where railways, immense buildings, and clearances of all kinds, are diminishing the space for the poorer classes to live in with fearful rapidity, entailing consequences which have been well described by Lord Shaftesbury from his personal knowledge. Speaking in the House of Lords of the destruction of the dwellings of the poor by railways, in the face of a natural increase of the city population, and a yearly immigration in addition computed at from thirty to forty thousand, he said: 'First look at the financial effects. There is a large population of workmen, such as shoemakers, tailors, printers, and dockyard labourers, who cannot remove from their place of employment without their occupations being wholly destroyed. Next, there is the change in the accommodation and its price. The proprietors of the meanest houses, seeing the great demand, raise the prices so that poor people who before lived in two rooms at a comparatively low rate are forced to pay much higher rents, and have further to put up with the indecencies and discomforts consequent upon sleeping eight, nine, or even ten in the same room. This is the story, not of hundreds, but of thousands. And see, moreover, how the change affects their social condition. Their burial and sick clubs are broken up, their reading-rooms destroyed, their social meetings for what is called social improvement are rendered no longer possible, and they are forced into other neighbourhoods where they find none of these comforts, and are in addition highly unwelcome arrivals, from the fact that they come still further to burden a labour market already overstocked, to raise rent, and to reduce wages.'

After alluding to the shocking scenes he had lately witnessed in one of these wretched refuges of the displaced poor, the noble lord added: 'One very decent woman said to me, "We are just over the main drains, and the walls are so ruinous that Jack and I take it by turns to sit up at nights, for the rats come up in such numbers that we are afraid that if we do not, they may carry off the baby." But why did the man remain? Because he knew that if he left his dwelling he could not find another in the neighbourhood, and would lose his employment.'

This frightful situation of things is every month becoming more frightful. Six years ago there were nearly three millions of people in London. The whole population of England doubles in about fifty-two years; but the chief increase is in the large towns, and most of all in the metropolis, where most of all the space for human habitation rapidly decreases. We are thus coming to a deadlock both in country and in town for want of bare room for the people to live in, while there is land enough and to spare. Already the population is degenerating both in town and country. The barrister threading the crowded lanes and courts between the Strand and Lincoln's Inn has noticed year by year the signs of a degenerating race upon old and young, and now they, too, have been displaced to swell the numbers in some more crowded and more squalid haunts. In the country, the degeneracy of the race is its most striking feature ; intelligence is almost extinct among the rural poor ; and in no other civilised land, and even in few savage lands, has any class of human being a look so cheerless, so unreasoning, so little human, as the English agricultural labourer, without the light either of intelligence or of animal spirits in his sullen face. But the working-classes are not the only sufferers. Already the dwellings of the middle classes in great cities not only are becoming dear beyond their means, but are beginning to disappear altogether ; and they too will find before long that there is no room for them in either country or town, and that they have before them only the hard choice of the ancient Britons. And the danger threatens a higher class still. A landless and houseless population will ere long be brought face to face with a few thousand engrossers of the soil, who seldom can sell or divide it, or make adequate leases of it if they would, but who will be charged with the consequence—with making 'pleasure-ground,' as the *Times* recently called it, of all the land in the kingdom, while the nation has not enough for bare existence. Nor does the danger beset all classes only from within. We are coming closer year by year to both Europe and America ; and if we are to hold a place, not to say as a great, but even as a small independent State, we must find room for the nation to grow, and to grow in health and strength ; we must find room for increasing numbers of men to live as men, and not as rats.

It is this land question in both country and town, traceable in both to the same source, which legislation must solve to rescue the nation from degeneracy, revolution, and subjection; but it is a question which the present legislature is unable to solve—not that it is insoluble by legislation (if it were, it would be all the more awful), but because, upon the one hand, the sufferers, whose energy and invention would be exerted to the utmost, are unrepresented or misrepresented in Parliament; and because, on the other hand, a class, which is omnipotent in Parliament on all questions relating to land, inherits its opinions as well as its estates, and naturally but unwisely imagines its interests concerned in maintaining things as they are; regarding all those who would do anything effectual to remedy the evil, though it threatens themselves and the existence of their estates, as its authors. In a speech on the question of intestate succession to real estates, Mr. Lowe declared: 'The present state of our law with respect to land is the result of a series of conflicts in which the landed interest has invariably been on the illiberal side, and has as invariably been overborne and conquered by the feeling of the country.' It is because 'the landed interest' is conscious of this that it seeks to exclude the feeling of the country from representation in Parliament.

Et est qui vinci possit, eoque
Difficiles aditus primos habet.

But it is surprising that a statesman, with the opinion just quoted of the legislative qualities of landed proprietors, should not see in the land question an unanswerable argument for reform, instead of an argument against it. In a speech on the extension of the franchise, Mr.

Lowe said: 'Look at the land question alone. In America nobody covets land, because he can get as much as he likes. But here the case is different; nothing is easier than to get up a cry about land; and at this moment it is generally believed upon the Continent that there is a law in existence under which the possession of land in England is confined exclusively to the aristocracy.' It is just because the supply of land is so limited by nature in England, that it is necessary that it should not be limited artificially, and that a parliament which will not remove the artificial limitation needs a reform. In America, 58,000 square miles kept out of the market by the state of the law would hardly be missed from the market; but in England there are only 58,000 square miles altogether.

It is to the reform of the law of landed property and the reform of Parliament for that end, that we must look for the solution of the land questions which present themselves alike in country and in town, and the same reforms will go far to solve both. To find dwellings for the overgrown population of the metropolis, for example, we must make outlets for industry elsewhere; we must remove the causes of the displacement of the rural population—of a perpetual influx of extreme poverty into the principal cities—of the little land which enters the market being artificially dear, and of the greater part never entering it at all from one century to another. If the unnatural congregation of multitudes in extreme poverty in one spot could be stopped, the question of dwellings for the poor in the metropolis would lose the chief of its terrors for the future. The evil has indeed been enormously increased by the merciless encroachment of companies powerful in Parliament, and with the instinct of 'the landed interest' on their side. Everything is possible in engineering, and the energy and skill which laid a cable under the Atlantic could have carried every metropolitan railway under ground. There is, again, no mechanical reason why an increase of space for the population of London should not be made upwards, in substantial houses ten, twenty, or thirty storeys high; but there must be a foundation left to build on; a forced competition must not make the rents of such houses exorbitantly high; and the tenants, on the other hand, must not be paupers, too poor to pay even a moderate rent. And the state of the law of landed property, and the system founded upon it, are the main causes of all the pauperism in England.

The law of landed property is, moreover, the radical cause which makes our jurisprudence a byword in the civilised world and prevents the possibility of reducing it to a simple and intelligible code. Thus the political question of Reform, which has been shown to be also a great economical question, involves a great juridical question besides. And the solution of the chief difficulties of both the economical and the juridical question may be found in measures which would not diminish but greatly enlarge the rights of property, properly understood, in which, however, cannot be included the right to deny them to men's successors, or to appropriate the property and votes of their tenants.

Even Dr. Johnson, notwithstanding his bias in favour of regulations tending to place hereditary leaders at the head of mankind, foresaw that the time would come when 'the evil of too much land being locked up' would have to be dealt with. But his was the not very philosophical way of thinking to which another very learned man in our own age was inclined—that cure is better than prevention.* For want of prevention the evil has now reached the magnitude only imperfectly described in these pages, and we are driven to seek at once for cure and prevention.

There are three different methods recorded in history to make choice from. One is the French law of partition of family property among all children alike—an expedient which deserves no higher commendation than that it is better than the feudal system of disinheriting all the children but one. A second method which suggests itself, with higher reason on its side, is a limitation of the amount of land that any single individual shall take by inheritance. Such a measure, however shocking to present proprietary sentiments, could not diminish the real happiness, it may safely be asserted, of one human being in the next generation; nor can it be confidently pronounced that the mischief resulting from the long retention of a restriction of a

---

* *Boswell.*—' I expressed my opinion that the power of entailing should be limited thus: that there should be one-third, or perhaps one-half, of the land of a country kept free for commerce; that the proportion allowed to be entailed should be parcelled out so that no family could entail above a certain quantity.' *Johnson.*—' Why, sir, mankind will be better able to regulate the system of entails when the evil of too much land being locked up by them is felt, than we can do at present when it is not felt.'—Boswell's *Life of Johnson.*

different kind upon the possession of land may not yet be found such that some such measure will be of necessity adopted, to make room for the natural increase of population. But it would be a remedy which only a violent revolution could at present accomplish, and what we want is a remedy which needs only an adequate reform of Parliament for its accomplishment. And if neither the French system of partition nor the agrarian system of the Gracchi is to be our model—if the feudal model is set before us only as a warning—we may yet find a model in the general tendency of English law reform since the system was established which first limited property in land to a particular line of descent in a particular number of families; for that end depriving each successive proprietor of the chief uses of property itself. The feudal landowner forfeited the right to sell his own land, to leave it by will, to let it securely, to provide for his family out of it, to subject it to the payment of his debts; he forfeited, therefore, the chief rights of property, taking only in exchange a right to confiscate the property of his tenants. The whole movement of English jurisprudence relating to land ever since may be summed up as an effort to restore to landowners the just rights of proprietorship on the one hand, and to protect tenants from the unjust right of confiscation on the other. In a memorable speech on the reformation of Parliament, three-quarters of a century ago, the illustrious scholar, Sir William Jones, rested his main argument on the following ground: 'There has been a continual war in the constitution of England between two jarring principles—the Evil Principle of the feudal system, with his dark auxiliaries, ignorance and false philosophy; and the good principle of increasing commerce, with her liberal allies, true learning and sound reason. The first has blemished and polluted wherever it has touched the fair form of our constitution. . . . What caused the absurd yet fatal distinction between property personal and real?—the feudal principle.' This argument errs only in representing the struggle as one of feudalism with commerce alone; it has been a struggle with the interests and instincts, not only of commerce, but also of natural affection, morality, and justice. The view taken by Sir W. Jones resembles that of Adam Smith, already referred to, which attributes all the progress of Europe to a gradual victory of the commerce of towns over the feudal institutions of the country. The progress, however, which has actually been made, so far as it is due to the influence of commerce, is due to its action, not only in and by the towns, but in the bosom of feudalism itself—in the commercial wants and necessities of the feudal lords of the soil, as well as of their tenants and their neighbours in towns. But we must go further and add, that not only the commercial side of human nature, but also its moral side, in the breasts of the feudal proprietors themselves, rebelled against a system which sacrificed the whole family save one, and all its dependents, to maintain the line of feudal succession.

From the moment when the power of bequeathing and alienating lands, which the civilised jurisprudence of Rome had introduced into England, was abandoned for the barbarous and retrograde rule of male primogeniture, an unremitting struggle began, to recover the ancient and legitimate essentials of property, by regaining testamentary powers on the one hand, and breaking the fetters of entail on the other. With regard to the former—the efforts and devices adopted to regain the right of testation over lands—we may apply, *totidem verbis*, to England the description an eminent jurist has given of the origin of wills among the Romans : ' We might have assumed, *à priori*, that the passion for testacy was generated by some moral injustice entailed by the rules of intestate succession ; and we find them at variance with every instinct by which early society was cemented together. Every dominant sentiment of the primitive Roman was entwined with the relations of the family. But what was the family ? The law defined it one way, natural affection another.' * The writer referred to adds that the system of *fidei commissa*, or bequests in trust, was devised to meet the disabilities imposed by ancient law on the proper objects of natural affection. But the Roman law at least embraced in the family all the children in the line of agnatic descent, whereas the feudal system confined it to one single and perhaps remotely related descendant —the heir-at-law. The device resorted to in England to remedy this still grosser outrage on nature was the same as in Rome—the invention of uses or trusts.' †

* Maine's ' Ancient Law.'
† ' I hold that neither of these cases was so much the reason of uses as another reason in the beginning, which was, that the lands, by the common law of England, were not testamentary or devisable.'—Lord Bacon's Reading on the Statute of Uses.

No more conclusive proof need be given of the total incompatibility of the feudal rules of inheritance with the wants of society, than that, whereas the Statute of Uses was passed in the reign of Henry VIII., expressly in order to put an end to testamentary and other dispositions by uses away from the line of feudal descent, only five years afterwards it was found necessary to pass the Statute of Wills, which begins with a recital that the king's subjects, as daily experience shows, cannot 'discharge their debts, or after their degree set forth and advance their children,' and proceeds to enact that two-thirds of lands held in military tenure shall be thenceforward disposable by will. Nor could the restriction on the remaining third survive the favourable experience of its abolition by an ordinance of the Commonwealth, of which the Act of Charles II. was a mere copy.

The history of entails presents a similar record of a revolt of the feelings and wants of human nature against the principle of descent which still governs the transmission of the bulk of landed property in England at this day. For 200 years after the statute De Donis restored the feudal restrictions, which landholders had already found means to shake off, continued attempts were made in Parliament to obtain the repeal of that statute, the consequences of which are well described in an old treatise commonly ascribed to Lord Bacon, in terms which have lost little of their application since: 'By a statute made in Edward I.'s time, the tenant in tail could not put away the land from his heir by any act of conveyance, nor let it nor encumber it longer than his life. But the inconvenience thereof was great; for by that means the land being so sure tied upon the heir as that his father could not put it from him, made the son to be disobedient, negligent and wasteful. It hindered men that had entailed lands, that they could not make the best of their lands by improvement, for that none upon so short an estate as his own life would lay any stock upon the land that might yield rent improved. Lastly, those entails did defraud many subjects of their debts, for that the land was not liable longer than in his own time.' Two centuries after the statute of Edward, the method of barring entails by recoveries was introduced by the judges, and that fiction was succeeded by the Statutes of Fines in the three following reigns.

In the foregoing and many similar efforts of our law, which we have not space to detail, one constant aim and movement is discernible—to neutralise and evade, by shifts and artifices, the feudal restrictions on the rights of property in land, and its free alienation, lease, division, and bequest.* But it may be laid down as a general proposition in the philosophy of law, that wherever, in the law of an advancing society, a perpetual effort and tendency manifests itself in a given direction by a succession of devices and changes, the general aim of those changes is essential to progress, and the tendency represents the spirit of progress itself —the spirit of civilisation struggling with the old spirit

* For example, powers of leasing entailed lands, and charging the inheritance with improvements—a mode by which the law attempts to restore indirectly and partially the rights of property which entails directly withhold.

of barbarism. The ground of this proposition is simple, and it is one especially strong in the case of a country so tenacious of custom, so suspicious of speculative reason, as England—that the expedients and changes in question are such as society is forcibly driven to by the personal experience of its members, and the demands of human nature and daily life. But the proposition is applicable only to the general aim and end of the efforts we speak of, not to the means.

The means adopted to rid land of its fetters were in the first instance the fiction of uses and trusts, out of which grew the baneful division of our jurisprudence into a double system of equity and law.* And this was only the beginning of a new evil superadded to

* In a recent debate in the House of Lords (Feb. 1870) the division between law and equity seems to have been referred to as caused by the division of courts. The author ventures, however, to maintain that the division of courts was the consequence, not the cause, of the inadequacy of the common law, and the consequent rise of a supplementary system of equity. The chief causes of the division may be enumerated in order as follows:—

First: and especially, the feudal restrictions on the testamentary disposition and alienation of land, rendering it unavailable for many of the wants of its successive holders, and so leading to the device of uses and trusts, which the Court of Chancery eagerly stepped in to enforce.

Secondly: defects in the remedies of the common law courts, or in the nature of the protection and reparation they could decree.

Thirdly: defects likewise in their mode of trial, especially as regards the evidence of parties to suits.

Fourthly: opposition to the Roman Law—opposition in reality to ecclesiastical powers and pretensions on the one hand, and to arbitrary government on the other, with both of which it became identified.

Fifthly: personal ambition and professional interests on the part of the founders of the system of equity.

Sixthly: the influence of scholastic logic.

The influence of the personal interest of the founders of equity on the growth of the system has been instructively pointed out in a learned and interesting essay by Mr. Neate, published in the volume of the Social Science Association for 1868.

the old; for the new pieces which lawyers have put into the old garment of our law have only made its unfitness for the wear of civilised life greater than before. Lord Bacon, after observing that 'the main reason of uses at the beginning was that lands were not by the common law testamentary or devisable,' adds that, since the statute, another reason was 'an excess of evil in men's minds affecting to have the assurance of their estate and possession to be revocable in their own times, and irrevocable after their own times.' The object of settlements in tail, renewed in each succeeding generation, is to accomplish ends still more inconsistent—to give each generation a free disposition over land, yet to bind the land from generation to generation in the feudal line of descent—to give all the family property to the heir, yet not to ignore those claims of nature and justice which feudalism, in its naked and ₊consistent barbarity, boldly set aside. The consequence is the practical retention of the old evil of perpetual entails, and along with it the new evils of heavy incumbrances on land, of increased incapacity of its owners to improve, of an unparalleled complexity and uncertainty of title, and of a division between law and equity carried into interminable fresh ramifications.

There is one way to remedy the old and new evils together, and at once to purge our jurisprudence, and to emancipate land from its burdens and trammels—and that is to extinguish the force of settlements as binding and irrevocable instruments, save so far as a provision for a wife is concerned; to put family settlements, save as to a wife, on the same footing as wills, *ipso facto* void upon marriage, and revocable by any subsequent conveyance or will; to enact that each successive proprietor shall take the land he succeeds to free from any restriction on his rights of proprietorship; and further, to make provision that all lands left burdened with any charges shall be sold immediately on the death of the owner to pay off the incumbrance. A moment's reflection might satisfy any unprejudiced mind that settlements impose unjust and impolitic restrictions, as well as pecuniary burdens, upon the owners of land. Take the case of a re-settlement, for example, in which the son joins with his father. It is commonly supposed that the son acts with his eyes open, and with a special eye to the contingencies of the future and of family life. But what are the real facts of the case? Before the future owner of the land has come into possession—before he has any experience of his property, or of what is best to do or what he can do in regard of it—before the exigencies of the future or his own real position are known to him—before the character, number and wants of his children are learned, or the claims of parental affection and duty can make themselves felt, and while still very much at the mercy of a predecessor desirous of posthumous greatness and power, he enters into an irrevocable disposition, by which he parts with the rights of a proprietor over his future property for ever, and settles its devolution, burdened with charges, upon an unborn heir, who may be the very person least fitted or deserving to take it. To make a settlement void upon marriage, unless so far as relates to a provision for the wife, is only to apply the principle of jurisprudence which, under the old law of wills, made marriage and the birth of a child—and which, under the present law, makes marriage alone—the revocation of a will. It is plainly absurd to make an arrangement for children irrevocable, which is entered into before they are in existence, and, therefore, before their claims can be weighed and provided for justly. It would for the same reason be insufficient to enact, as one eminent writer has proposed, that no estate should be vested by settlement in an unborn child;* since immediately on the birth of the first son, a settlement in conformity with that restriction, yet open to the objections just stated, might be made.

To complete the emancipation of land from artificial restrictions on its distribution and use out of the feudal line of descent, it is necessary to assimilate its devolution in the case of intestacy to that of personal property. Every mischief and injustice which settlements leave uncommitted, the law of primogeniture steps in to accomplish. In assimilating in this and other respects the law of real to that of personal property, the legislature will be only promoting a movement which has characterised civilisation both in ancient and modern times. 'The idea,' in the language of Mr. Maine, 'seems to have spontaneously suggested itself to a great number of early societies, to classify property into kinds. One kind of property is placed on a lower footing than the others, but at the same

* 'The Economic Position of the British Labourer,' p. 51. By H. Fawcett, M.P.

time is relieved from the fetters which antiquity has imposed upon them. Subsequently the superior convenience of the rules governing the transfer and descent of the lower order of property becomes generally recognised, and by a gradual course of innovation the plasticity of the less dignified class is communicated to the classes conventionally higher. The history of Roman Property Law is the history of the assimilation of *res mancipi* to *res nec mancipi*. The history of property on the European continent is the history of the subversion of the feudalised law of land by the Romanised law of movables; and in England it is visibly the law of personalty which threatens to absorb and annihilate the law of realty.'*

Every step which has been made to communicate to land the alienability by which personalty was early distinguished, has been a step in the path of the assimilation of real and personal property law. The process of assimilation may be traced in the invention of uses, the fictions of fines and recoveries, the Statute of Wills, the abolition of military tenures, and (by a long series of piecemeal reforms) the subjection of inherited land to the debts of its former possessor.†
But, as has already been said, a tendency persistently evinced in the modifications of law in a progressive community carries on its face the proof of its necessity and good policy. The principle of feudal descent, which is the root of the two monstrous anomalies of

---

* 'Ancient Law,' p. 273.
† For a remarkable example of the assimilation of real and personal property law, see 27 & 28 Vic., chap. 112, as to judgments.

English jurisprudence—the divisions of law and equity, and of real and personal property law—is the root also of the artificial limitation of land; and at once to reform our jurisprudence, and to set land free from restrictions against national industry and life, we must strike at the root instead of lopping off branches one by one, as has hitherto been done by a territorial and half-feudal legislature. This being done, the remaining steps to facilitate the commercial transfer of land are obvious and easy, and it could be readily shown that history supplies the same argument in their favour which applies to the reforms already suggested. These steps are (in addition to some stated already)—first, the compulsory registration of all dealings with land in a registry open to the public at a trifling expense; secondly, a new Statute of Limitations, greatly shortening the period within which non-claim shall perfect the title of the present possessors, who might otherwise be injuriously affected by registration; and thirdly, the sale of all encumbered estates, or of enough to defray the incumbrances, with a parliamentary title to the purchasers.

One more measure is requisite to remove the restrictions which limit artificially the trade and manufactures of towns to particular spots—namely, to revise and alter the regulations of the Customs, which confine the import and export trade of the country to particular harbours, exclusive of several well adapted by nature for commerce. It is, of course, well to diminish, as far as can be done without injury to trade, the collection of duties; but the present restrictions undoubtedly hurt the revenue as well as the trade of the country.

Finally, there is a matter with which, above all, only a Reformed Parliament can deal effectually—the insecurity of tenure, of which the mischief of game may be considered as part. The insecurity of tenure is a public calamity, purposely maintained to deprive tenants of the political power and independence given to them by law ; and if some more direct remedy be not applied to remove it, the makeshift of the ballot will be used.

THE ENGLISH LAND QUESTION, 1870.

THE land systems of England and Ireland, though closely analogous in many respects, as regards both history and structure, present, nevertheless, some features of striking dissimilarity. The prominent Irish land question is one relating to agricultural tenure; though it is so because the system in its entirety has prevented not only the diffusion of landed property, but also the rise of manufactures, commerce, and other non-agricultural employments. In England, on the other hand, notwithstanding monstrous defects in the system of tenure, the prominent land question is one relating to the labourer, not to the farmer, and to the labourer in the town as well as in the country. The chief causes of this difference are—first, the violent conversion of the bulk of the English population into mere labourers long ago; and, secondly, the existence of great cities and various non-agricultural employments, created by mineral wealth, and a superior commercial situation, but confined to particular spots by the accumulation of land in unproductive hands, by the uncertainty of the law and of titles, and by the scantiness and poverty of the rural population on which country towns depend for a market. An immense immigration into a few great cities has accordingly been the movement in England corresponding to emigration from Ireland; and no less than 5,153,157 persons, by official estimate, will, in the middle of the present year be gathered into seven large towns—London, Liverpool, Manchester, Birmingham, Leeds, Sheffield, and Bristol; 3,214,707, or one-sixth of the total population, being concentrated in London alone. A twofold mischief has thus been produced by the English land system—in the wretched and hopeless condition of the agricultural labourer on one hand, and the precarious employment and crowded dwellings of the working-classes in large towns on the other.

There is no lack of considerable writers and politicians to assure us that this situation is the natural result of commerce and economic laws; but, alarming as it is, it would be much more so, were such a conclusion generally held; since no reforms could then be looked for, either to diminish the existing misery, or to avert the future catastrophe it threatens; and, in fact, the situation must actually become worse with every forward step in industrial progress, if that conclusion be well founded.

It is, therefore, no matter of mere theoretical or historical interest to ascertain its actual causes; although, even from that point of view, it engages the profound attention of economists on the Continent, struck by the contrast which the distribution of both land and population in England presents to what is found in every other part of the civilised world. 'England,' says a distinguished Englishman on the

Continent, referring particularly to the researches of a German economist,* 'is the only Teutonic community, we believe we might say the only civilised community, in which the bulk of the land under cultivation is not in the hands of small proprietors; clearly, therefore, England represents the exception and not the rule.'† It would surely be strange if the exception were the result, as Mr. Buckle asserted, of 'the general march of affairs;'‡ and if industry and commerce, which are peopling the rest of the world with landowners, had, as a more recent writer expresses it, 'severed the people of England from the land.'§ The present author presumes to affirm that the exceptional situation of England, in place of being the natural consequence

* See the work hereafter cited of Herr Erwin Nasse, Professor of Political Economy in the University of Bonn, on 'Inclosures of Commons in England.'

† 'Systems of Land Tenure.' Germany. By R. B. D. Morier, p. 322.

‡ 'The history of the decay of that once most important class, the English yeomanry, is an interesting subject, and one for which I have collected considerable materials; at present, I will only say that its decline was first distinctly perceptible in the latter half of the seventeenth century, and was consummated by the rapidly increasing power of the commercial and manufacturing classes, early in the eighteenth century.... Some writers regret this almost total destruction of the yeoman freeholders, overlooking the fact that they are disappearing, not in consequence of any violent revolution or stretch of arbitrary power, but simply by the general march of affairs; society doing away with what it no longer requires.'—*Buckle's History of Civilization in England,* i. 569.

§ 'I shall now proceed to trace historically what the economic causes were which have severed the people from the land.'

'It is the commercial and not the feudal spirit which in England has worked against peasant properties. Wipe out the commercial element from English history, and you wipe out those causes which have worked *against* peasant proprietorship in England. But for the commercial element, the feudal system in England would probably have remained in full force as in other countries, and the English peasants have become peasant proprietors.'—*The Land Question,* by Frederic Seebohm. 'Fortnightly Review,' February, 1870.

of commerce and industry, is the product of a violent and unnatural history on the one hand, and of laws existing at this day most adverse to both commerce and industry on the other.

The history of the revolution by which that result has been brought about is so copious and minute that many volumes might be filled with it, though only its principal steps can be presented here. As may be inferred from the two passages just cited,* it has unseated two ancient classes of small landholders, the peasantry and the yeomanry, as, for brevity, we may name the two rural classes below the landed gentry. The encroachment, too, on the domains of both began at the same time and in the same manner, and has been prosecuted to its consummation in a great measure by a similar process. Each, however, of the two classes has had also its own special history of extinction; and while the poorer class, the peasantry, have never been suffered to recover, even for a generation, the ground from which they have been driven century after century, there was in the case of the wealthier class of yeomanry, along with their dispossession, an opposite movement, which down to the last hundred years continued to recruit their numbers.

Briefly enumerated, the chief causes by which the peasantry—the really most important class—have been dispossessed of their ancient proprietary rights and beneficial interests in the soil are the following :—

(1.) Confiscation of their ancient rights of common,

* See the last two notes.

which were not only in themselves of great value, but most important for the help they gave towards the maintenance of their separate lands.

(2.) Confiscation to a large extent of their separate lands themselves, by a long course of violence, fraud, and chicane, in addition to forfeitures resulting from deprivation of their rights of common.

(3.) The destruction of country towns and villages, and the loss, in consequence, of local markets for the produce of peasant farms and gardens.

(4.) The construction of a legal system based on the principle of inalienability from the feudal line, in the interest of great landed families, and incompatible with either the continuance of the ancient or the rise of a new class of peasant landholders.

(5.) The loss, with their lands and territorial rights, of all political power and independence on the part of the peasantry; and, by consequence, the establishment and maintenance by the great proprietors of laws most adverse to their interests.

(6.) Lastly, the administration by the great landowners of their own estates in such a manner as to impoverish the peasantry still further, and to sever their last remaining connection with the soil.

These different causes have necessarily been mentioned in succession, but in reality they have often operated simultaneously. The one first stated was the first, however, to operate on an extensive scale, and the reader's attention is therefore asked to it first.*

Some centuries ago the greater part of England was still uninclosed, and to a large extent subject to common use; the lord of the manor being himself a co-partner, as it were, both in the system of husbandry followed on the arable land and in the pastoral and wood rights enjoyed in common. Round each village, as a general rule, lay in the first instance a little territory of tillage land, divided into individual shares, but cultivated on a common system, and subject also to 'commonable' rights on the part of the individual holders—rights, that is to say, to pasture in common on the stubble after harvest and on the fallow grass. Beyond this arable territory, thus partly enjoyed in common, lay another territory, used entirely in common; the pasture rights, however, on the portion nearest the tillage land being usually 'stinted,' or

---

* Professor Nasse begins his treatise, already referred to ('Ueber die mittelalterliche Feldgemeinschaft und die Einhegungen des sechszehnten Jahrhunderts in England'), with the following words:—'In the agrarian history of the nations of Central Europe, there is no event of more importance, or vaster in its consequences, than the dissolution of the ancient co-partnership in the use of the soil for husbandry, and the establishment in its stead of separate and independent farms. But this revolution has a special importance in the case of England, contributing largely, as it has done, to the extrusion of small landholders, and to the foundation of that preponderance of large property which in turn has had so great an effect on the constitutional history of that country.' The author is indebted to Herr Nasse both for this most instructive treatise, and for oral information on the subject of inclosures. Herr Nasse, it may not be amiss to state, is far from being unfriendly to large estates or large farms, either in his own country or in England.

strictly limited in respect of the number and kinds of animals allowed to feed on it, while on the remoter portion each of the commoners might graze, in summer at least, as many animals as he could feed in winter from the produce of his separate fields. These rights are expressly recognised by the early statutes as legally belonging to the commoners, and are said to have often been sufficient to enable each of them to graze not less than forty sheep, besides as many cows as he had winter food for. Taken together, the common and 'commonable' rights constituted no small part of the villagers' means of living, and it will appear hereafter how the loss of them entailed on many of them the further loss of their separate holdings, and contributed to thin the ranks even of the wealthier class among them—the yeomanry. The first encroachment was made by the Statute of Merton (20 Hen. III. c. 1), which stated that many great men of England complained that, after affording to the freeholders of the manor the requisite pasture appertaining to their holdings, there was a residue of waste, wood, and pasture, which was unprofitable. The statute granted, therefore, to the lords of the manor the right to inclose such residue, the remedy of a suit for insufficiency of pasture before the judges of assize being reserved to commoners alleging it. This statute was confirmed in the next reign, and extended from the freeholders of the manor to neighbouring commoners; and the recitals of the second enactment show how unpopular the new inclosures were, the ditches and hedges being destroyed by night. Our legal records show, moreover, that many suits were actually brought by commoners for insufficiency of common. But we may judge what were the ordinary chances of success on the part of villagers against 'great men' in those days of judicial corruption, and how far it was prudent for tenants and poor neighbours, especially when already impoverished by stint of pasture and of fuel, to wage war against the lord of the manor. They must often have been made to feel that a half is more than the whole. The island, too, especially after the great plague, was wide compared with the people; and it was not until the inclosing movement, beginning with the rise in wool at the close of the fifteenth century, that extensive hardship was inflicted on the rural population. In the sixteenth century it spread vagrancy and pauperism throughout the country, and gave the peasantry of England a Poor-law in exchange for their ancient patrimony. Mr. Morier pertinently remarks that the inclosures of the sixteenth century are usually spoken of as though denoting merely the conversion of arable into pasturage, and the consolidation of farms, 'without reference to the primary fact which governs the two, namely, the inclosure, not of arable land as such, but of *commonable* arable land.' Mr. Morier refers to losses of their separate holdings on the part of the villagers, to which we must presently refer; but it is important to bear in mind that, along with the 'commonable' arable land inclosed, an immense extent of common pasturage and woodland was withdrawn from the peasant and added to the domain of the great landholders. During the minority of Edward VI., the

Protector Somerset appointed a Royal Commission ' for redress of inclosures,' to inquire into the grievances and usurpations with which the country rang; and Hales, the most active member of this Commission, while denouncing in the strongest terms the wrongs of which the great proprietors were guilty, expressly limited his invectives to such inclosures as encroached on the common rights of others, observing that inclosures of private property were more beneficial than otherwise. 'The miserable and unsatisfactory result of this Commission,' says Professor Nasse, ' originally hailed with intense delight by the rural population, is sufficiently well known. The power of the nobility in the country was so great, and the hand of the executive so weak, that in some cases the witnesses summoned did not dare to appear, and in others, those who had given truthful evidence were subjected to ill-treatment by the landlords. If the Protector's extraordinary Royal Commission could not effectually resist the power of the ruling class, it may naturally be inferred that the protection of the ordinary courts could not much avail the sufferers. Their rights rested on the customs of each estate, to be proved by the rolls in the hands of the lord of the soil, and they were liable to forfeiture by an indefinite number of acts on the part of the copyholders. The small copyholders were doubtless unable to substantiate their rights in courts of law, opposed by expert lawyers. Latimer, in fact, charges the judges with injustice and receipt of bribes, and says that money was almighty, even in courts of justice. A period of such tremendous revolution in Church and

State as the reign of Henry VIII. could certainly not have been favourable to the protection of customary rights. Such a sudden change as the secularisation of the Church lands must have shaken the whole traditional order of property. Thus, a pamphlet published in 1546 complains that the new owners of Church property generally declared the ancient rights of the copyholders forfeited. They were compelled either to relinquish their holdings, or accept leases for a short period.'

The inclosures of the sixteenth century, violent, unjust, and sweeping as they were, form, as the last sentence from Herr Nasse indicates, no more than one great chapter in the history of the confiscation of the patrimony of the English peasantry. It did not fall within the scope of his essay to pursue the history of the whole movement beyond that period, but he says of it : ' Powerful as it was, it then reached its aim but to a limited extent. The small landowners did not all disappear in the sixteenth century. The majority of the freeholders doubtless held their ground, and even the copyholders were not all driven out or converted into tenants for terms of years. Lord Coke could declare in the seventeenth century that one-third of England was copyhold. The revolution thus inaugurated has lasted down to our own days. Sometimes the progress has been slower, sometimes faster, until by degrees the close connection in which the two phenomena, inclosure and expulsion of the peasantry, originally stood, has ceased.'

It has ceased only with the almost complete expulsion of the peasantry from the soil; but although the Inclosure Acts of the last century and a half have withdrawn, in addition to what had been lost before (and with hardly any compensation to the sufferers), a further amount of common territory, estimated as equal to one-third of the total area now under cultivation,* the inclosure movement from first to last—from the Statute of Merton to the last Inclosure Act—has been but one of many processes by which the consummation has been reached. That it is entitled to the prominence Professor Nasse gives it, is nevertheless sufficiently clear. As he observes, there were two courses which might have been pursued with advantage instead

* The first Report of the Royal Commission on the Employment of Women and Children in Agriculture states:—'According to the estimate made by the Select Committee of the House of Commons on Emigration in 1827, and the calculations of Mr. Porter in 1843, 7,175,520 statute acres had been inclosed in England and Wales since the first Inclosure Bill in the year 1710 up to the year 1843. To these since 1843 have been added 484,893 acres, as appears by the Annual Report of the Inclosure Commissioners for 1867; making together 7,660,413 statute acres added to the cultivated area of England and Wales since 1710, *or above one-third part of the total of* 25,451,626 *acres in cultivation in* 1867. . . . The inclosure to this extent since 1710, *in very many cases without any compensation to the smaller commoners,* has withdrawn from the agricultural labourer means which would otherwise have been open to him of adding to his resources by the exercise of ancient rights attached to his dwelling, or by the acquisition of new rights and privileges upon the waste in connexion with new dwellings, as new dwellings increased with the increase of the agricultural population.' The amount of compensation given to the smaller commoners may be judged from the statement of Lord Lincoln in the House of Commons in 1845, that in nineteen cases out of twenty the Committees of the House had neglected the rights of the poor. Poor commoners, he said, could not come to London, appoint highly paid counsel, and produce evidence in support of their claims; and the Committees of the House had remained in perfect ignorance of them.

of detriment to the commoners. Either the ancient system of joint husbandry (which was unquestionably wasteful) might have been transformed into a system of farming for the common benefit, adapted to the improvements and requirements of the age; or there might have been an equitable distribution of land, which would have bettered the position of every commoner. As it was, the peasantry lost not only the benefits derived from rights of commons over the greater part of England, but that loss, in numerous cases, entailed the loss of their separate fields. They had lived on the produce of the two, and their husbandry was based on it. They were the more unequal to the augmented rents and fines demanded of them, that they had lost the sustenance of their stock, and the more unequal to defend their lands and holdings in a court of law against injustice. They lost moreover their local markets in villages and country towns, which decayed with the decay of husbandmen, or were violently pulled down for the inclosure of the ground on which they stood within the great proprietor's domain.* This was not all. The small proprietor, the freehold tenant, the copyholder, and the tenant for years were ejected from their own fields as they had been from their commons. 'When some

* Sir Thomas More complained :—' Noblemen and gentlemen, yea, and certain abbots, not contenting themselves with the yearly revenues and profits that were wont to grow to their forefathers and predecessors of their lands, leave no ground for tillage. They inclose all into pastures; they throw down houses; they pluck down towns, and leave nothing standing. And as though you lost no ground by forests, chase lands, and parks, those good holy men turn all dwelling-places and all glebe lands into desolation and wilderness.'

covetous man,' says Harrison, 'espies a farther commodity in their *commons*, *holds*, and *tenures*, he doth find such means as thereby to wipe out many of their occupyings.' * Bishop Gilpin complained that the great landowners scrupled not to drive people from their property, alleging that the land was theirs, and turning them out of their shelter like vermin. Sir Thomas More declared that tenants were 'got rid of by *force* or *fraud*, or tired out by repeated injuries into parting with their property.' And Mr. Morier sums up the dealings of the great proprietors with the villagers' fields (with which their own lands lay mixed under the ancient system of common husbandry) as follows: 'In the most favourable cases, the withdrawal of one-third or one-half of the land from the "commonable" arable land of a township—such half or third portion consisting in many cases of small parcels intermixed with those of the commoners—must have rendered the further common cultivation impossible, and thereby compelled the freeholders and copyholders to part with their land and their common rights on any terms. That in less favourable cases the lords of the manor did not look very closely into the rights of their

---

* Is this the species of 'commercial element' to which Mr. Seebohm refers in the sentence—'Wipe out the commercial element from English history and you wipe out those causes which have worked *against* peasant proprietorship in England'? 'Fortnightly Review,' February, p. 230. The italics are Mr. Seebohm's. It may be well to call attention to the fact, which Mr. Seebohm in one part of his argument seems to lose sight of, that the terms 'holds' and 'tenures' comprehend freeholds, and every form of landed proprietorship, as well as of tenure by lease and copyhold. Every estate in land, as well as every leasehold, was and is a tenure, although landed proprietors have found it convenient to forget it.

tenants, and that instead of an equitable repartition of land between the two classes, the result was a general consolidation of tenants' land with demesne land, and the creation of large inclosed farms, with the consequent wholesale destruction of agricultural communities or townships, is well known to every reader of history.'*

Severed from the village community which had once stood together, however feebly, against invasion of their common rights; impoverished by the loss of pastures for his cattle and sheep, and of fuel for his house, in a time of rising prices; deprived, too, of a market within reach for what produce remained to him to sell—how was either the petty landowner or the small freehold or copyhold tenant to make good defence against the tremendous weapons with which English law armed, as it still does, the lord of the manor against the villager? Shakespeare informs us how it was that lawyers had become great landowners in his time:—

'*Hamlet.* Why may not that be the scull of a lawyer? Where be his quiddits now, his quillets, his cases, his tenures, and his tricks? Why does he suffer this rude knave now to knock him about the sconce with a dirty shovel, and will not tell him of his action of battery? This fellow might be in 's time a great buyer of land, with his statutes, his recognisances, his fines, his double vouchers, his recoveries. Will his vouchers vouch him no more of his purchases than the length and breadth of a pair of indentures? The very

---

* 'Cobden Club Volume,' p. 321.

conveyances of his lands will hardly lie in this box.'* Not to speak of the risks of 'an action for battery' against a powerful noble, if he chose to have him knocked on the head, how was the copyholder to produce a box of conveyances in the control of the lord himself? Was it likely that the small proprietor could outwit the lord's sharp lawyer, with 'his cases, his tenures, and his tricks'? The burning hatred which the peasantry of his own time felt towards the ministers of a legal system by which they were oppressed and ruined, breathes in the language which the great dramatist puts in the mouth of Cade and his followers.† And as the old race of village landholders disappeared before the usurped inclosure, the disseisin, the ejectment, how was a new race to rise in their stead, or to become 'great buyers of land' like the lawyers? How was a new race of peasant proprietors to spring up in our own time, once it had become extinct, under perils surrounding the purchase of land thus described by Lord St. Leonards:—

'This danger compels *every* ‡ purchaser to require a sixty-years' title, by which sellers and buyers of land are put annually to an enormous expense.' § 'Was this 'enormous expense' likely to be defrayed by a

---

* *Hamlet*, Act v. Scene 1.

† '*Dick*. The first thing we do, let's kill all the lawyers.

'*Cade*. Nay, that I mean to do. Is not this a lamentable thing, that of the skin of an innocent lamb should be made parchment? That parchment being scribbled o'er should undo a man? Some say the bee stings; but I say 'tis the bee's wax; for I did but once seal to a thing, and I was never mine own man since.'—2 *Henry VI*. Act iv. Sc. 1.

‡ Italics in original.

§ 'Handy Book on Property Law.' By Lord St. Leonards. 8th ed. p. 88.

peasantry reduced to the condition of agricultural labourers on the verge of pauperism?

With their lands and their commons, it should be remembered, the rural population lost all political weight; the great proprietors could legislate respecting land and the people upon it as they thought fit. While prices were rapidly rising in the sixteenth century, landlords in Parliament, and landlords in the parish, fixed the rates of wages; and in our own time, landlords in Parliament maintained a Poor-law which made it the direct interest of landlords in the parish to turn the peasantry out of their cottages, and to suffer no more cottages to be built. The very poverty to which they had been reduced by centuries of encroachment, became a motive for expelling them altogether. 'The year 1775,' it is stated in the Report of the Royal Commission before cited, 'is noticed as the period from which a marked change for the worse in the condition of the agricultural labourer became visible. The change was attributed to inadequate wages compared with the cost of the necessaries of life, to the consolidation of small farms, to the loss of privileges by inclosures of commons, and also to the loss of small portions of land which had contributed to the labourer's resources, and which his necessities compelled him to sell. . . . In "The Case of the Labourers in Husbandry," published in 1795, it is stated: "Cottages have been progressively deprived of the little land formerly let with them; and also their rights of commonage have been swallowed up in large farms by inclosures. Thus an amazing number of people have been reduced from a comfortable state of independence to a precarious state, as mere hirelings, who, when out of work, immediately come upon the parish."* When this stage had been reached, parochial policy dictated that the cottage should follow the garden, and the peasant's last interest in the soil was extinguished.

The peasantry of England have, in short, been dispossessed of their ancient connexion with land by a series of confiscations and encroachments—by a legal system devised for the sole behoof and to consolidate the power of great proprietors—and by proceedings in exercise of this power so acquired, which have resulted in an agrarian economy even more unnatural, more hurtful, and more demoralising than that of Ireland. The dispossession of the English peasantry has not, indeed, like that of the Irish, been aggravated by religious persecution, or by the tyranny of race; but it has been more complete, and it has left them in a yet lower position in the social scale.

The history of the yeomanry presents some different vicissitudes, and also some common features, when regarded side by side with the history of the peasantry. Yeomen, as well as peasants, were deprived of rights of commons, of great assistance to their husbandry, and of considerable value. They, too, in ages of violent usurpation and legal injustice, lost many members from their ranks; but their hold on the land was less

---

* 'First Report on the Employment of Women and Children in Agriculture, 1869,' pp. xvi., xvii.

easily loosed, and for centuries there was, moreover, an opposite movement. Farmers were enriched by leases, and became buyers of land; and the ranks of the order were recruited from the towns as well as from the country. Citizens and shopkeepers, and even artisans, sought investment in land; and a document, ascribed to Edward VI., complained that the grazier, the farmer, the merchant, became landed men, and that the very artificer left the town and lived in the country. M. Guizot justly remarks that the great division of lands, through the ruin of the feudal aristocracy, and the growth of commercial wealth in the sixteenth century, is a social phenomenon which has not attracted sufficient attention. And the movement did not entirely cease for two centuries more. It was not, indeed, until after the publication of the 'Wealth of Nations,' that the long leases which, as its author states, commerce had introduced, and under which the tenant-farmer had frequently risen to become a landowner, disappeared; and that the farmer sank into the dependent of the great proprietor, who was thus enabled to make and maintain such laws relating to land and its tenure, as well as its ownership, as he thought best for his own consequence, profit and pleasure. By the close of the last century, moreover, by far the greater part of the land had come under strict settlement in the feudal line, and comparatively little has ever entered the market since. What little has entered the market has been more and more an article of luxury, not of business—sought for the social consequence or the political power attaching to the monopoly of land, or for the country pursuits of the sportsman, not of the farmer. Landed property has been deprived, by the risks and expenses attending dealings with it, of its natural value for the cultivator, as being naturally the most secure and attractive, the most immediately and cheaply accessible investment for his capital, labour and time, and the most marketable commodity, because of its universal utility, should he wish to raise money on it or sell it; while, on the other hand, it has been invested with an artificial value for those who seek in it mainly political and social predominance or amusement. Among the causes which the Chief of the Statistical Department in France assigns for the increasing subdivision of landed property, in addition to the increasing wealth of the peasantry, is *la suppression du cens électoral*,* because the larger estates no longer carry with them the monopoly of political power, which a limited suffrage formerly gave. In England it is precisely the reverse: land for the last hundred years might advantageously be bought for the command of votes,† or for social rank, or even for pleasure; but it has been a most perilous investment for farmers for profit, and the more so the more they laid out on the land, and the less they left over for law expenses and litigation. M. de Lavergne, in his 'Rural Economy of Great Britain,' correcting a French notion that land in England never changes hands at all, points to the advertisements, and remarks: 'These ad-

---

* 'Statistique de la France.' Agriculture, 1868. P. cxvii.
† No small number of Peerages in the United Kingdom owe their creation to the purchase of lands with borrowed money for the purpose of commanding votes.

vertisements usually run as follows : " For sale, a property of — acres in extent, let to a substantial tenant, with an elegant and comfortable residence, a good trouting stream, beautiful lawn, kitchen and flower gardens, in a picturesque county." ' This is really a fair sample of the sort of land which most frequently enters the English market ; by far the greater part never entering it from one century to another. ' A small proprietor,' said Adam Smith, ' who knows every part of his little territory, who views it with all the affection which property, especially small property, naturally inspires, and who, upon that account, takes pleasure in not only cultivating but in adorning it, is generally of all improvers the most industrious, the most intelligent, and the most successful.' ' But,' he added, ' the law of primogeniture and perpetuities of different kinds prevent the division of great estates, and thereby hinder the multiplication of small proprietors. The small quantity, therefore, which is brought to market, and the high price of what is brought thither, prevent a great number of capitals from being employed in its cultivation and improvement, which would otherwise have taken that direction.' It is not, however, a high price that would prevent the purchase of land by the farmer, or even by the labourer, if its transfer were cheap and safe. It does not prevent it in Belgium, Germany, or France ; it is the risk and cost legally attaching to what little is sold, and the unsuitability of that little, which prevent it in England. ' I appeal to your lordships,' said Lord Westbury, speaking on the transfer of land in 1862, 'does any of you know anything about your titles to your estates? Is there not dwelling upon every estate, or rather sitting upon the shoulders of every land proprietor, a solicitor, who guides him in all things, controls him in all things. Talk of a priest-ridden country! That we are a lawyer-ridden country, with regard to the conditions of real property, is a truth beyond the possibility of denial. What has thrown light upon every subject of knowledge? It has been the introduction of printing. Why has not printing been introduced into legal deeds? Why is it that you have presented to you a mass of parchment, so repulsive in its character, so utterly forbidding in its condition, its language, and even the style of its writing, that you surrender yourselves in despair? You do not know what you are signing.'*

It is not, however, the lawyer, but the large proprietor, seeking to re-establish in a commercial age the territorial system of the middle age, who has kept land out of commerce, surrounded it with prohibitions, pitfalls and snares, devoted it to the maintenance of family pride, hidden all his dealings with it in darkness, and committed them to writing in characters symbolical of the period to which in policy and spirit they belong. With such a land system before us, such a history behind it, and such marks of that history in its every detail, is it possible to maintain that 'it is the commercial and not the feudal spirit which in England has

* Compare with these remarks those of Jack Cade, respecting parchments and signatures, cited *supra*.

worked against peasant properties'? What is it but the commercial spirit, a commercial jurisprudence, an open land market, the progress of trade, manufactures and mines, the increasing demand for and the increasing profits of minute cultivation, together with that natural love of land which every disciple of Adam Smith must include among the economic laws determining human pursuits, that augment every year the number of peasant properties bought in the market in Germany, Belgium, and France? It is doubtless true that, under a just and natural system, and with perfect free trade in land, there would have been a disappearance of some peasant and yeoman properties, and a departure of others from former owners and families. Failures, casualties, deaths, the decline of domestic manufactures, changes in husbandry and in markets, changes in the localities of towns and in trade, both internal and foreign, the attractions of towns, the tastes of particular men, succession to land by women*— these and other natural causes would, undoubtedly, under a sound system, have caused a natural and continual flow of small properties, of both yeomen and peasants, into the market. But this outward flow could not have been confined to the small properties, and there would always have been an opposite current. The profits of ground under the master's foot, the natural attractions of agriculture and country life, the love of independence, the accumulation of savings

* It deserves remark, however, that women make excellent farmers both in England and on the Continent, when they can devote their time to it. In the dairy districts of England the wife is a more important person than her husband.

among a large rural population promoted by the possibility of such an investment, the ideas and tastes engendered by a numerous class of small proprietors, the diffusion of land by a just law of succession, would have filled many of the vacant places of those who dropped out of the ranks, and added new regiments to the whole number.*

But only one current has been suffered to flow in respect of small estates—an outward current, largely swollen in former times by force and fraud, and in

* 'Great complaints are made that the class of farmer-owners—the old yeomanry—has largely diminished. There can be no doubt that this class of people would have been from time to time renewed far more than it has been, had land come more freely into the market. It is obvious that, if not renewed, any such class must gradually disappear through deaths, extravagance, and the countless chances and changes which must occur in every class' (*Thoughts on Free Trade in Land*, by William Fowler, M.P. 1869. Longman). This treatise contains a great amount of information in a very small compass. But the present author cannot concur in Mr. Fowler's next observation on the foregoing topic, unless limited to England *under its present legal system:* 'But a more powerful influence has been in operation, inasmuch as it is clear that a man with only a moderate capital can in England use his capital better as a farmer than as a proprietor as well as farmer, because he will thus have all his money free for use in his trade as a cultivator; in short, of having a large sum locked up at a low rate of interest in the price of his land.'

Under a good legal system the price of the land need not be locked up. The owner can either borrow on it easily, safely and cheaply, and either farm more intensively, or take adjoining land and farm more extensively. M. de Laveleye has answered by anticipation Mr. Fowler's argument, in his excellent book on the rural economy of Holland :—' M. Roscher prétend que le fermier appliquera à faire valoir la terre plus de capital que le propriétaire, parce que celui-ci devra consacrer à l'achat du fonds une somme considérable, que le premier peut employer à augmenter l'intensité de la culture. Cette remarque est spécieuse; je ne la crois cependant pas fondée. En effet, celui qui aura acheté le fonds peut lever sur hypothèque la somme nécessaire pour améliorer sa culture; il paiera alors sous forme d'intérêts ce qu'il aurait payé comme fermage, et il aura cet énorme avantage, qu'il profitera exclusivement de toutes les améliorations, en qualité de propriétaire, sans risquer de les voir tourner à son détriment à l'expiration du bail.'—*La Néerlande.* Par Émile de Laveleye, p. 147.

modern times by unjust legislation and a barbarous jurisprudence; while the number of large estates has been artificially maintained by restraints on their division and sale, and the current towards them artificially swollen by the political power and the consequence attached to them. In place of a natural selection having determined the extinction of the small proprietor, the very struggle for existence would have lent to the peasant powerful aid against his more indolent rival. But what trade could survive if, besides being loaded with heavy penalties and restrictions, it were closed against all new comers? What army could outlast a campaign if, while exposed to cruel losses and hardships, the posts only of officers falling could be filled?

A learned writer has lately advanced the proposition that agricultural tenure in England, after passing from the mediæval form of tenure at will into freehold and free copyhold tenure, became and continues to be a hereditary tenure; and that the main difference between the English and the Irish land systems lies in the permanent tenure established in England and the precarious tenure existing in Ireland.* The truth is,

---

* 'In this country, by force of the old traditions of freehold tenure, and the tendency it had created in favour of permanent occupancy, and by force also of the universal custom of tenant-right, perpetuity of tenancy was *practically*, though not legally, secured . . . . ; and hence, as a learned author states (Mr. Dixon's *Law of the Farm*), the same farms descend in the same families generation after generation, sometimes century after century, in some cases for four hundred years . . . . Had there been no disturbing causes, the English law might have operated in Ireland, as in England, to produce that result. But the civil wars, and confiscations which ensued, placed the landlords as a body in opposition to the mass of

that the great bulk of the tenants of England, and with them no small body of small proprietors, sank long ago into the condition of agricultural labourers, or migrated to towns—such towns as the loss of a country custom and the accumulation of land in uncommercial hands did not destroy or prevent from coming into existence.

An enormous disproportion of the English population has thus been forced by the land system into a few large cities, and thrown upon precarious employments for support. Manufactures and trade are not only precarious in being subject to sudden vicissitudes and collapse, but in a more general respect, on which Adam Smith has emphatically dwelt.* The English

the people, and the penal laws which followed prevented the latter from acquiring any desirable interest in land. Thus the relation of landlord and tenant was never, as in England, based upon an inheritable tenure, originally established by law, and then perpetuated by custom, and protected by tenant-right.'—*History of the Law of Tenures of Land in England and Ireland.* By W. J. Finlason, Esq., Barrister-at-Law, Editor of Reeves' *History of the English Law.*

* The capital that is acquired to any country by commerce and manufactures is all a very precarious and uncertain possession till some part of it has been secured and realised in the cultivation and improvement of the land . . . . No vestige now remains of the great wealth said to have been possessed by the greater part of the Hanse Towns. The civil wars of Flanders, and the Spanish Government which succeeded them, chased away the great commerce of Antwerp, Ghent, and Bruges. But Flanders still continues to be one of the richest, best cultivated, and most prosperous provinces of Europe. The ordinary revolutions of war and government easily dry up the sources of that wealth which arises from commerce only. That which arises from the more solid improvements of agriculture is much more durable, and cannot be destroyed but by those more violent convulsions occasioned by the depredations of hostile and barbarous nations, continued for a century or two together, such as those that happened for some time before and after the fall of the Roman empire, in the western provinces of Europe.'—*Wealth of Nations,* book iii. c. 4.

labourers, too, whom our land system crowds into towns, have not that subsidiary and durable resource which town labourers on the Continent are steadily gaining under their land system; nor have English labourers that providence and frugality which continental land systems nurture.

The Irish land question is of more importance politically than the English for the hour, but it is not so economically even for the hour; and it is so politically for the hour only. Economically, the emergency is much greater at this moment in this than in the other island; the main land question here relates to a poorer class than even the Irish tenantry, and there is a much greater amount of material misery and actual destitution in England, traceable mainly to its own land system, though aggravated by that of Ireland and the consequent immigration of poverty.

The day is not distant when the supreme question of English, as of Irish politics, will be whether the national territory is to be the source of power and luxury to a few individuals, or of prosperity and happiness to the nation at large? and whether those few individuals or the nation at large are to determine the answer?

WESTPHALIA AND THE RUHR BASIN,* 1868–1869.

In few places are the old world and the new, the world of immobility and custom, and the world of change and progress, seen in closer proximity and contrast than in Westphalia; a province now heading the rapid march of Prussian industry, yet preserving not a few broad features of the Germany of the past. By the side of the peasant of the olden time, whom the conservative economist Herr Riehl, in his dread of revolution, regards as the emblem of all that is sound in the age, and the sole safeguard of the future of Germany, are the engineer, the miner, and the manufacturer, whom English economists, unable to boast of their own peasantry, are commonly better inclined to put forward as the types of the age, and the pledges of the future. The Basin of the Ruhr, occupying the middle region of the province, and reaching beyond it to the Rhine, is the chief seat of Westphalian mining and manufacturing enterprise; the mountains and valleys of Sauerland and Siegerland† in the south are the

* Reprinted from the 'Fortnightly Review,' March, 1869.
† The general name of Sauerland is given to the mountainous region of Westphalia south of the Ruhr Basin. The country watered by the Sieg bears the name of Siegerland; the greater part of it, however, lying beyond Westphalia in the Rhine Province.

strongholds of ancient rural life. But the genuine *bauer* is not extinct in the Ruhr Basin; and the train glides, the tall chimney rises, and the miner sinks his shafts and drives his adits among the southern hills. The prevailing characteristics, nevertheless, in the south are still those of rustic simplicity, and we may give to antiquity in our description the precedence it will not long survive to claim.

The scenery of southern Westphalia is eminently picturesque in the sense to which Mr. Merivale limits the term, as denoting effects due not to the imagination of the spectator bodying forth the forms of things unseen, but simply to the picture which nature herself puts before the eye. The traveller does not bring, but finds the charm of the landscape in steep wood-clothed hills and winding vales, with cottages and gardens clustering here and there. Most refreshing to the eye of the traveller from parched England last summer was the deep verdure of these valleys, though it was a year of drought also Westphalian. The perfection of the irrigation, the works for which serve also for draining, is celebrated over the continent of Europe, affording a practical refutation of the doctrine of some insular writers that peasants cannot accomplish such works. The rainfall is equal to that of Ireland, and it falls with such violence that all the elements of fertility would be washed off the hills but for the care with which they are planted; while the *bas-fonds* below would be now soaked into morasses, and now baked into aridity, but for the skill with which the descending streams are collected and distributed.

It is scenery, however, it must be confessed, which lacks for the most part the charm of variety. Each turn of the road presents a picture of considerable beauty, but generally a repetition of the one just left at the other side of the hill. It is everywhere, too, picturesqueness on a small scale. The eye seldom meets the horizon in those pent-up valleys; and the mountains which enclose them rarely are high enough to tempt an ascent through the woods and shrubs which impede it, or to reward it with an extensive prospect if made. Now and again they form a fine natural amphitheatre, but even then the panorama is strictly confined. Like the social life of the people, the scenery owes much of its character to geological causes. Devonian rocks emerging in contorted forms from beneath the Ruhr Basin compose the hills; the main valleys run across the strike, the side valleys parallel to it; and the country is thus everywhere cut into deep glens enclosed within high narrow ridges. If, however, 'the grandeur of vastness,' which Mr. Merivale describes as the most powerful element in American landscapes, is here totally absent, there is a resemblance to American scenery which a stranger might hardly expect to find so near Rhineland, the country of feudal memorials and tower-crowned heights. Rarely does the ancient castle (more rarely still the modern) look down on the village. Siegen is an 'antique city,' but is without a rival; and it occupies the position of a great capital, though it has but seven or eight thousand inhabitants. The peasant proprietor is the chief potentate here; the wood cottage his cow and pig share with himself may be the most sumptuous dwelling beheld in a long day's walk. Country gentlemen there are none ; a few noble proprietors may be heard of, but they are absentees, their castles usually half in ruin, or clumsily patched, and inhabited by an agent or by retainers. The post coach—which, like the livery of the post-boy, never is cleaned—is, save an occasional cart, the only vehicle one meets along the principal roads ; and, besides carrying the letters it did, until the new Ruhr-Sieg Railway was lately completed, the whole parcel delivery as well as passenger traffic of the district, though it holds but four passengers.

Here and there a new house of stone or brick is now seen—it is near a railway station that such an innovation is most likely to appear—but as a general rule the village cottages differ only in size, and are constructed as follows :—A framework of timber, painted black, is filled in with wattles and clay, whitewashed outside, the black stripes of the wood contrasting effectively with the white walls, and giving an external appearance of ornateness and neatness, by no means sustained by the real condition of things either within or around the house. Seen from without, too, most of these cottages look lofty and spacious ; but the room for the family is really small, the upper part serving as a hay-loft or barn, and half the lower being pig-sty, cow-house, and stable, if a horse is kept. Small, indeed, is the attention to cleanliness or comfort in any part of the dwelling ; the English visitor finds that dirt is not peculiar to the Irishman's cabin. No approach to the drawing-room furniture and luxury, the piano, &c., of which Herr Riehl deplores the appearance in some parts of Germany, has yet made its way into Westphalia, south of the Coal Basin. Like their cottages, and the hills and valleys around them, the villagers too have a family likeness, at which Riehl must rejoice, as the very embodiment of primitive custom and unbroken uniformity of life. The artist, he says, who would paint mediæval German faces with historical truth, must take his models from among the peasants, whose features, in some districts, resemble at this day the effigies of princes and nobles in churches of the thirteenth century. Michelet, interpreting such a phenomenon, might regard the resemblance as a proof of actual consanguinity on the part of the peasant with exalted personages of an earlier age. ' Le serf en moyen âge, est-il libre? Sa femme en pratique n'est pas plus sienne que l'esclave antique. Les enfants, sont-ils ses enfants? Oui et non. Il est tel village où la race entière reproduit aujourd'hui les traits des anciens siegneurs.'

If there really is a family resemblance of this kind to mediæval grandees on the part of the Sauerland peasantry, one must own that it is not more flattering to the beauty than to the morality of the former, for the latter are not a comely race. In plain truth, from the baby (and the villages swarm with babies in a manner formidable for the France of the future, if hopeful for the manufacturer in the Ruhr Basin) to the grown man or woman, there is an all-pervading ugliness, which no visitor can fail to remark. Other causes, however, than a common ancestry of oppressors, may account for the family likeness, as well as the rude looks and manners of these villagers; and one seeks some other explanation, the more that there was in Westphalia one class of peasants with peculiar freedom and rights of self-government; although there was likewise a large class of serfs, and old men are still to be met who remember being called 'sclaven' in their childhood. Freemen or serfs, however, they all suffered alike from war, invasion, and rapine; and the blood of the conqueror and the freebooter may thus be mingled with theirs. But the general likeness comes, doubtless, in part of a legitimate family relationship, for some names are so common that their possessors are distinguished by numbers.* The severe out-door labour which all the women undergo, is another cause of coarse-featured resemblance, and is at the same time in all probability the main cause both of the persistent boorishness of the people, and of the uncleanliness of their houses. Captain Burton comments with satisfaction on the superior physique of German over both Brazilian and American women, which he traces to out-door labour. 'Not a few,' he says, ' of the (Brazilian) women possess that dainty delicate beauty which strangers remark in the cities of

* Speaking of a similar circumstance in his own department of La Creuse, in the centre of France, M. Léonce de Lavergne says:—' Chaque village a dû être à l'origine la résidence d'une seule famille, car les habitans portent presque toujours le même nom.'—*Économie rurale de la France.* The present writer was likewise struck, in traversing the villages of La Creuse, by a physical resemblance of the villagers; but these, unlike the peasantry of Sauerland, are a very good-looking race, due probably to a happier history, and lighter labours in the field on the part of the women.

the Union. The want of out-door labour shows its effect as palpably in the Brazil as in the United States. The sturdy German *fraus* who land at Rio de Janeiro look like three American women rolled into one. Travellers are fond of recording how they see with a pang girls and women employed in field-work. But they forget that in moderation there is no labour more wholesome, none better calculated to develop the form, or to produce stout and healthy progeny.'* The due moderation, however, is not observed in the mountains of Westphalia, nor in many other parts of Germany; and Herr Riehl himself is driven to admit that the looks of the women suffer from the severity of their labours. The imposition of heavy field labour upon women is no doubt traceable in part to primitive German life, or the primitive division of employments —man, the warrior; woman, the labourer. But modern causes preserve the custom: the younger men are absent in the army; and those who have served their time, are tempted from the farm by the mines and manufactures around them. In Siegerland it is not uncommon for peasants to be co-proprietors in a mine which they work at themselves. Female husbandry becomes thus the cardinal feature in the rural economy, and the great extent of ground under meadow and wood makes such husbandry possible, the amount of tillage being small. The rich irrigation of the valleys yields four or five cuttings of grass, from which the cattle get the greater part of their food; and the hill-

---

* 'Explorations of the Highlands of the Brazil,' i. 392.

sides are cropped for the most part only in the year after the removal of the wood, which is their main growth; the 'wood-rights,' like the 'water-rights,' being carefully guarded, and every *gemeinde*, or commune, having both its 'wood-overseer' and its 'water-overseer.' Several causes combine to make wood here one of the principal objects of husbandry: the infertility of the hills, the continued rise for two centuries in the price of wôod, and the great demand for bark for tanning, which is one of the chief local industries —skins coming for the purpose to Siegen from all parts of the world. It is the old custom, however, to estimate a peasant property by its amount of meadow land, though the hill-side attached to it may be three or four times as large. A plough as old as the time of Arminius is a sign of the tenacity with which ancient custom is still clung to in this hitherto isolated district; and the introduction of improved agricultural machines will greatly lighten the labours of the women, by enabling the men to get through a much greater amount of work during their periodical visits to the farm.

The persistence of ancient custom is doubtless attributable in part to the environment of the physical world. Mountains have played a great part in shaping the history of mankind; they have been staunch guardians of customs, and obstacles to new ideas and arts. There is a literal truth in Shakespeare's phrase, 'mountainous error,' which may perhaps have been present to the fancy of the poet, though the connection between mountains and custom in this literal sense is the converse of that in his verse.* But higher mountains than any in Sauerland or Siegerland can no longer shut out movement or change. Already the manufacturer's villa rises along the iron road which joins Siegen with the Basin of the Ruhr; the steam-hammer resounds in the valley of the Lenne; and long trains laden with sulphur from the Siegena mines leave the station of Grevenbrück for the markets of all central Europe. It is happy for Westphalia that the future of Germany does not depend, as Herr Riehl contends, on the immobility of the peasantry—the steadfastness of their adherence to immemorial usage. The order of things which rests on such a basis is apt to give way of a sudden, like the mountain and 'mountainous error' which the railway removes. It is on peasant property in land, not on peasant custom, that the stability of Germany rests; and sixty years ago Prussian statesmen arrived at that conviction. 'Prussia saw with terror, in 1808,' says Gustav Freytag, 'how insecure was a State which had so great a claim on the bodies, and so little on the hearts, of its people.' The worst traits of the German *bauer*—his boorishness, his obstinacy, his laziness at work for another—belong to the past; they are the vestiges of ages of barbarism, servitude, and military oppression; while his best qualities—his sobriety, honesty, and thrift for his family—are the offspring of peasant property.

That the future of Germany rests on the peasant is

* 'What custom wills, in all things should we do it,
The dust on antique time would lay unswept,
And mountainous error be too highly heaped
For truth to over-peer.'—*Coriolanus*, act ii. sc. 3.

but half true; and so far as it is true, it is so for a different reason and in a different manner from what Herr Riehl has in view. It is so because property and education are elevating his condition and enlarging both his understanding and the sphere of his affections. He has gotten a country in the room of a master. But the future of Germany rests also with the miner and the mechanic; and the region of Westphalia from which we can best augur it is the Basin of the Ruhr,* where the *bauer* flourishes most, and where mining and manufacturing are carried on on a scale which, for Sauerland and Siegerland, is as yet only a prospect. 'If you would see what Germany is doing,' said M. Emile de Laveleye to the writer, 'go to the Ruhr Basin;' and during the visit which followed the suggestion (though made chiefly in reference to the intelligence of German enterprise, and the wisdom of Prussian government), he was often reminded of the attention which M. de Laveleye shows in his works to the physical geography, the geology especially, of the countries whose economic condition, productions, and industrial occupations he describes. The mountains of South Westphalia with their mineral wealth, the coal measures of the Ruhr Basin, and the diluvial flat to the north, with its rude bogs and moors, divide Westphalia into three distinct economic, as into three geological, regions. It has been the doctrine of some eminent writers, Auguste Comte at their head, that the influence of nature's powers, and of local conditions,

* Called also the 'Westphalian Coal Field,' though its bounds extend westward far beyond the limits of the modern province of Westphalia.

such as soil, climate, &c., over human society, decreases as civilisation advances. But the truth is, that the number and force of physical causes operating on the condition of man increase with human progress, and as local resources are brought more and more into play. A new age opened for mankind when iron was discovered, and the influence of iron on the fortunes of nations becomes constantly greater. The gold of California and Australia had no influence on the original inhabitants; twenty years ago it was still inoperative on mankind; it would have continued so but for geology and navigation; it has by their aid created two nations who, it is already evident, must have no small share in shaping the future history of both hemispheres. Coal played no significant part in English history a century ago. It has since trebled the population, shifted the political centre, and produced a social revolution. The coal of the Ruhr Basin had no effect on the fortunes of Westphalia fifty years ago; fifteen years ago its effect was but trifling; it has since raised the province to the first rank of industrial Europe. The whole tendency of increasing physical knowledge is to discover new natural forces and agents, for man's use or abuse, and to bring into action—for good or for evil—the special resources of every locality.

There is, indeed, one class of local physical forces of which the influence on man decreases as his knowledge and power advance,—those of which the mountain may be taken as the symbol,—the forces of obstruction and isolation. The mine, on the other hand, may be regarded as the symbol of physical forces which gain influence as civilisation advances; and the railway—itself the child of the mine—removes the mountain and opens the mine. An analogous distinction applies to the study of nature. Mr. Arnold, writing on German education, argues that 'the study of nature is the study of non-human forces, of human limitation and passivity. The contemplation of human force and activity tends constantly to heighten our own force; the contemplation of human limitation and passivity tends to check it.'

The contemplation of natural powers by which man was imprisoned and baffled tended no doubt to reduce him to immobility and stagnation; it is not so with that study of nature which shows how dominion over nature may be acquired, and prompts to the acquisition. The mine is the creature of geology, as the steam-engine is of mechanics. This reflection was brought forcibly to the writer's mind on arriving in the Ruhr Basin from Sauerland. A few hours after he had been wearily watching one afternoon a set of labourers in the valley of the Lenne, lifting stones lazily one at a time from a roadside quarry into a cart, which half the number of men might have filled in a fourth of the time, he found himself by the side of a coal-mine near Dortmund, from which a steam-engine was pumping several thousand feet of water a minute night and day, while around was a colony of miners—English, Irish, and Germans—all looking the incarnation of activity and force, though with striking differences of physical type, and among them the President of the Prussian Mining and Iron Works Company,* a man

* Mr. W. T. Mulvany. To this gentleman, and to his brother Mr. T. J.

to whose enterprise, energy, and sagacity the Ruhr Basin owes not a little of its extraordinary progress in the last fifteen years. It was like passing from 'a land in which it seemed to be always afternoon,' to one in which there was no night.

Forty minutes by express from Dortmund and one is at Essen, in the centre of the coal-field, surrounded by manufactories and foundries, but chiefly remarkable for the great cast-steel works of Mr. Krupp, who may well be regarded as the representative man of the Ruhr Basin. He began business at the age of fifteen, with two workmen and a small local market, and twenty years ago his establishment was still a small one. Now the buildings form in themselves a considerable town; the steel-works alone give employment to upwards of 8,000 men, who with the families of those who are married, make a population of 25,000 maintained by this single establishment, exclusive of 2,000 men in Mr. Krupp's employment at coal-mines near Essen, at blast furnaces on the Rhine, and at iron-pits on the Rhine and at Nassau. The steel-works included in 1867, 412 melting-furnaces, 195 steam-engines, some of them of a thousand horse-power, 49 steam-hammers, 110 smiths' forges, 675 different machines; and all these numbers now are exceeded. The works are connected by special lines of railway above fifteen miles in length, and the gasworks of the establishment are equal to those of the city of Cologne. 'The administration,' as Mr. Samuelson says, 'is like that of a small State.

Mulvany, the author is under much obligation for information and guidance in the Ruhr Basin.

All the heads of the technical departments are pupils of the various polytechnic schools in Germany. The commercial staff includes a jurist, by whom all contracts are settled and legal questions determined. The foremen have all risen from the ranks.' Unfortunately Mr. Krupp is not only a representative of the prodigious progress of industry in the Ruhr Basin, but an example of the influence of political causes on its productions—a class of causes which most English economists seem deliberately to ignore, although they are among the chief conditions determining the occupations and wealth of mankind. In 1866 the steel produced at Mr. Krupp's works was valued at nearly a million; but the greater part was probably material of war. Yet there is good reason to believe that even at his works the amount of production would be greater were this a world of good government and peace; and what would be the increase in the other manufactories of the Ruhr Basin, whose business is dependent on peace? It may be affirmed as beyond question that the only impediment to Prussian progress is war; and although the blame hitherto has rested chiefly, not on the government of Prussia, but on the military despotisms surrounding it, Prussia itself is now in a condition to cast the sword into the scale of peace, and is responsible accordingly. In most respects the Prussian government has, it must be admitted, been for half a century singularly sagacious and beneficent, and there is one point in which its wisdom is specially illustrated in Mr. Krupp's works. He has but few Prussian patents, —these, too, only for considerable inventions; and the discrimination with which patents are granted in Prussia is alone sufficient to enable Prussian manufacturers to distance before long those of a country in which to make even the slightest change is now attended with danger, in which it is perilous in the highest degree either to patent a great invention or to work it without one. Prussia is fast acquiring all the peculiar advantages to which England owed her earlier superiority—coal, iron, mechanical invention, and good means of communication—and adding to them conditions of success, of which England is deprived by her own laws—including what Bacon has called 'a law of neglect.' The chief point to be considered in comparing the prospects of England and Prussia is not their present relative condition, but their relative condition now as compared with what it was twenty years ago. Twenty years ago the Ruhr Basin was nowhere in the industrial race; now it produces nearly half as much coal as the great northern coal-field of England: twenty years ago it had only just completed a single line of railway; now the Basin is a network of branches, connecting, not only the towns, but the principal manufactories and collieries with the three main lines which traverse it. The following figures show the rate at which the production of coal has advanced:—

Date	English tons*	Date	English tons	Date	English tons	Date	English tons
1851	1,771,454	1856	3,510,502	1861	4,964,621	1865	9,276,685
1852	1,921,962	1857	3,635,256	1862	5,701,201	1866	9,329,503
1853	2,146,275	1858	3,898,502	1863	6,300,981	1867	10,526,015
1854	2,670,099	1859	3,793,356	1864	8,146,433	1868	11,226,747
1855	3,252,323	1860	4,276,254				

* The Prussian *tonne* is a measure of capacity, and varies therefore in

The immense increase of production shown in these figures is mainly attributable to the introduction of railways and the low charge for the carriage of coal. Down to 1851 the Ruhr and the Rhine were the only means of transport in districts beyond the immediate neighbourhood of the collieries, and the greater part of the coal was of an inferior kind, raised where it came to the surface by small collieries along the Ruhr. In 1851 the Cologne-Minden Railway came into use for the transport of coal, and led not only to deep-pit sinking, and the discovery of seams of superior coal in other parts of the basin, but also to the establishment of iron-works and other manufactures, affording a local market for the coal. To this local market, down to 1859, it was in a great measure confined. In that year the charge for railway carriage of coal for long distances was reduced to one *pfennig* per *centner* (a tenth of a penny per cwt.) per German mile,* and the above figures show the subsequent increase of production. The railways and coal-mines render each other reciprocal service; the carriage of Westphalian coal is now one of the most important branches of traffic on several of the chief Prussian lines, and the low rates at which it is carried enable it to find a distant market. The projected reduction of the rate for the transport of iron ore to the same tariff as that for coal, when carried into effect, will greatly augment the market for coal as

weight as applied to different articles—coal and iron, for example. The quantity of coal in a *tonne* is about one-fifth of an English ton. In some of the reports in English blue-books the *tonne* is translated 'ton,' which may mislead readers.

* The German mile is about $4\frac{3}{4}$ English.

well as for manufactures of iron. Until the last few years the Ruhr Basin excelled only in the manufacture of steel; but its iron manufactures are now of the highest quality. The chief difficulty with which the iron manufacturer has hitherto had to contend is the great cost of the carriage of the ore from the mines in Siegerland, the Rhine Province, Nassau, Hesse-Darmstadt, and Hanover. The iron-mines are situated for the most part in mountainous districts, some not yet approached by railways, others without even roads to connect them with railways or rivers, the ore being often drawn by oxen or cows, when dry weather permits, across fields or through woods to the nearest road. Nevertheless, under all these disadvantages, the iron manufactures of the Ruhr Basin have trebled in amount in the last ten years; the improvement in quality is even greater; and the iron-works of Duisburg may soon become as celebrated as the steel-works of Essen.

Of the progress of textile manufactures, Elberfeld affords a striking example. A correspondent of the 'Times,' who recently described it as 'fifteen years ago a manufacturing town, containing 6,500 inhabitants,* sinking lower and lower into the slough of pauperism,' ascribes its emergence to a prudent change in the system of pauper relief. But prevention is better than cure, though many English politicians seem unable to comprehend it. The system of poor-relief has doubtless had its effect; but the extinction of the causes of poverty, and the increase of employment in manu-

---

* Query, 36,500? The population of Elberfeld must have amounted to at least 36,000 at the time referred to.

factures, have been the principal cause of the diminution of pauperism in Elberfeld-Barmen, now a town of 100,000 inhabitants. The descent of peasant lands by custom to the eldest son in several of the provinces of Prussia—Westphalia for example*—was formerly a source of constant pauperism in the towns, which, before the great recent development of manufactures, were unable to absorb in industrial employment the immigration of the younger members of the family. But the extension of industry of late years has been such, that, but for war and rumours of war, it is probable that pauperism (which has, in fact, greatly decreased, notwithstanding a great increase of population) would be extinct in the Ruhr Basin.

The relation between capital and labour is naturally one of the points to which an English economist's attention turns in contemplating a region which has so

* The present province of Westphalia, being composed of a number of different districts, formerly under different sovereign princes, lay and ecclesiastical, had formerly a great variety of laws and customs, some of which are still retained in particular towns and districts. By a law passed in 1860, and not retrospective in its operation on prior marriages, the law of descent is as follows. A community of property is established between man and wife, unless otherwise stipulated by marriage contract, respecting which also there are certain restrictions and stipulations. On the death of either, the survivor is entitled to a fixed proportion, and the children to other fixed proportions, depending on the number of children; but no actual division of the property takes place until the death or second marriage of the surviving parent, unless a previous division has been provided for by a disposition made by both parents. The surviving parent has also a right to retain the whole property on payment to the children of the value of their shares; and other provisions respecting the distribution are laid down to prevent the necessity of parcelling lands. Usually the parents settle during their lifetime which of the children is to take the land, and how the shares of the others are to be paid off, and the family property is very rarely divided.

great an industrial future before it. Since the recent change in the Prussian law permitting combinations of workmen, there have been a few strikes, but regular trade-unions have not yet been organised in this part of Prussia. Nevertheless the younger employers—and they are probably more *en rapport* with the spirit of the times than their seniors, whose ideas on the subject are based on experience of the past—seemed to the writer, wherever he had opportunities of inquiry on the subject, strongly impressed with a conviction that the relations of employer and employed are about to assume a new phase throughout Germany. It is a remarkable fact, however—and one which proves that the former state of the law was not by any means the only cause of the amicable relations between capitalists and workmen—that Mr. Krupp—in business for forty years, and with not less than 10,000 men for some years in his employment—has never had a dispute with a workman; a fact doubtless ascribable in a great measure to the admirable institutions and regulations for the benefit of the workmen, of which an account will be found in a pamphlet published in Paris, in 1867, entitled ' Aciérie de M. Fried. Krupp, à Essen : Institutions et Dispositions établies dans le but d'améliorer la situation morale et physique de ses ouvriers.' By one of the provisions of the establishment, every workman becomes entitled, after twenty years' work, to a retiring annual pension of half his last year's salary. and after thirty-five years he may retire on full pay. Such regulations, however, effective as they must be, do not appear to explain the extraordinary concord and order perpetually maintained in this enormou establishment. From 1,000 to 1,400 men are frequently engaged at one operation, such as casting an ingot; they work as one man; and the same harmony and regimental order prevail throughout. It is doubtless traceable in part to the military training which every Prussian receives. But even at coal-mines, where the same regimental order is not required, and where the upper miners were English, I was assured that they preferred to have Germans to work with; the preference being founded on the superior docility and sobriety of the Germans. It is curious to find local prejudices stronger than national ones among English miners in the Westphalian coal-field. A north-countryman who works amicably with the Germans, will resent the intrusion of a Cornishman. 'They are not Englishmen, they are Cornishmen,' said an English miner to me of two poor fellows who had come over on an unsuccessful expedition for work. On the other hand, as regards the effect of Prussian military training and State supervision on the national character, there are occasions on which the superior individuality of the Englishman is conspicuous. A very large coal proprietor in the Ruhr Basin, employing many English as well as Germans, assured me that when an accident occurs the Englishman will do on the moment the best thing to be done, while the Germans stand at attention waiting for orders, probably given to them promptly by their English comrade. As an individual, the Englishman *is*, if I may venture to express such an opinion, naturally superior to the German. His history down to the last fifty years was a much happier one, his personality was more respected, and, what is no small matter, he was and still is (leaving out the agricultural labourer) better fed. Among the Germans at the Westphalian mines the type of the Englishman appeared to me by comparison heroic and majestic. Germany has only had sixty years of emancipation from serfdom, little more than forty of deliverance from perpetual war; her military training (useful as it would be for a short period) is beyond measure oppressive when protracted for three years; and peasant property has not yet had time to produce its best results. 'Les Allemands sont trop gouvernés,' says M. Emile de Laveleye, 'mais bien gouvernés—les Français trop gouvernés et mal gouvernés.'

If, however, there are institutions in Prussia which impair in certain respects the free action of the individual man, and the spirit of self-reliance, there are others which tend eminently to foster self-control, intelligence, providence, and several of the best essentials of true individuality.* The superior sobriety of the German is one constant manifestation of self-command—of a self-command which accompanies him throughout his day's work as well as in his leisure,

---

* As regards the effect of education upon the capabilities of the workman, I have been told by some English employers that an English workman who has been engaged about a part of a machine for a year, though very likely more handy than any of his German comrades, will probably have no conception of it as a whole, while the Germans have it all in their heads, and can draw it, so that they are more ripe for promotion, or to set up for themselves.

rendering him much less liable to make careless blunders or to run reckless and useless risks. The inferiority of the Englishman, in this respect, arises not only from the want of intellectual education, but still more from the absence of that motive for general thrift and forethought, the prospect of succeeding to, or of buying, a piece of land and a house, which is the material basis of much that is best in the continental nations. The workman in the town does not feel himself severed from the country, or doomed to remain a mere day-labourer so long as he can work. It is characteristic of the difference between England and Germany that a *good* means in the latter an estate in land, a *bauer-gut* a peasant property in land, while in England the only goods in popular thought are perishable articles.

In the Ruhr Basin the wealth of the peasantry has, like that of the manufacturers and miners, and in a great measure in consequence of that of the latter, enormously increased in the last twenty years, and the so-called *bauer* is sometimes a man worth above 15,000*l*. The daughter of one of these men, near Dortmund, married the other day, and received 20,000 thalers (3,000*l*.) down as her marriage portion, besides which she will become entitled to 4,000*l*. more on her father's death. In the houses of such wealthy farmers, the modern furniture, the piano, and the 'female accomplishments' of which Herr Riehl deplores the introduction, may be found: though the farming is still generally rough, and the uncourteous manners of a time when the *bauer* hated the gentleman as an oppressor survive—like the moat round the country gentleman's house.

Among the peasantry, the smaller class of proprietors here, as in Sauerland and Siegerland, are for the most part dirty and slovenly in their houses and farmyards; and an Irish gentleman living amongst them remarked to me, 'They seem of the Irish small farmer's opinion, that, " where there is muck, there is luck."' Cleanliness has no nationality, it is the growth of freedom, self-respect, and prosperity; and it will rapidly grow in Westphalia with the development of its resources, the ingress of knowledge and change, and the increase of general wealth. Not long ago the same plough referred to before as of the age of Arminius was still in use in the Ruhr Basin, and all the implements of the farm were of a primitive kind. Now steam threshing-machines are common, lent or hired from one farm to another; though we are often positively assured in England by writers who seem to affect never to have been out of it, that peasant properties, small farms, and machinery are incompatible.

Westphalia, the Ruhr Basin in particular, may be regarded as the type of Germany, of its unhappy early history, its recent good government and rapid progress, the vast future before it, and the formidable competition before England. 'If you would see what Germany is doing,' said M. de Laveleye, 'go to the Ruhr Basin;' but the chief lesson to be learned regards what Germany is about to do. What will the Ruhr Basin be in another twenty years? All the elements of England's earlier industrial superiority, coal, iron, mechanical power, are, as before said, rapidly becoming the common property of Germany, which brings with them to the development of its great natural resources, moral and intellectual advantages due to no national superiority on the part of the Germans, but to greater sagacity and foresight on the part of their statesmen. Of England, moreover, though not of Germany, Herr Riehl's maxim is true, that the custom of the peasant is the sole foundation of present order, the sole safeguard against future anarchy. And the peasant is driven to the town.

WESTPHALIA AND THE RUHR BASIN, 1869-1870.

THE marks of South Westphalian progress, since the previous year, which met the eye last autumn in the valley of the Lenne—the increase of houses of brick and stone, of people, carts, public conveyances and private carriages on the roads, of new faces of a different type near the stations, of villas and factories by the riverside—made a scene so changed that the first impression conveyed was that the truer a description of the south of the province, as it appeared a twelvemonth before, the farther from truth was it now. Such, however, was soon seen not to be the case beyond the immediate vicinity of the great thoroughfare of the new business and life of the region, the railway. Not far from it were roads even more lonely and silent than the year before; and the very new highway of progress which had so transformed and augmented the industry of the valley through which it winds its own course, had extinguished altogether the simple industries of valleys adjacent. Rivers formerly determined in a great measure the economy of the whole district; its metal manufactures were carried on by the aid of water-power, and planted themselves in the river valleys; the men congregating there, while the dry valleys were left during most of the year to the husbandry of women, or to nature.

Iron and copper works of a primitive kind, together with charcoal-burning, gave formerly a considerable amount of employment in places where they are now dying out before coal and steam in the distance. In the valley of the Bigga, a river adjacent to the Lenne, there was a few years ago a good deal of metal production which the Ruhr-Sieg Railway has arrested, but which a branch line is expected soon to resuscitate on a grander scale. Even in the Lenne valley itself, although many tall chimneys have risen, though the steam-cylinder is fast driving out the water-wheel, and the steam-hammer the old tilt-hammer, the production of textiles by power has not yet begun; and a good part of the clothing business is done as it was in the middle ages. The shoemaker still goes round the farmhouses and the mines in the neighbourhood with the implements of his trade; the owner of the premises supplying the leather, and the stock of shoes being made on the spot, as the author has had ocular proof. The weaver, too, makes his periodical call at the cottage, and works up the thread which the housewife has spun from her own flax, dried in the sun—the process here substituted for steeping.

But if the manufacturing side of South Westphalian industry is far as yet in degree, if not in time, from the complete revolution that awaits it, the agricultural side is altogether unaltered. It is not here that M. Emile de Laveleye can find evidence of the superiority of the German over the Celt as a cultivateur d'élite; unless, indeed, for his admirable irrigation and draining, which are however of no modern date. All along the Ruhr-Sieg line itself, as poor oat crops were seen last August as one could wish never again to behold in Ireland. In fact, the only tolerable crop the author saw, turned out on inquiry to be the produce of seed imported from Ireland. The snow is seldom off the ground before the end of February, when all the labour of the family is needed to put in at once the more important rye and potatoes, so the oats are sown too late. The rye itself is not a magnificent success; and most of the wheat consumed in the valley is imported from Hungary. The harvest returns for the year 1869, recently published by the Prussian Minister of Agriculture, place Westphalia lowest but one among the departments for the yield of the principal grain crops, wheat, rye, barley, and oats; Schleswig-Holstein coming first, and the other provinces ranking in order as follows—Pomerania, Prussia, Hanover, Rhine Province, Brandenburg and Saxony, Silesia, Hesse, Posen, Westphalia and Hohenzollern. In some of the provinces, the seasons doubtless in a great measure determined this order; but in the South Westphalian hills, the sterility of the soil and the system of husbandry together, must ensure feeble cereal returns. Above the left bank of the Bigga an isolated plateau of Devonian limestone appears like a geological island surrounded by rocks of Lenne-schiefer;* and here

---

* Under this plateau lies in the Biggathal the smart little town of Attendorn, overlooked by the ancient schloss of a wealthy nobleman who never comes near it, and whose wife, it is said, has never seen it.

much heavier grain crops were to be seen than anywhere else around, just before the last harvest. But although the immediate cause of the light harvests of Sauerland is the general sterility of the soil, it is certain that Flemish husbandry would produce very different results. The ultimate cause is that the women have to do almost all the farm work, including the feeding of cattle, in addition to the work of the house, which includes the spinning of thread and the mending of clothes; and, considering all they have to do, they do it surprisingly well.

Besides their ordinary labours in and out of doors, the women do likewise the extraordinary work of the place when a sudden emergency arises, such as a fire. They run to the house and form in double line, one side handing up buckets of water, while the other side hands down rescued articles. Even in the town of Siegen, this is the usual course when a fire takes place; the women supplying the water and removing property, while the men, save those working the engine, stand by looking on. Fires are of frequent and destructive occurrence in the villages, from the number of thatched roofs separated only by small gardens. Every cottage seems to be insured; but if fire insurance has its economical side, it does not consist in a tendency to diminish the number of fires. Slated roofs are now increasing under a law prohibiting new thatches within a certain distance of other houses, and by degrees the old incendiary will disappear altogether.

In spite of the scanty harvests and the indifferent husbandry of South Westphalia, it would be a serious mistake to suppose that its rural economy offers an argument against a system of property which doubles the income of the family by the addition it makes to the earnings of the man at his trade, more than doubles the happiness of the whole family, notwithstanding the hard work it throws on the women. It would be better for the man to give up his trade than his land. He has indeed to import his wheat from Hungary, but he is able to pay for it; and the high prices of meat, butter, milk, vegetables, and house-rent, which are such grievous calamities to the English labourer, are to him sources of profit. Although the German nation is not one remarkable for attention to personal appearance, the children in these villages are all comfortably clothed, and are never seen bare-footed, as both children and adults too often are in the plain of the Rhine, where so many families are without a *bauer-gut*. In these villages, too, it should be remembered that many of the people are themselves the children of serfs—of *sclaven*, as the author has heard them say; a term which, though not the correct one, for their legal status was not that of slavery, shows how abject their condition really was, and from what prostration they have risen under their land system to independence and comfort, in a period during which the peasantry of a great part of England have socially and economically sunk.

The rate of wages in Sauerland and Siegerland varies considerably in different places, and is generally lower than in the Ruhr Basin. One employer has for several years, to the author's knowledge, paid 30 per cent.

more for labour at one mine than at another about five-and-twenty miles off; the reason being that he cannot buy out the small proprietors round the mine where the rate is highest, and many of them, on the other hand, object to receiving his labourers as lodgers —no bad evidence of the independence of their position. Another cause of inequality of wages as compared with the rates at the coal-mines in the Ruhr Basin, lies in the cost of carriage from the iron-mines in the southern hills to the railway stations, and again the much higher railway tariff for iron ore than for coal. Coal comes out of the mine ready for use; iron ores on the contrary contain only a variable percentage of iron, and are valueless until after a costly process of smelting. The inferior ores, therefore, which are necessarily extracted along with the higher qualities, would not repay the present cost of transport to the place of manufacture, and therefore do not even repay the cost of extraction. An iron-mine so situated cannot pay the same rate of wages as a coal-mine in the Ruhr Basin, with its own branch line to a railway, or to an iron factory in connection with it. Whatever conclusions Ricardo's hypotheses may lead to, the real economic conditions of production and distribution have nowhere equalised wages, profits, or rent; they have, in fact, in recent times produced new inequalities through the different rates at which industrial development has proceeded in different localities, the different natural advantages of different localities, and the rise of such a multitude of special industries and such continual change in their conditions, that omniscience only could estimate their prospects, or enable competition to equalise them. In the case of the iron-mines of Sauerland and Siegerland, however, the projected reduction of the railway freight for iron ore and the construction of good roads to the mines, may raise wages to the rates at the coal-mines in the Ruhr Basin; but migration to the latter, although some takes place, does not do so, and cannot, because the iron-mine cannot afford it, yet is not abandoned.

Admirable maps are published from year to year showing every mine and railway in the region over which the elastic name of the Ruhr Basin continues to stretch, with the extension of mining industry north and south of the Ruhr. But only a map indicating every new house and factory, and all the new preparations for building, mining, and manufacture, could give a representation on paper of the gigantic growth of this young industrial world since the author described it but a year ago. Villages grown into towns; towns spreading to meet one another; embryo towns and villages emerging; the population increasing under one's eyes with the immigration of workmen from more distant parts of Prussia, from Bohemia, from these islands themselves; miners from Cornwall, Wales, and the north; weavers from Lancashire and Ulster; capitalists coming even from France; everything — save that long unworkmanlike pipe which disgraces the German nation — displaying a rapidity of industrial movement which we are accustomed to associate with the pace of America only. The causes of this prodigious advance are partly mechanical doubtless; cheap and abundant coal and a good system of railways must soon change the face of any region. And the industry of this district appears to derive considerable advantage from the combination in some of the largest establishments of the business of coal-mining with that of iron and steel manufacture, contrary as that may appear to the division of labour. The iron-works are supplied with coal coming straight from the mine at very little additional cost, and the coal-mine in turn has an immediate demand for its produce. The railway again which brings iron ore to the factories from the Rhine Province and the south of Westphalia carries back coal and coke and gets a return traffic for the same waggons. The textile manufactures again of the Basin have a steady demand from a great mining and iron-factory population around them, as well as from a considerable rural population deriving great profits from the large market for agricultural produce.

To the mechanical causes of the rapid progress of this part of Prussia must be added political, legal, and moral causes; the confidence in peace springing up with the decline of despotism in France, the education, intelligence, and sober and orderly character of the German people, with a land system superior to any other in its facilities of transfer, and securing (as happily many others do) a wide distribution of landed property. Coal-mines and steam locomotion, however well combined, cannot raise costly factories and buildings on ground which entails, obscure titles, and a tortuous technical and dilatory jurisprudence mark out as feudal territory; nor will even an extensive foreign trade, with its changes and chances, supply the place of a brisk and increasing home market afforded by a large, contented, and well-to-do population in both town and country around.

The Prussian land system, resembling the French and the Belgian in respect of the simplicity and security by which a transfer is effected—a signature in the presence of a notary, followed by an entry in a local registry, being all that is requisite—is superior to either the French or Belgian in point of economy; the duty being but one per cent., and the notary's fee a mere trifle. Some idea of the impediment the English system of conveyancing puts in the way of industrial progress may be gathered from the fact that the capitalist in the Ruhr Basin grumbles at having to pay one per cent. in addition to his purchase-money for an absolutely safe and marketable title; and that, after all, one per cent. is a considerable tax. Suppose a manufacturer pays 10,000*l*. for an advantageous site for a factory, with ground for his workmen's houses and his own residence, he is not in a better position to pay 100*l*. to the Government for having so many other hundreds to pay to the vendor, and being called on immediately for heavy additional disbursements to complete his operations before he can get any return. In France, in a similar case, he would have above 600*l*. to pay to the State instead of but 100*l*.; he would, however, then be as safe as in Prussia. In England, supposing title and settlements to permit of a sale in the place desired, after searches, opinions, and conveyance, and the subsequent outlay of perhaps 100,000*l*. in his business, the purchaser may discover that he has invested only in a ruinous law-suit.

The accessibility of landed property to all the other classes of the community, however, may not appear at first sight otherwise than disadvantageous to the capitalist, who finds them formidable competitors in the land market, and by no means easily tempted to part with what land they have got. The author has known land sold in the Ruhr Basin at above 1,200 thalers a morgen, at an auction at which all the bidders but one were farmers and labourers. Land here, as elsewhere in Western Europe, gets more and more into the hands of the diminutive buyer. The wealth of the peasant increases; the mine and the factory themselves add largely to his wealth, and render him a more formidable rival as a land buyer; they both make land better worth buying for cultivation, and enable the cultivator to lay by more for its purchase. The miners, too, and the town workmen accumulate savings; and their first investment is usually a plot of ground for a house. The man borrows the money to build the house, if his savings are short of that mark; and his wife and children cultivate the garden while he works at his trade, until he pays off his debt, or lays by for another investment in land. The easy transfer and general diffusion of land accordingly raises its price against the rich buyer in the Ruhr Basin, as its close monopoly on the contrary does in England; but in the former, the capitalist, as well as the workman and the peasant, has the benefit of perfect security; and he has an additional compensation in the order, sobriety, and diligence of his workmen on the one hand, the home market of a prosperous population on the other. It is not too much to assert that manufactures could not have made the stride they have done in the last fifteen years either in Germany or in France without the aid of their land systems, and the consequently increasing home market for the productions of the power-loom, and the industries to which it gives activity in turn.

Now that the war-cloud seems to have dispersed, the capitalist of the Ruhr Basin sees but one other cloud in the horizon—in the attitude which labour is beginning to assume, and the power of organisation over all Germany, of which already it displays no doubtful indications, although the trade-union is a very recent growth. That a fundamental change in the relations between labour and capital throughout Europe is approaching seems beyond doubt; but whatever the issue, it will not on the Continent be the issue at the same time of a conflict between an insignificant number of persons with immense property and an overwhelming number with none; a conflict, it should be observed, which becomes all the more decisive in favour of numbers, when the only weapon employed is Universal Suffrage.

A VISIT TO LA CREUSE, 1868.*

IT has often been said of late years that Paris no longer is France; that, looking to the show on all sides of mere imperial splendour and power, the influx of strangers from all parts of the world, and the obscurity of the social and intellectual elements of which it once was the focus, it may be the capital of the empire, the metropolis of the world; but the capital of the French nation, the centre of national genius and life, the representative city, it is not. There is, on the other hand, however, a sense in which Paris is now France, in a greater degree than ever before. The town has grown, while the country has shrunk in the composition of France, and the town (especially the chief town) is now made up of elements gathered from the farthest parts of the country. Instead, therefore, of saying that Paris is not France, it is better to say that not only France but Paris itself must now be studied in the remotest departments, to understand the changes which have taken place in both under the empire. A true political picture of the capital, with its new palaces and boulevards, and the enormous increase in its numbers, would exhibit La Creuse in the background, with its

* Reprinted from 'Fraser's Magazine,' February 1869.

desert hills, its mean hamlets, and its vanishing peasantry. The most primitive and isolated of all the departments — the very name of which is not found in Murray or Bradshaw — it has much to tell of the general state of the great kingdom of which it seems so insignificant a part, of that transformation of a rural into an urban population, which is one of the most portentous revolutions of the age, and of the means by which, and the cost at which the modern splendour of the metropolis has been created. Those too who care to see what still remains soundest in France, in the heart of its people and in the character of its institutions, side by side with sad proofs of the change which has passed over both in the last twenty years, will find their account in a visit to La Creuse. They will find themselves, as it were, in a border land between old and new France, recalling with a new meaning the name of La Marche, which it bore as a province.* Without a railway until the other day, ill-provided with roads, and its narrow valleys blocked up as it were in culs-de-sac by the peculiar formation of its mountains and hills, it has remained in many respects unchanged since the middle age. The Revolution itself passed it by almost untouched: it is to this day so secluded from the world that all the inhabitants of a village will turn out to gaze at a stranger; yet its male population is the

* Referring to the ancient name of La Marche and the peaceful character of its peasantry in all past time, so unusual with *Borderers*, M. de Lavergne says, in the brief sketch of La Creuse contained in his ' Économie rurale de la France:'—' Quoique rappelant les *borders* d'Écosse, on n'y recueille aucune des traditions belliqueuses qui se rattachent d'ordinaire à ces frontières entre la plaine et la montagne qu'on appelle des marches.'

most migratory in France; the greater part of its grown men are rather Parisians than peasants of their native hamlets, spending three-fourths of the year in the capital—of whose newest quarters they are the builders in the most literal sense—and passing only the winter months in the rural commune, in which official tables of population enumerate them.

The passenger by the new railway forming the base of a triangle, of which the apex is Paris, and St. Sulpice Laurière on the line to Limoges, and Montluçon on that to Vichy, are the other extremities, crosses the whole breadth of La Creuse between the departments of La Haute-Vienne and L'Allier; but he might perhaps gather from that cursory view a very erroneous impression of the character of a region, the barrenest parts of which are concealed by the cuttings of the line, while bright chestnut groves and deep woods of oak and beech seen under a summer or autumn sun give to much of the landscape a rich and smiling appearance. Even from the railway, however, glimpses of the real desolation and wildness may be caught. One may see, for example, from the carriage a woman tending cattle or sheep, knitting at the same time a stocking or a waistcoat, while under her arm is the signal for the train—at once shepherdess, manufacturer, and railway official. Tracts of land again may be discovered here and there in a complete state of nature, owned for the most part by village communities on that primitive system of common property, of which Maine seems not to have looked for examples so near the centre of western civilisation.* Along the whole line, too, towns are conspicuous by their absence. Gueret itself, the capital of the department, is hardly more than a village to an Englishman's eye, inferior in both architecture and numbers to not a few English villages: indeed, with the solitary exception of Aubusson, which has but 6,000 inhabitants, yet is the seat of a manufacture of tapestry of ancient celebrity, the 'towns' of La Creuse are all villages, the 'villages' hamlets, often of no more than four or five cottages. To see however in a few hours the real nakedness of the land, the magnificent scenery it nevertheless possesses, and an oasis in the desert deserving on more than one account particular notice, the traveller would do well to leave the railway from Paris at St. Sulpice Laurière (where it joins the line which traverses La Creuse), and make an excursion to the village of St. Goussaud, perched on the summit of a mountain, from which the eye may sweep far beyond the limits of the department to the dark Puy-de-Dôme frowning over Clermont-Ferrand in the Auvergne.

Looking down on La Creuse itself, the eye ranges not over one great hollow—as a name taken from the river, which has hollowed a channel through its mountains of granite, might seem to denote—but over innumerable hollows and heights, with here and there amidst forests and mountain heath, a grey patch which marks the thatched roofs of a poor hamlet, and the presence of human life. Descending from St. Goussaud, a drive of six or seven miles brings to the foot of the ancient

* 'Ancient Law,' chap. viii.: The Early History of Property.

castle of Peyrusse, a picturesque ruin, the history of which (it is almost the only thing in La Creuse with a history) runs back to the wars of Pepin the Short; and which, from a precipitous rock, looks down on a mountain-glen formed by the river Thorion,* with few rivals for grandeur and beauty in France. The chief interest, however, of the scene for an Englishman will probably be found in the fact that it is beheld within the demesne of the author of the most celebrated works on the rural economy of both England and France—M. Léonce de Lavergne, who, in a district so unreclaimed that the wolves are not yet expelled from his woods, and the wild boar comes from time to time to devour the produce of his fields, pursues the careers, rarely united, of a political philosopher, a country gentleman and a farmer. The purport, indeed, of the 'Rural Economy of Great Britain and Ireland' cannot be fairly understood without knowing that it is the work on the one hand of a political philosopher weary alike of revolution and of despotism, and on the other hand of a landed proprietor and large farmer, eager to spread the practice of agriculture, and of residence on their estates, among the owners of large estates in his own country. It is in this spirit that M. de Lavergne has held up before France the example of English institutions and customs. Nothing could be more alien from his mind, or from the general doctrine of his writings, than an intention to depreciate the French system of peasant property and small farming—of which we find him, only the other day, summing up the results in a review of the

* Taurion, as it is otherwise spelled.

Enquête agricole in the 'Revue des Deux Mondes:' 'Tout le monde accepte la petite propriété nonseulement comme une nécessité mais comme un bienfait. On reconnaît qu'elle est favorable et à la production rurale et à la sécurité publique.' Similar statements abound in his numerous works upon agriculture and land; and they come with double force from one who, being himself a large landowner, is surrounded by peasant proprietors, to whom, circumstanced as they are, he has hitherto almost in vain set an example of careful and scientific cultivation. Were one looking for a broad contrast to Flemish husbandry, one would find it on every side around the demesne of Peyrusse. Within it nearly every plant, for which the farming of Flanders is famous, may be seen in luxuriant growth—beet-root, turnips, carrots, Jerusalem artichokes, rape, hops, flax, hemp, besides sarassin, rye, and other cereals, except wheat, which (as in Flanders) has but small success at Peyrusse, on account of the natural poverty of the soil.* The system followed by M. de Lavergne includes, however, a much greater proportion of pasture than is practised in Flanders, and the greater part of his land is under wood, to which a considerable tract of mountain heath must be added to give an idea of the contrasts of elaborate cultivation and wild scenery

---

* M. de Lavergne seems to share a common opinion that the soil of Flanders is naturally rich, judging no doubt from the French portion, which is so. But M. Emile de Laveleye, speaking of his native soil, says:—' Parmi celles que l'homme a mises en culture, il s'en trouve peu d'aussi ingrates. Le sol tient presque toute sa valeur non de la nature, mais du travail de l'homme. C'est dans cette région peu favorisée que l'on trouve l'agriculture flamande avec tous les caractères qui la distinguent.'—*Économie rurale de la Belgique*, pp. 10-37.

within his own boundaries. The truth is that some of the crops at Peyrusse are grown only for experiment and example. The produce of one farm will not raise up a market; the hops of a single grower will not create a brewery; and the chief produce of the lands of some of his neighbours is heather and furze, on which, along with the withered branches of trees and shrubs, their lean cows have (though they have to do the work of both horses and cows) to make out a good part of their winter keep. M. de Lavergne himself, contending singly with nature, would have little reward for repelling her entirely from his precincts. Hills clothed in purple and gold add much to the picturesqueness of the scenery, if they do little for the farm beyond furnishing the cattle with a part of their litter—for which heather and furze are here put to use. The chief revenue of a large proprietor in this wild district must come neither from the produce of his own farm, nor from that of his tenants, but from the sale of his trees in the market of Limoges, where wood is the chief fuel employed in the manufacture of porcelain. Hence it is that so much of M. de Lavergne's ground is covered by forests, which, besides yielding a revenue to himself, afford covert to innumerable foxes, not a few wolves, and occasional troops of wild boar on their way to his potato-fields. Foxes, wolves, and wild boars, one hardly need say, are not preserved for sport in a country of peasant proprietors; but one large owner cannot exterminate them, and his poor neighbours will not waste time or powder and shot upon animals not good for food. They are, in fact, mostly old men and women, whose sons and brothers are absent in Paris, or in some garrison town, and whose chief sport is catching fish in their hands in the river which flows under Peyrusse.

Exploring the byroads around it—roads meriting the execrations bestowed by Arthur Young a hundred years ago on the roads of his own country—one finds oneself from time to time in one of those rude villages of which a picture is drawn by M. de Lavergne himself in a passage which also describes the distribution of land in La Creuse. 'Out of a total of 550,000 hectares, 150,000 at most belong to persons above the peasant class;* with estates of 30 hectares on an average, cultivated by métayers. 300,000 hectares are owned by a multitude of peasants, with 5 or 6 hectares to a family; the remaining 100,000 hectares belonging to them in common as village communities. The villages around which their little estates are grouped, contain generally ten or twelve houses, with about fifty inhabitants. Beheld from a distance, these little republics, half hidden in chestnut and cherry-trees, have an appearance of brightness and peace which makes one dream of the golden age. As you approach the illusion vanishes. Miry and impracticable roads, thatched roofs so close that one spark sets them all in a blaze, rooms without air or light, in which all the beds lie in a heap, the cow-house part of the dwelling,

---

* '150 ou plus appartiennent à des bourgeois.'—*Econ. rurale de la France*, 3rd ed., p. 386. The word *bourgeois* does not here mean what we commonly understand by it; it includes all who are independent of manual labour for their livelihood. In this sense, a country gentleman, like M. de Lavergne, is a *bourgeois*.

all the passages covered with manure; one can hardly comprehend how human beings can live in such hovels! The rest of the economy is of a piece: the furniture of the most primitive kind; for clothing, the wool of the flocks, and the hemp the shepherdess has spun.' Nevertheless these rude dwellings are palaces compared with the mud cabins of the Irish peasantry; they are built of solid stone from the inmates' own quarry, the chestnut and cherry trees around them are the cottagers' own; they are often mantled with clusters of grapes. No rent-day threatens the cow which shares the roof with distraint, and it is the wool of her father's own sheep, the hemp of his own land, of which the shepherdess makes the family clothing. Here and there, too, the neat farming of a little plot shows that the example of Peyrusse is not altogether thrown away, and that civilisation might find its way into the poorest hamlets of La Creuse, but for a ceaseless drain of its manhood and strength, rendering impossible that natural progress of opulence which plants manufactures and trade round the farm, and expands by degrees the village into the town. St. Goussaud is the only village for many miles round Peyrusse in which a shop catches one's eye—a shop for the sale of Government tobacco; not an inappropriate emblem of the artificial character of the trade which the department is exhausted to maintain. In place of building towns within their own borders, Paris is the town the poor peasantry of Creuse are helping to build; its *travaux de luxe* are constructed by men whose families are without the means of civilised existence. The shepherdess seen from the railway was the symbol of the economic condition of a region whose fields are untilled for want of strong arms, which has no retail trade, even of the commonest articles of clothing, and which is unable to man the railway it has gotten at last, or even, if the expression may be pardoned, to woman it adequately. La Creuse is one of sixteen departments of which the population has decreased under the empire in every *arrondissement*; the number of its inhabitants is actually less at this moment than it was before the Revolution, even according to the official enumeration, which is far from showing the real depopulation, since, as before stated, the greater part of the grown men are absent most part of the year. Describing in 1856 the effects of the public expenditure upon building in Paris, added to the blood-drain of the army, M. de Lavergne declared from personal knowledge, 'La Creuse and the adjoining department of La Limousin, from which the masons are brought, have scarcely any able-bodied men. Cultivation is literally suspended.' In that year the number of masons brought from La Creuse alone was estimated at 50,000, out of a total population of 279,000 of all ages and sexes : in 1866, the total had decreased to 274,000 ; it is now further reduced, and a doubled conscription threatens to consummate the depopulation of the department.*

* When M. de Lavergne, in an 'Essay on Peace,' published in 1855, sarcastically remarked, that 'if it be a fine thing to have 500,000 men under arms, it would be a much finer thing to have a million,' he probably did not foresee that it would come to be thought so. The Emperor himself probably did foresee it, since his published works show that he meditated it long before the Empire.

The levy of 100,000 fresh conscripts a-year falls of necessity chiefly on the rural population, because the peasants are too poor to purchase exemption. Three-quarters of the men who have died in the service in the last twenty years, three-quarters of the men still under the colours, M. de Lavergne affirms, have come from the country, adding that 'peasant property is the chief sufferer, for a poor cultivator whose son is taken from him is ruined.' Accordingly the decline of the rural population of France is ascribed by M. de Lavergne chiefly to the military drain: 'Par là s'explique la plus grande partie du vide, l'émigration ne vient qu'après.'* But La Creuse suffers under imperial rule more than most other departments, for while it must contribute its full quota to the military contingent, it loses a yet larger part of its best strength by emigration to the capital. There are, indeed, people in France who, following English precedent, explain all the movements of labour by demand and supply, the tendency of wages to an equality, &c., and who are ready to argue that the peasantry follow their own interests in going to the towns, and that it must therefore be the best thing for the country. There is, they urge, a demand for builders in Paris, and a supply of poor labourers well fitted for building in La Creuse, where there is no demand for their labour; wages are much higher in the capital than in remote parts of the country; emigration is the process by which they are raised in the latter to the metropolitan level. But the truth is that the old formula of demand and supply

* 'L'Enquête agricole.' *Rev. des Deux Mondes*, Nov. 15, p. 409.

never explains anything: it merely states over again in vague general terms the facts it is put forward to explain. Why is there so great a demand for building in Paris? Why none in La Creuse? Why are wages so much lower in the latter than in the former? How can the emigration of labourers create capital and profitable employment behind them? On each side of La Creuse lie flourishing industrial cities—on its eastern border Montluçon, the entrepôt of a great coal basin; on its western border Limoges, 'the potteries' of France; yet no emigration takes place to either, nor does the one solitary seat of manufacture in La Creuse itself, Aubusson, obtain any increase of population from the country around it. In political constitution and in system of government lies the real explanation of many economic phenomena both in England and France, which political economy, treated as 'a deductive science,' can never explain.

'It starts,' we are told, from the principle that every man knows his own interest best, and if let alone will pursue it, and it follows that principle out into all its ramifications.' * But what is the interest of an Imperial Government? Does an emperor always know his own interest best? And if he follows it into all its ramifications, how are the interests of the country he governs likely to be affected? One-third of the whole expenditure of the State, it has been computed, takes place in Paris; another third in other large towns; but one-third, therefore, is left for all the rest of the country, from which the whole is mainly derived.

* 'Spectator,' Oct. 10, 1868.

Comparing the relative public burdens of country and town, M. de Lavergne finds that the former bears three-fourths of the taxation—furnishes three-fourths of the troops—and gets one-third of the expenditure; and dividing, again, the country into two regions, it is found that the half in which La Creuse is situated has only one-third of the railways and roads. Again, in one year, of which we have the official statistics, the public expenditure in Paris is set down at upwards of 31,000,000*l.*, in La Creuse at 150,000*l.* Not a regiment is stationed at La Creuse, while its scanty resources and labour are heavily taxed to garrison Paris, as well as to build its new streets. Then how can the emigration of their own sons and brothers, to build those new streets, enable the peasantry of La Creuse to compete in the labour market with an Imperial employer, who has unlimited command over funds to which they are themselves compelled to contribute? Or, how is the capital of the manufacturer in Aubusson increased by the outlay by M. Haussmann and Marshal Niel of millions in Paris? On the contrary, the expenditure in the metropolis of funds collected by loans and taxation from all parts of the country, has prevented the construction of railways, roads, and other much-required public works, in remote parts of the country, which would have led to the influx of improvements and capital, and a rise in the prices of produce, by which the demand for labour and the rate of wages would have been raised in La Creuse. As it is, looking to historical evidence of the condition, in former centuries, of the whole central region, of which La Creuse is now by far the poorest part, M. de Lavergne does not hesitate to pronounce that it would have been better for the whole centre had the rest of France disappeared in a cataclysm. The inhabitant of Paris eats, on the average, ten times as much meat as an inhabitant of La Creuse or La Corréze, and much better meat. The Parisian eats the best wheaten bread, and drinks wine every day, whilst both are almost unknown to the peasant of La Creuse. In the reign of Francis I., on the contrary, the comparative condition of the central provinces (of which La Creuse appears to have been the happiest) was thus described by a writer whose report M. de Lavergne fully accepts :—' Les provinces intérieures ont les mœurs plus douces que les autres. Elles se nourrissent aussi beaucoup mieux. C'est du bœuf, du mouton, beaucoup de porc frais ou salé, du gibier, de la volaille, des fruits, toutes choses que le pays produit en abondance.' *

It is sometimes contended, however, that the institution which causes the vast emigration of the French peasantry to the towns, from impoverished departments like La Creuse, is peasant proprietorship. How, it has been asked, is the owner of a few acres to make it worth a labourer's while to remain in his employment? Those who so argue forget that the number of small properties not only places an equal number of men in a much happier position than they could occupy as labourers for hire, † and makes a better provision than

---

* 'Économie rurale de la France,' p. 406.

† In the concluding part of his work on the rural economy of France, summing up its general results, M. de Lavergne says of the small properties—' Deux millions possèdent en moyenne 6 hectares. Ceux-là

a workhouse for their old age, but removes so many competitors from the labour market, and really raises wages instead of depressing them. But for small properties, all the present proprietors would be added to the number of men in want of employment; all, instead of half, of the men of La Creuse would be driven to emigrate. So far as landed property is concerned, it is its non-division—not its subdivision—which impoverishes La Creuse; and the non-division is owing to the neglect of a government otherwise occupied than in promoting improvements in remote parts of the country, which add no immediate éclat or visible strength to an empire. Reference has been made to the quantity of land in La Creuse belonging in common to the villages. 'I do not hesitate to say,' M. About pronounces, 'that almost all the valueless land in France belongs to impersonal beings—the State, the communes, or the charitable institutions. . . . . . . If a number of villagers own twenty acres in common, you may predict that the ground will be neither drained, manured, nor cultivated. Every one will take all he can out of it; no one will spend a sou of capital, or a quarter of an hour's labour on it. Sell the village common to yonder poor shepherd with a dozen sheep, and those twenty acres will soon produce 500 hectolitres of corn.' *

The common lands of La Creuse are, in fact, never

---

jouissent d'une aisance véritable. Leurs biens se divisent par des héritages, mais beaucoup d'entre eux ne cessent d'acheter, et en fin de compte, ils tendent plus à s'élever qu'à descendre dans l'échelle de la richesse.'

* 'Le Progrès,' pp. 188-9.

cultivated, unless in seasons of unusual scarcity; and the ground is manured neither before nor after the crops which are then snatched for the common use of the village. It was explained to the present writer that the chief cause of the sensation produced by his own appearance in the villages of La Creuse, was the village common. Not conceiving the idea of a traveller for pleasure or information, the only reason that could be conjectured for his visit was a desire to buy land. But the buyer of a villager's separate estate would take along with it a share in the common land; and for one cow or one sheep that his predecessor fed on the common, might feed four, becoming thereby the common enemy of the village. Hence the acquisition of additional stock, and the entrance of new capital, are alike viewed with disfavour.

It is not too much to say that every neglect, as well as every act, of the Imperial Government which diminishes the peasantry of La Creuse, and the capacity of its soil to support an increase of numbers, is a public calamity to France, and even to Europe. From time immemorial it has been a region in which crime has been almost unknown,* and the gentle yet manly virtues of the race are visible in their features and form—peacefulness, affection, courtesy, sobriety, honesty, with manly independence and physical vigour. It is this race which Imperial policy is fast eradicating from its native soil, and transforming into a crowd of restless roving town

* In his crime charts (1833), M. Guerry says of La Creuse—'On a compté chaque année d'après la moyenne un accusé pour attentats contre

operatives and dissolute garrison soldiers. The depopulation of La Creuse is but a striking example of the gradual extinction throughout France of Jacques Bonhomme, who was all that the name imported. The rural population of France is now scarcely greater than it was at the beginning of the century, while the urban population has increased from six millions to sixteen, and of the numbers enumerated as belonging to the country, no small part now consists of an element infected with the vices of the camp and the city. Not only all France, but all Europe has reason to join in the eloquent invocation in which M. de Lavergne implores those who direct the destinies of France to leave to it Jacques Bonhomme.

'Dans toutes nos grandes crises historiques, le paysan français, si bien personnifié par Jacques Bonhomme, a toujours fini par nous tirer de l'affaire. Remontez aux croisades, aux guerres féodales, aux guerres contre les Anglais, aux guerres de religion, aux guerres d'Italie, aux guerres de Louis XIV, aux guerres de la Révolution et de l'Empire : c'est Jacques Bonhomme qui répare sans cesse le mal fait par d'autres. C'est encore Jacques Bonhomme qui a supporté tout le poids de la dernière révolution et de la dernière guerre, c'est lui qui a héroïquement subi sans se plaindre l'épreuve douloureuse de la disette ; c'est lui qui ne se lasse pas de fouiller le sol natal " avec une opiniâtreté invincible," comme dit La Bruyère, et qui en tirera certainement de nouveaux fruits. Il ignore les jouissances du luxe,

---

les personnes sur 37,000 habitants. C'est environ quinze fois moins que dans la Corse ! '—Mahon's *History of England,* chap. xlvi.

les gains du jeu, les ambitions fiévreuses, et possède encore les mâles vertus et les instincts productifs de ses pères. Laissez-le faire ; il vous rendra bien vite, sans faste et sans bruit, sinon ce que vous avez perdu, du moins ce que peuvent créer des richesses nouvelles, le travail et l'économie. Si les autres classes de la société française, riches, bourgeois, artisans de villes, valaient pour leurs rôles ce que Jacques Bonhomme vaut pour le sien, ce n'est pas l'Angleterre, c'est la France qui serait depuis longtemps le premier peuple de l'univers.'*

* 'L'Agriculture et la Population.' Par M. L. de Lavergne. Second Edition, 1865, pp. 343–4.

A SECOND VISIT TO LA CREUSE.

THE author has elsewhere remarked that the land system of France cannot be estimated fairly without reference to the political conditions under which it has been tried. And of all the departments of France, La Creuse presents the most striking example of their influence. An extreme instance, it is true, it is nevertheless a typical one of the obstacles which the policy of the last eighteen years has opposed to the tendencies of the age to carry rapid improvement into the most backward rural localities; while it illustrates also the effects of earlier misgovernment. The cardinal doctrine of the first authority on French rural economy in the lectures, of which the suppression of his Chair in 1852 prevented the oral delivery, is that the town is the most powerful agent in improving the country.* He has lived to see the influence of the town pass like a pestilence over his own department, depopulating its villages, and leaving its fields to relapse into waste. The number of men and boys migrating annually

* 'Rural Economy of England, Ireland, and Scotland.' Translated by a Scotch Farmer, pp. 167-8. The gentle allusion in the Preface to this work to the suppression of his chair is as characteristic of an author remarkable for amiability as for extraordinary capacity and knowledge, as the act itself was characteristic of the principles and tendencies of despotic government.

to the capital and other large towns for the greater part of the year has been generally computed in the department itself at about one-fifth of the entire population; and even official reports refer this enormous migration to the extravagant expenditure on building in Paris and other great cities by the Government, and the municipal authorities carrying out Government policy.

The first transformation of the simple peasant of La Marche—the old province with which La Creuse is nearly coextensive—into a builder of palaces is not indeed to be laid to the charge of the present empire; and the report of the 'Enquête agricole' in the few tardy pages which, out of many thousands in its numerous volumes, have been devoted to La Creuse, alludes not without truth to an 'émigration séculaire et traditionnelle;' though it does not refrain from adding that 'the current which carries its population to the towns has now assumed an alarming intensity.' The movement began, however, more than two centuries ago with the architectural splendour of an earlier despotism at Versailles. In a still earlier age the peasantry of France were accustomed to gather into the nearest towns for security from pillage; and the invasions of the English in the fourteenth and fifteenth centuries, followed by civil war in the sixteenth and seventeenth, caused a continuous aggregation round local centres. But that was local concentration, not emigration, and the last half of the reign of Henry IV, 'the only king France ever loved,' afforded an interval of tranquillity and prosperity to the country which was followed at once by diminished crowding to the towns, and the growth of numerous villages. Brief was that period of sunshine for the peasant. On him fell the burden alike of the pomp and luxury of despotism, of its wars of stupid ambition, of its blunders in legislation, administration, and finance, and of its drain of all the wealth of the country to the capital. The immigration of the noble and even the middle class consequent on its policy of centralisation was of necessity followed by an immigration of labourers and mendicants seeking subsistence. The servile obligations which bound them to the soil, the difficulties of the road, the obstacles to employment created by trade guilds and regulations of industry, the prohibitory edicts of the kings—alarmed at the growth of Paris, without perceiving either its causes or its real danger—their own miserable poverty, and their physical and mental prostration from hunger and suffering, forbade the less energetic of the peasantry to wander from their villages and huts, but the more vigorous and enterprising forced their way to the cities. 'Ceux qui résistent,' wrote Quesnay of the effects of the sufferings and insufficient food of the country population, 'qui conservent la santé, et acquièrent des forces, qui ont de l'intelligence, se délivrent de cet état malheureux en se répandant dans les villes. Les plus débiles, les plus ineptes, restent dans les campagnes, où ils sont aussi inutiles à l'État qu'à charge à eux-mêmes.' The poorest by nature and the most isolated of all the provinces was La Marche, but its pure air and water and their own simple virtues gave its inhabitants hardy frames, and fitted them for labours requiring both strength and dexterity. After the building of Versailles they continued accordingly to furnish Paris with its chief supply of masons and bricklayers, and a genius for building became hereditary in the men of La Marche or La Creuse.* Between 1815 and 1848, the average number of emigrants—using the word in the French sense—was computed at little short of 25,000. But in place of doubling that number, the last twenty years ought to have greatly diminished it—by opening up the resources of the department; by enlarging local employment and raising wages; by lowering the cost of cultivation, while adding to the value of its fruits; and cheapening imports to the consumer, while enhancing the prices of exports for the producer.

It is nowhere disputed that there have been causes which have caused an immigration from many rural districts in France into the large towns. New manufactures and increasing trade have offered employment, and new facilities for migration have given easier access. But this natural immigration was in itself a sufficient reason for not adding an artificial one. The Creuse peasant moreover has never taken to manufactures or trade; he loved at all times his village better than the city, as his annual return to it for the winter, and his final return for the rest of his life, gave proof; and he was too robust a foot-traveller to dwell on the difficulty or the ease of the journey. Sheer

---

* The immigrants from La Marche were confounded in Paris with those from Limousin; and the Creusois *maçon* is still traditionally called a Limousin in the capital.

poverty, caused by the sterility of his native soil and its remoteness from markets, forced him to seek a harvest from brick and stone in the city which he could not reap from his own fields, as poverty forced the Irish peasant to reap his harvest in England and Scotland. The main object of the migration of the Creusois was moreover to accumulate enough to spend his last years in a cottage, and with a small farm of his own. 'These village youths,' says M. de Lavergne, ' all sought to become proprietors like their fathers, and the money obtained by the migration went entirely in the purchase of land. The last residue of the large domains was thus more and more cut into shreds.' He adds, it is true, that the small estate of the peasant was itself frequently subdivided by succession; legal expenses and mortgages too often swallowed up the best part of its scanty produce; and after all their efforts, not a few saw the land so dearly acquired escape at the last from their hands.* But all these evils would have rapidly disappeared before an improvement in cultivation and a rise in the price of its produce; for it is observed throughout France that the subdivision of peasant properties among children by succession diminishes instead of increasing as the owners themselves increase in prosperity. To this circumstance in part, it may not be amiss to observe, is to be attributed some apparent inconsistency in the remarks of M. de Lavergne on the amount of subdivision. When his 'Économie rurale de la France' was written, commerce was less active, agricultural

* 'Économie rurale de la France.'

prices were lower, the peasantry were less wealthy, and subdivision among children was commoner than it is now. Another cause is that the partition of the separate parcels of a small property, which a mischievous reading of the Code brings about, does more harm in some places than in others; and M. de Lavergne described things as they came under his eye through the country. In La Creuse the increase of rural wealth from its own resources in the last fifteen years ought to have removed almost all temptation to leave it. The very railways—one of whose chief sources of profit is the migration, and from whose books in a great measure the estimate has been formed that in more than one year the number of emigrants has exceeded fifty thousand—ought themselves to have arrested the movement. Writing before La Creuse had a railway across it (and it would have had one much sooner but for less useful constructions elsewhere), M. de Lavergne said of the line from Paris to Limoges, which passes its western frontier: 'The general economy of the department formerly rested on the sums brought back by emigrants. Now we hear of industrial enterprises, of public works to be constructed on the spot, and of agricultural improvements to be undertaken. A fortunate circumstance comes at the moment to favour these new tendencies. The Creuse has no railway through it as yet, but the line from Paris to Limoges touches it at one extremity. The opening of this line has lowered the price of lime 50 per cent., at the same time that it opens new facilities for the transport of cattle to the metropolis.'

Lime is the chief ameliorator of the granitic soil of the Creuse, and it is only one of many means of improved husbandry which the railways bring at much diminished cost. At the same time the farmer now gets a great addition to his profits in the price of his produce. The price of meat in the towns of the department has doubled in ten years; eggs are now selling at 1 franc 30 centimes the dozen at Aubusson, where residents remember the dozen as costing only the 30 centimes.* The Abbé P. Labrune, Archiprêtre d'Aubusson, published last year a work on the migration from his department, which establishes by many striking facts the gain which might accrue to it from employing productively at home the labour which is unproductively lavished on Paris. At the gate of his own town, Aubusson, he points to some land the produce of which, fifteen years since, fetched but 60*l.*, while in 1869 it fetched 600*l.* At Évaux, a much less considerable place, and farther from railway communication, Count de Montignac has now an income of 1,000*l.* a-year from an estate which twenty years ago brought him only 120*l.* In another instance, the value of the annual produce of land has risen from 36*l.* to above 360*l.* The Abbé argues from these and many more examples that the emigrants, almost all of whom are either small landowners, or their sons, could have earned more by their own farms and employment within the department than they have done in Paris.†

---

* This is stated on information from the spot in the present month, February 1870.

† The Abbé in his calculations of the relative wages in Paris and La

And while the Creuse peasant can sell almost everything he raises at greatly advanced prices as compared with former years, he can buy many things—implements of husbandry, articles of clothing, tea, sugar, and holiday wine, considerably cheaper than formerly. Instead, therefore, of the peasant having been drawn to the town, the town should have come to him; the streets of Paris, instead of luring him from his fields, ought to have been supplied with a part of their produce, and towns should have grown round him and rewarded his labours with a liberal home market. Yet Gueret, the capital, remains a mean country village, with a few large public buildings in the middle, and immediately surrounded by hills producing nothing richer than heather. Agricultural statistics show that La Creuse ranks far below even the most desert department of Brittany, both in the total value of its crops, and in the yield per hectare. But it ranks second among the departments for its number of sheep, and at the head of all for cattle and sheep together; an economic condition which, taken in connection with the absence of towns and manufactures, the small area under crops, and the emigration of the best strength of the population, affords a not uninstructive parallel to the condition of Ireland. Not the less is it so, that there is a broad contrast in the causes; for it

Creuse puts the rate in the latter at two francs a day. The 'Agricultural Statistics' for 1861–2, published in 1868, put it at 1 franc 72 centimes. The present author, when in the department a few months ago, found different rates in different localities, and even within the same commune.

See on the great disparities of wages in France, 'Études sur la Monnaie.' Par Victor Bonnet, 1870. pp. 63–4.

is not its land system which has depopulated La Creuse, and arrested both cultivation and trade. On the contrary, M. de Lavergne can say: 'Sans le lien de la propriété qui les retient, ils seraient tous partis.'

The Abbé P. Labrune earnestly warns the Government of the peril to itself from the sentiments prevalent among the army of workmen it has assembled in Paris. Immigrant workmen, he observes, have been mixed up with every revolution in Paris for a century. Among examples of the change which is taking place in the character and sentiments of the emigrants from the Creuse, he refers to one young man who, before going to Paris, was one of the most inoffensive in the commune. Now his language is: 'Il n'est besoin ni d'empereur, ni de rois, ni de juges, ni d'armées, ni de notaires, ni de prêtres, ni de ces gens qui ne font que gêner la liberté. Les propriétaires sont de grands voleurs, dignes de la corde ; le moment est venu où on leur rendra justice.' The articles of this new creed may possibly not be all so very unsound as the worthy Abbé may think ; although it is not one which promotes the stability of an Imperial Government. Unfortunately it confounds things.

M. Élie de Beaumont cites with approval in the Introduction to his work on the 'Geological Map of France,' a dictum of the great naturalist, Cuvier, respecting the influence of geological conditions on the life and thought of man, and the impossibility of the inhabitant of a region of barren granite, like La Creuse, becoming similar in habits and ideas to the occupant of a fertile limestone soil : 'Nos départemens granitiques produisent sur tous les usages de la vie humaine d'autres effets que les calcaires; on ne se logera, on ne se nourrira, le peuple, on peut le dire, ne pensera jamais en Limousin ou en Basse-Bretagne, comme en Champagne ou en Normandie.' The railway which carries lime at a reduction of 50 per cent. ought in reality to have assimilated the physical conditions of life in La Creuse in no inconsiderable measure to those of fertile Normandy. Instead, however, of coming to live and think like a prosperous Norman peasant proprietor, who is least of all things desirous of hanging all the owners of property, the Creuse peasant is coming to think, like some hundred thousand other workmen in Paris, that he would be a good deal better off himself if they were all attached to the cord. Even in Normandy itself, the labourer who has worked in Paris has some subversive ideas. Not long ago one such, seated in a diligence, and apparently well to do, found serious fault with the author for having hands less horny than his own, and intimated that such a state of things was too intolerable to continue.

However, the attractions to Paris are less than they were, through a cessation of public buildings; and it is estimated that about 4,500 fewer emigrants left La Creuse in the year which has just closed. The author himself during a visit to the department last autumn was struck by an appearance of more men in the fields, and an increased breadth of cultivation; and subsequent inquiry satisfies him that such was the case in localities which did not come under his eye. As the German peasant calls his little possession land a *Gut*, so the

French peasant calls his own a *bien*; and it is a good, not only to the peasant himself, but to a Government which has done little to deserve it. The land system of France alone saves the Government from an immigration into the capital equal to that which the land system of England produces in London, and much more rapid in its political consequences.

THE PEASANTRY AND FARMS OF BELGIUM, 1867.*

BELGIUM, the ' old cock-pit of Europe,' as it was called, has lately become the chief battle-ground of a controversy in which, though never likely to be fought in blood, and assuming the peaceful guise of an economic discussion, some think they see the beginning of a revolution that will leave behind it few traces of the order of things the quarter of a century of battles that closed at Waterloo was inaugurated to maintain. Pregnant or not with so great a future, the controversy, in connection with which the rural economy of Belgium is constantly appealed to, concerning the respective effects of large estates and large farms on the one hand, and peasant properties and *la petite culture* upon the other, is one on many accounts deserving the attention of both the politician and the theoretical economist. As to the latter, the very existence of political economy, as an accepted branch of philosophy, is at stake, if we are to believe a writer justly commanding no little attention in the world of political letters, who affirms that the professors of what claims to be a distinct branch of science are in irreconcilable conflict

---

* Reprinted from 'Fraser's Magazine,' December 1867.

about its first principles and most general laws, citing among other examples the questions—'Are small farms or large farms best?' 'Does the peasant proprietor thrive?'*

That some fundamental economic doctrines are collaterally involved in the questions thus somewhat ambiguously expressed will not, we imagine, be disputed; but we venture to add, that an economist can no more be expected to decide the questions themselves from the first principles of political economy, or the general laws of production, than a mathematician to say, from the first principles of mechanics and the general laws of motion, whether large or small ships of war are best for naval engagements—or whether rifles or cannons will decide the fate of battles in future. To borrow a phrase from Mr. Mill, with which his economic readers are familiar, what the writer referred to calls first principles are in truth last principles. And political economy, like all other branches of science,

---

* 'Economists, it is believed, have worked out a system of general truths, which any shrewd man of business can readily apply. We are very proud of our great writers who have created this science. . . . . But when we come to study the science, we certainly do not find this agreement among its professors. There are hardly ten generalisations on which the writers are at one, and that not on the details but on the first principles, not on intricate points of practice but on the general laws of production. Who is right about currency? What are the laws of population? Are small farms or large farms best? Does the peasant proprietor thrive? Let us suppose these questions asked from a body of economists, and we should have them at cross purposes in a moment. Indeed we find ourselves not in a science properly so called at all, but a collection of warm controversies on social questions. What would be the state of medicine, if physiologists were hotly disputing on the circulation of the blood?'—'The Limits of Political Economy.' By F. Harrison. *Fortnightly Review.*

especially those which are of recent birth, is a progressive investigation, not a completed one. It might take for its motto Bacon's 'Prudens interrogatio dimidium scientiæ;' and its weakness, where it is weak, is the weakness, not of decrepitude, but of youth, and proves only that it has a wide field and future before it. To answer inquiries such as their critic proposes, economists, in addition to carrying the first pages of their text-books in mind, ought to question the plains of Flanders, and the mountain-sides and valleys of Switzerland and Lombardy; indeed, the rural economy of every country they can visit besides their own. They ought, moreover, to regard such inquiries as most useful, because they add the book of nature to their studies; for every branch of human science, to whatever the stature it has grown, gathers, Antæus-like, fresh vigour from falling back on earth, from which Newton himself learned the movements of the heavens. In immediate connection with the very controversy just mentioned, a late distinguished astronomer not long ago illustrated the importance of terrestrial observation by replying to persons who argue that a system of husbandry which prospers in Flanders might prosper in Ireland: 'There is no analogy between small farming in Belgium and in Ireland. A visit to Belgium would at once have dispelled the illusion. In Belgium there is a fine climate for the growth of cereals; the soil is usually a sandy loam, producing the finest wheat crops. The country is rich in minerals. Iron is raised in immense quantities, and applied to every useful purpose; there is a great manufacture of artillery and small-arms. More coal is raised than in all France, manufactures abound, there is industry in every shape. What a contrast to Ireland, where wheat may be said to grow almost by sufferance in average, and to fail altogether in bad seasons.'*

We join in the noble astronomer's recommendation of a visit to Belgium, if only for the purpose of dispelling an illusion betrayed in this very passage: one shared by not a few persons remarkably well informed on other subjects; and arising apparently from thinking of Belgium at a distance in the lump, mixing up the agriculture of the Flemings with the manufactures of the Walloons, the soil of Hainaut and of the south of Brabant with the farms of Flanders, and the sandy regions traversed by the Scheldt and Lys with the iron and coal in the valleys of the Meuse, the Sambre, and the Trouille. The truth is, that Belgium is far indeed from being one uniform whole; least of all is it such a whole as described in the passage just quoted. It is, on the contrary, a country remarkable for broad contrasts. The visitor finds two races, speaking different tongues, intermingling but little, jealous of each other, and, as a general rule, inhabiting different halves of the kingdom: of these races, one, occupying the northern half, famous now for its husbandry alone, though once as famous for pre-eminence in manufactures; the other, backward for the most part, by comparison in agriculture, but holding a foremost position in manufactures which is of modern date. He sees

---

* 'The Relation of Landlord and Tenant in Ireland and other parts of the United Kingdom.' By the Earl of Rosse. Murray, 1867.

regions adapted to different products, and agriculture in every stage of its progress, from the first to the latest; and what strikes him more, he sees the most perfect and the most productive cultivation where the soil is most sterile by nature, and where there is no mineral wealth whatever to create for the farmer great industrial markets; while, on the contrary, agriculture is found backward, not in rude regions alone, still haunted by wolf, wild boar, and deer, but within easy reach of rich and busy mines and a flourishing manufacturing industry.

We say agriculture is seen in all its stages in Belgium. M. de Laveleye describes them as four: in the first of which half of the arable land always lies fallow; in the second the fallow comes only every third year; in the third fallow is superseded altogether by a constant rotation of crops; finally comes the practice followed in Flanders, according to which the ground not only is never let rest, but gives two crops in the year. Of these four methods the first is still commonly practised in the Belgian province of Luxembourg. Not many weeks ago we saw the smoke ascend from burning patches here and there upon the Ardenne hills, of the wild mountain vegetation of ten or fifteen years, preparatory to two or three successive cereal crops, after which the ground is left again to nature for a decennial interval or more. This is the ancient practice which, in M. de Laveleye's picture of the rural economy of Ardenne, gets the name of *essartage*,* and which in France is called *écobuage*.

---

* 'Économie rurale de la Belgique,' 2me éd. pp. 206–8. The region called Ardenne in M. de Laveleye's pages occupies about three-fourths

But earlier stages of the natural march of industrial progress, as Adam Smith has classified them, meet the eye in Ardenne. The first of all is, as he says, the hunting and fishing stage, after which comes pastoral life, agriculture next, and, lastly, manufactures and the varied industry of towns. Of these, the pasture of cattle in the rudest fashion is the chief pursuit of man in Ardenne, and the poor animals are half starved in winter. But a great part of this wild country may in fact be said to remain still in the hunting and fishing stage, for not only do fish and flying game abound, but the forests are alive with deer and boar, and the wolf still holds his own. Macaulay tells that the last wild boars in England, preserved for royal sport, were slaughtered by exasperated rustics during the civil wars. Close to the very line of railway from Spa to Luxembourg, the country-side was up in wrath before our eyes, last August, to hunt the boar. And even in the adjoining region of Entre-Sambre-et-Meuse, traversed by several railways, and not remote from swarming hives of human industry, exceeding bitter cries came from the peasantry to the Government to defend them from troops of invading *sangliers*. A Belgian journal published the following piteous appeal:

'On écrit de Gochenée (Florennes):—"Nos environs sont infestés de sangliers qui causent aux agriculteurs des dommages incessants et irréparables. Il faut être sur les lieux pour apprécier l'étendue et l'importance des ravages. C'est depuis sept ans environ que ces animaux sauvages ont fait leur ap-

of Belgian Luxembourg, with part of the province of Liége, south of Spa.

parition en masse chez nous. Ils parcourent en bandes les forêts voisines de la commune, où ils trouvent un abri assuré, après les déprédations nocturnes.

'" Depuis la plantation jusqu'à la récolte, ces bêtes fauves ne cessent de faire la guerre aux champs de pommes de terre. C'est la nuit qu'elles choisissent pour exercer leurs rapines. Le sanglier voyage volontiers par bandes. Aujourd'hui, ils vous culbuteront quelques centaines de plantes de pommes de terre dans un champ, demain dans un autre ; parfois, la même nuit, dans cinq ou six champs différents à la fois.

'" Que dirai-je des champs de seigle ou d'orge situés à proximité des bois ?—A peine le grain commence-t-il à mûrir, que les sangliers arrivent. Ils se jettent de préférence sur les parties les plus belles et les plus épaisses, ils forment des javelles, les couchent à terre, dévorent les épis, se vautrent dans la paille, courent de çà de là, et vous mettent la récolte dans un état lamentable.

'" Que mettra le laboureur dans son champ, après la pomme de terre ainsi ravagée ? Du seigle, le plus souvent. Eh bien, pour glaner la pomme de terre oubliée dans les sillons, le sanglier vous retournera un champ tout entier : avant la fin de l'hiver, pas un pied carré n'aura échappé à ses atteintes.

'" Que faire ?—Voilà sept ans que cela dure, et réellement nous avons subi de grandes pertes à cause de cela. Toute la population demande à cors et à cris que le gouvernement, protecteur naturel de nos propriétés, et auquel nous payons régulièrement l'impôt, intervienne et prenne des mesures promptes et expéditives pour nous délivrer de ces animaux destructeurs." '

Where such complaints are heard, however, Adam Smith's third period of husbandry has been reached; in Ardenne the wild boar has scope enough without obtruding within the precincts of human cultivation. He may roam the very 'forest of Arden,' which Murray's 'Handbook' says recalls so well Shakespeare's description of its scenery, that one might dream of meeting there the banished duke in sylvan court. And in truth, the natives of Ardenne in general may, in comparison with the ever-toiling Flemings, whom they contemn, be said, like the duke's companions, 'to fleet their time carelessly as they did in the golden time.' M. de Laveleye remarks upon their hospitality to strangers. But hospitality is a primitive virtue, sometimes accompanied by that primitive development of the intellect, which takes forms considered blamable where industry has arrived at the advanced commercial stage at which honesty is accounted the best policy. The tourist who comes for sport is welcomed, but as the people of the place themselves observe, it is *toujours le dernier venu*, supposed to come with the most open hand, who gets the peasant's heartiest aid, and the village host will sometimes balk his sport for private ends. A very pleasant innkeeper caused us, not long ago, to miss a boar-hunt that he might not miss us at his *table d'hôte*, and if his charges were low in proportion to the prices of an untravelled place, he seemed to think he might requite himself for entertainment at so light a cost by indirect and ingenious means. But Ardenne is the heir of all the ages; the railway which traverses it, and which brought a Belgian lady in a bloomer dress to an hotel at Viel Salm some weeks ago, bids prices advance and primitive virtues and arts retreat, together with the wild boar, before the commercial stage of human progress, which Flanders had reached at the opposite side of Belgium, centuries ago.

There let us cross, and in the famour Pays de Waes, of which St. Nicolas is capital, look upon woodland scenery of another sort from that which Ardenne boasts. 'On se croirait d'abord,' says M. de Laveleye, in one of his inimitable pictures,* ' dans une vaste forêt, tous les chemins sont plantés d'arbres, tous les champs en sont entourés, tous les fossés bordés. La vue est bornée de toutes parts.' Like the forests of Ardenne, the woodland here teems with animal life, but the wild boar was ages ago transformed into the fat hog; the wolf has been supplanted by the dog, which, if a large one, too often draws his master's cart; large dogs at least, along with large proprietors, find England beyond doubt the happiest land. For deer, there is a

* In a report to the Institute of France upon M. de Laveleye's 'Économie rurale de la Belgique,' M. Léonce de Lavergne justly observes: 'M. de Laveleye est un écrivain en même temps qu'un agronome. Les tableaux s'animent sous sa plume, et qu'il décrive la culture jardinière des Flandres ou les bruyères de la Campine, les riches moissons du Brabant ou les plateaux arides du Condroz, les cimes sauvages de l'Ardenne ou les grandes prairies des *polders*, l'effet du paysage n'est jamais oublié. On dirait une succession de tableaux flamands; on y retrouve ces horizons bas et verdoyants où ruminent paisiblement des vaches, ces chaudes écuries tout encombrées de fourrages et d'animaux, ces intérieurs rustiques, ces grands bois, ces bestiaux à l'abreuvoir, qui revivent sous les pinceaux de Paul Potter, de Wouvermans et de Berghem.'

goat that gives six quarts of milk a day, and for smaller game, tame rabbits for the London markets swarm in the cottages. In Ardenne, lean kine grazing hungrily are seen in herds; here fat cattle are still more numerous, but the roadside traveller never sees a cow, unless, when morning and evening children lead the tranquil animals from their stalls to graze a short while upon the little grass-plot by the tiny farm. In Ardenne the farm peasantry live, not from poverty, in squalid huts of slate-stones rudely plied, which stand out naked and bleak on the wayside. Here, the neat cottage of the poorest labourer retires within a trim enclosure, and adds a modest ornament to the scene of gay and luxuriant garden cultivation, glimpses of which are caught between the thickly planted poplar and willow trees, and which M. de Laveleye reproduces to the life as follows : ' Sans énumérer toutes les plantes auxquelles le cultivateur donne ses soins, on peut citer comme cultures industrielles le colza, la cameline, le pavot, le houblon, le lin, le chanvre, la chicorée ; comme cultures alimentaires le froment, le seigle, le sarrasin, les haricots, les pommes de terre ; comme cultures fourragères et racines, le trèfle ordinaire et le trèfle incarnat, les féveroles et les vesces, l'avoine, les pois, les choux, les betteraves, les navets, les carottes, etc. La variété de ces récoltes donne aux campagnes en toute saison un aspect riant, un air de luxe et de parure. Jamais l'œil attristé ne s'égare sur de vastes guérets, comme dans les pays riches où domine la culture du froment. Aussi quand le cultivateur flamand, habitué au spectacle de ses champs toujours verts, aperçoit les immenses plaines nues de la Picardie ou même de certaines parties de la Belgique, il se croit transporté dans un désert, ne comprenant pas que c'est la nature ingrate de sa propre terre, qui l'oblige à recourir à des cultures si diverses.'

We quote this passage not for its life-like descriptiveness alone, but because it also places before the eye the proper objects and methods of *la petite culture*, and corrects a misconception on the subject common in this country, which both does great injustice to the Flemish farmer, and teaches a wrong lesson in husbandry. The misconception we refer to is, that the success of *la petite culture* in Flanders is due, as Lord Rosse put it, to a soil and climate eminently favourable for the growth of cereals, wheat in particular. The truth is, that the soil is naturally unfavourable to every crop without exception, but most of all to wheat; and, moreover, that not cereals, but productions of which butter and flax may be taken as representatives —that is to say, house food for cattle to be converted into animal food for man and plants, such as flax and hemp for man's clothing and use—are the true objects of *la petite culture*. We were particularly struck by the rarity of the little patches here and there of wheat this summer in the Pays de Waes, though M. de Laveleye's statement was fresh in our minds that— in the light soil of Flanders wheat, however richly manured, gives a poor return; the chief object of cultivation is not cereals, but flax and butter, so much so that the best farmers sell hardly any of the little grain they grow, and use it for the consumption of their cattle.*

In fact, in a seven years' course of husbandry, with 'intermediate crops,' or more than one crop a year, wheat usually comes up but once, and then only forced by rich manure. If the tourist would judge what the soil is fit to grow without the most elaborate spade culture and the most copious manuring, let him take advantage (as we did, following a suggestion in M. de Laveleye's pages) of the occasional glimpses of its native character as shown by the cuttings of a railway side by side with the richest cultivation. Let him, for instance, look round the roots of the lean firs beside the station of Mille-Pommes, the next station to St.-Nicolas, in the heart of the Pays de Waes. What would an English large farmer give for land like that? what could he make of it? What the Fleming will give for it, and what *la petite culture* can make of it, may be stated in figures. By the side of a cultivated hectare which would sell for 120*l.*, a hectare in a state of nature sells for 12*l.* But even these figures, cited by M. de Laveleye as an evident proof that the soil owes almost all its value to culture, do not fully exhibit the state of the case, unless it is borne at the same time in mind that the 12*l.* are given for the natural hectare only because it can afterwards be made worth 120*l.* by *la petite culture*. It is potential value only—or, in other words, room for the peasant to work in, space for his spade to turn in, and for the bestowal of his time, his thrift, and his long labour of love—that the hectare

* 'Économie rurale de la Belgique,' pp. 39, 48.

brings of its own. It has been said by a person in Ireland, who knows, what few persons either there or in England seem to do—the real meaning o *la petite culture*, that 'the house-keeping and house-feeding of cattle is its body and soul.' We should be more inclined to say that making the most of both space and time is its body and soul. It is a great error to suppose that a minute subdivision of farms is in itself a disadvantage to agriculture, which only extraordinary advantages of soil and situation can compensate. *La petite culture*, or minute farming, as it may be translated, contains in itself one of the most important conditions of its own success, in that it *is* minute. It is an old saying that there is no manure like the master's foot, and the master's foot is always on every inch of the tiny Flemish farm. 'Pas un pouce de terrain perdu,' was the remark of the French savant in agriculture, from the records of whose travels in Flanders half a century ago M. de Laveleye has quoted some exquisite passages. 'Le fumier,' says M. de Laveleye himself, speaking of the house-keeping of cattle, 'est recueilli avec infiniment plus de soin qu'en Angleterre, rien ne se perd, ni de leur litière, ni de leurs déjections liquides.' The principal characteristics of Flemish husbandry, says the same authority, are, first, the great variety of crops; secondly, the extensive practice of intermediate cropping; thirdly, the abundant use of the most active manures; and, lastly, the extreme minuteness of the farms.* But whoever examines the subject with attention will not fail to perceive that the

* 'Économie rurale,' p. 36.

three first of these characteristics have followed from the last. Minute care, minute economy, are the natural consequences: nothing is lost; the most is made of the least, and *multum in parvo* is the result. You see a peasant child gather the smallest tufts of grass along the road: they will presently make part of a rabbit; the rabbit will grow in time into a goat or pig; the pig or goat into a cow; the cow will multiply, and perhaps its produce may bring its master land of his own enough to feed several cows. It is the same with time as with space: the most is always made of it. The Irish farmer sows late; his land is wet and cold for want of drainage; and winter is too often upon him before his one exhausting crop is off the ground.[*] The Fleming takes time both by the forelock and the afterlock: the year sees him so early in the field, that it rewards him with a second crop, and his ground, being never left to rest, becomes as active as himself. 'Jamais les champs ne sont déserts, jamais le sol ne se repose. Il semble qu'à force de le façonner, l'homme espère lui communiquer une partie de son activité et

[*] An excess of moisture in the soil of Ireland is the chief agricultural defect, and fortunately it is in the power of our farmers to correct this evil. The thorough-drain will remove the water which consumes the heat of the sun, and allow the air to pass into the interior of the soil, warming it, and giving it that temperature which will cause the dormant seed to vegetate, and at the same time supplying to the young plant the gases required to promote its growth. Forty years ago, on a town land about two miles east from the Castlereagh hills in Down, the harvests were twelve or fourteen days earlier than in Castlereagh, where the farms are more elevated and exposed; but now, by superior cultivation, draining, manuring, &c., the case is altered, and the crops in Castlereagh arrive at maturity from six to eight days earlier than in the former locality.—*Lessons on Agricultural Chemistry*. By Professor Hodges, M.D.

de sa vie. En toute saison l'on voit des cultivateurs occupés à le labourer, le bêcher, le biner, le sarcler, le débarrasser des mauvaises herbes, à y transporter les matières indispensables pour le féconder, à récolter enfin les produits nombreux si péniblement obtenus. La déesse de la terre germanique, la farouche Hertha, ne ressemble guère à la Cybèle du midi aux fécondes mammelles, la bonne mère, *bona dea* ; ce n'est que vaincue par des soins continuels, par des sacrifices sans cesse renouvelés et toute baignée de leurs sueurs, qu'elle accorde quelques dons à ses laborieux enfants.'*

The traveller in the Lothians must no doubt be struck, as Lord Carnarvon says he lately was, by 'the chimney which every single farmhouse possesses, indicating an enormous development of agriculture by the aid of almost all the mechanical appliances which art and science can suggest.' We did not see one chimney of the kind the eminent nobleman referred to in a recent visit to the Pays de Waes, but we saw a multitude of chimneys of a different kind, indicating a still more prodigious development of agriculture by the aid of a higher power than steam. Steam threshing-machines are now common in Flanders, but agriculture does not reach its highest point by becoming a mere mechanical and chemical process : it is where it is a moral and intellectual process on the part of all the cultivators, where it calls into play both the powers of their understanding and the affections of the soul, that it seems to produce the most abundance, and that it certainly produces most happiness and good. The

* De Laveleye, 'La Belgique,' p. 40.

peasant in Flanders who is not the owner of the little plot he tills too often shows the lines of anxiety and the spareness of face and form that comes of sparing food—for both land and landowner are poor, and exact the most; but see him in the fields, watch him at his work, and you cannot mistake his cheerful interest in his toil : he loves the ground and likes his work. Sometimes you see his wife and daughter weeding beside him on their knees; but they weed with all their hearts, while the children make a play of their little helps to the family husbandry.* Whence comes this all-pervading love of the farm? It comes from the wide distribution of little farms; above all, it comes of a wide distribution of farms of their own among the peasantry—that is to say, of peasant proprietorship, with the sentiments and habits it creates, the example it sets, and the hopes it awakens. Half the small farmers of Flanders own at least a part of the land they cultivate. And what is of especial importance, the ownership of land is not confined in Flanders by legal restrictions and expenses to a caste, or a class, or a particular number of families. Its transfer is easy and cheap ; little plots are continually for sale, and the labourer is frequently a buyer; the notary does a flourishing business, though his charges are low. Hence it is that M. de Laveleye can say: 'Même quand la terre ne lui appartient pas, un lien très-fort attache le cultivateur flamand au sillon qu'il arrose de ses sueurs ;' hence that 'charme si puissant

---

* Unless for weeding flax and turnips, *hired* labour of women is rarely employed by farmers in Flanders—of children, we believe, never.

de la campagne qui agit profondément sur ces âmes rustiques.' The owners of land have made agriculture an interesting art; they have spread the love of practising that art, and the love of the soil on which it is practised, throughout a whole peasantry. No gulf is fixed between the landowner and the labourer, and the latter does not despair of winning a home and a farm of his own. A member of Parliament told an agricultural society in the north of England the other day that the condition of agriculture near Paris is 'as bad as possible owing to the small proprietors.' We are not writing here of France, or we might show that peasant proprietorship has done prodigies of good, though under peculiar obstacles, there; but as regards Flanders, we are prepared to affirm that, as Falstaff could boast of being not only witty himself, but the cause of wit in other men, the peasant proprietor may boast that he is not only a good farmer himself, bu the cause of good farming in other men. M. de Laveleye says, it is true, that the agricultural labourer in Flanders is, 'perhaps of all labourers in Europe, the one who, working the hardest, is the worst fed.' He is in reality not worse fed than many of his fellows in England,* and he is always well housed; but it is an additional testimony to the powerful attraction towards husbandry which peasant properties create, that the Fleming *is* so laborious and skilful a workman for so scanty a wage. He has not often the ruddy look of

---

* His bread is black, it is true, while the English labourer's is white, but it is pleasant to the taste, and we have found it very good stuff to walk on when other food was not readily forthcoming.

vigorous animal life which the produce of even sand can give him who has no rent to pay out of it (for we have seen many a blooming cheek in the fields and cottages of peasant proprietors); but he has never the hopeless, half-sullen, half-servile, jaded-animal look of the English agricultural labourer. He is, indeed, by no means a mere manual labourer; his mind and his heart are in his work, and at the same time he always keeps the future—that is to say, a farm of his own in the future—in sight. He has learned, too, in the neat cottages surrounding him from his childhood, those habits of cleanliness, care, and economy which make half the success of *la petite culture*, and which he will carry with him into *la grande culture*, if he succeeds in enlarging his farm. For it must not be supposed that the farms of Flanders are all small, or that large farming is unprosperous. It is true that *la grande culture* is of necessity less elaborately perfect, and that there is a tendency towards the subdivision of farms, because under *la petite culture* it is found that the sand yields a greater produce, and can pay a higher rent. Nevertheless, there is a good number of farms of considerable size on which an example is set with respect to the introduction of mechanical inventions; and which contribute to enlarge the ideas and exercise the thought of a rural population, all whose other mental education might almost be said to be *la petite culture* and the life of the rural commune. For little is done by the clergy, who have assumed the control of popular instruction, to promote it in reality, and much is done by them to impede it in any form but that which they sanction themselves. In addition to the superior happiness and independence of the peasant who has the management of a little farm, compared with the mere labourer, its management evidently tends to develope that practical sagacity and foresight, combined with a faculty of forming prompt resolutions on important matters connected both with the market and the farm, which the Flemish peasantry possess in an eminent degree. Then there is the life and activity of those charming villages which have grown up without number in Flanders, exactly in accordance with Adam Smith's theory of the natural progress of opulence—a point deserving of the more attention, since it has been contended that an indispensable condition of the success of *la petite culture* is the vicinity of large manufacturing centres of consumption, or at least of a market arising from a large aggregation, in some form, of other industries than that of agriculture itself. Lord Dufferin has stated this argument in the most forcible way : ' The provinces of Belgium where *la petite culture* prevails are thickly studded with large industrial towns and innumerable villages, and the land around is devoted to an extensive system of market-gardening only practicable in such localities. The facilities for obtaining manure are exceptional, and high manuring at the cost of from 10*l.* to 18*l.* to the acre, stolen crops, together with the cultivation of plants used in the adjacent manufactories, are the keystones of Belgian agriculture. To expect, therefore, that because holdings of four or five acres can be cultivated with advantage amid the densest population in Europe, of which the agricultural class forms less than one-half, a similar system can be introduced into Ireland with its sparse urban population, its restricted markets, and its limited manufactures, seems as unreasonable as to argue that because it pays Mr. Early Pease of Brompton to employ a press of hands and 50*l.* per acre in raising asparagus for Covent Garden market, a similar expenditure and similar method of cultivation should be adopted in the valleys of Wales and the straths of the Highlands.' *

In reference to this argument, it is a fact worth noticing, that the provinces of Belgium in which the principal manufactures of the country, with the towns in which they centre, are situated, are those which are considered *pays de grande culture*, and we lately ascertained that farms are increasing in size in the vicinity of some of the towns referred to. The following statistics of the machinery and steam power in Hainaut and Liége on the one hand, and of East and West Flanders on the other, taken from an official table for 1864, tell their own tale:

	Machines à vapeur fixes		Chevaux de force	
Hainaut	2,295	} 3,682	64,178	} 98,420
Liége	1,387		34,242	
Flandre orientale	646	} 873	9,756	} 11,845
Flandre occidentale	227		2,089	

Another important fact, for its bearing on Lord Dufferin's argument, is that the collapse of the staple manufactures of Flanders (since the spinning-wheel and the hand-loom have been superseded), and the transfer

---

* 'Irish Emigration and the Tenure of Land in Ireland.' By Lord Dufferin: pp. 167, 175.

of the sites and production to countries with superior mechanical advantages have led, not to a diminution of *la petite culture*, but to a more minute subdivision of farms. Sir George Nicholls was so much struck with instances of this, that he went so far as to attribute the origin of the present system of husbandry in Flanders to the decay of its manufactures and towns, in a well-known report to the English Government. 'The extensive manufactures which at no very remote period flourished in Belgium appear to have congregated a numerous population in and around the great towns. As the scene of manufacturing industry changed, this population was deprived of its employment, and compelled to resort to the cultivation of the soil for subsistence. This seems to have been the chief origin of the system of small farms which prevails, cultivated by the owner and his family, generally without assistance.'

We need hardly say that 'the system of small farms which prevails' is of no such recent date, but many centuries old. Sir G. Nicholls was, however, correct to the extent that the cause he refers to gave a further stimulus to the system, instead of paralysing it, as Lord Dufferin's theory would lead us to expect. Adam Smith, we may add, nearly a century ago emphatically pointed to the prosperity of Flemish husbandry, notwithstanding the decline of its cities, as a proof of the superior durability and self-sustaining character of agricultural prosperity, in comparison with that arising from the commerce and manufactures of towns: 'No vestige,' he said, 'now remains of the great wealth said to have been possessed by the greater part of the Hanse towns, except in the obscure histories of the thirteenth and fourteenth centuries. It is even uncertain where some of them were situated, or to what towns in Europe the Latin names given to some of them belong. But though the misfortunes of Italy in the end of the fifteenth and the beginning of the sixteenth centuries greatly diminished the commerce and manufactures of the cities of Lombardy and Tuscany, those countries continue to be among the most populous and best cultivated in Europe. The civil wars of Flanders and the Spanish Government chased away the great commerce of Antwerp, Ghent, and Bruges. But Flanders continues to be one of the richest and most populous provinces of Europe. The ordinary revolutions of war and government easily dry up the source of that wealth which arises from commerce only. That which arises from the more solid improvement of agriculture is much more durable.'

So much in respect to the large towns. But what, moreover, is the real relation between those 'innumerable villages,' and the perfection and success of small farming which Lord Dufferin—in support of his inference that Ireland has not the non-agricultural conditions essential to such agriculture—attributes to them? This inquiry deserves the more attention from the fact that Lord Dufferin's theory derives some colour of support from a remark of Mr. Mill's, that a country will seldom have a productive agriculture 'unless it has a large unagricultural population, which will generally be collected in towns and large villages.' * We do not

* 'Principles of Political Economy,' book i. chap. viii. Mr. Mill adds, however: 'Or the only available substitute, a large export trade

dispute the justice of this remark, but add to it Adam Smith's observation that where cultivation is carried on with proper security to cultivators, it creates for itself a large non-agricultural population around it. This is most happily confirmed in the case of Flanders. Its 'innumerable villages,' and the industry of the non-agricultural population they contain are beyond question the direct offspring of agriculture, the ministers and creatures of the cultivators. Take M. de Laveleye's description, the truth of which any one who visits the country may very easily verify by leaving the railway at any station between Antwerp and Gand, and walking a few miles on any road. 'The Flemish village is formed not of an aggregation of farms but of a combination of the industries required to meet the wants of the numerous population dispersed through the country. In the rural communes accordingly, there will be found grocers, bakers, confectioners, drapers, tailors, and dressmakers exhibiting in their windows engravings of the latest fashions, and even clockmakers and coachmakers. The aspect of the village corresponds with the conditions in which its industry is exerted. All shows a humble ease, obtained by economy, order, and care. Each village being, moreover, the dwelling-place of a certain number of small proprietors, constitutes a centre of local activity independent of the chief towns of the province. There are societies for instrumental and vocal music, literary societies, horse-racing societies which give prizes to

in agricultural produce to supply a population elsewhere,'—an available substitute with which Ireland is now provided.

the best trotters, agricultural societies, archery societies,
&c. There is not throughout the sand regions of
Flanders a locality so small and isolated as not to have
two or three such societies. In large villages there
will be found eight or ten.' An instance of the way in
which agriculture evokes by its side other industries
and new improvements which struck ourselves very
lately in a village with many good houses, was that
one of the best bore the advertisement in Flemish of a
vendor of guano and artificial manures. The very
variety and beauty of the houses in these villages is no
mean result of the cultivation of the country, and must
have a most beneficial effect on the minds of the rural
population. The grace of the dwellings of the wealthier
small proprietors, embowered in tiny pleasure grounds,
is beyond description. But the humblest workman's
cottage is exquisitely neat, and each has something
about it which gives it a character of its own. And
look within, look at the furniture, the bright ware, the
clock, the petroleum lamp, the chest of drawers and
its contents, and see what a quantity of auxiliary
industry agriculture has called into existence in the
house of the poorest of its village servants. Could there
be a more complete realisation of Adam Smith's description of the natural progress of opulence, and of
the home market which agriculture naturally creates
for itself, than the whole structure of a Flemish village?
'Smiths, carpenters, wheelwrights,' he says, 'ploughwrights, tanners, shoemakers, and tailors are people
whose services the farmer has frequent occasion for;
and as their residence is not, like that of the farmer,

necessarily tied down to a precise spot, they naturally settle in the neighbourhood of one another, and thus form a small town or village.'

The butcher, the baker, and the brewer, he adds, soon join them, together with other artificers and retailers; and the town or village thus constituted is ' a continual fair or market to which the inhabitants of the country resort to exchange the rude for manufactured produce;' an exchange which furnishes the townspeople or villagers on the other hand both with the materials of their work and their food. The constitution of the Flemish villages fully bears out this theory, and an analysis of the tables of ' professions ' or occupations of the population of the Flemish provinces will be found to add further confirmation to it. The immense number of persons, we may observe—nearly half the population—classed in the Belgian census as persons of no occupation (*personnes sans profession*), has puzzled some English statisticians, and is certainly an absurd and misleading classification. It really includes, in addition to the comparatively small number of persons who follow no occupation in consequence of their wealth, all the women and children who cannot or do not follow any occupation; a class which must in any country compose nearly half the population. To call all the babies *personnes sans profession*, is not simply pedantic; it leads to false estimates of the amount and nature of the industry of the people. If any one, however, examines the tables of occupations in the census, he will see that the great majority of the non-agricultural population of Flanders is engaged in operations arising directly out of agriculture; namely, either in furnishing it with what Dr. Chalmers calls 'its secondaries,' that is to say, its implements, clothing, and other requirements, or in the preparation for use and the carriage and distribution of its principal produce, animals, milk, butter, flax, hemp, tobacco, hops, beetroot for sugar, oil-plants, and grain. One little item of Flemish commerce is significant. The children of the peasantry feed rabbits in the manner M. de Laveleye describes,* and 1,250,000 skinned rabbits, valued at more than 1,500,000 francs, are annually exported to the London market from Ostend, while the skins are retained in the country for the manufacture of hats. Thus agriculture leads, after Adam Smith's theory, both to foreign trade and manufactures at home.

Moreover, now that steam factories are rising in Flanders, the excellence of its flax, and the industry and manipulative skill of its numerous rural population, may go far to compensate for the total absence of iron and coal as regards the manufacture of linen. Mines are not the only causes determining the sites of manufactures; an abundant supply of material and of labour from the country may more than counterbalance the absence of mineral power, as is strikingly shown in Belfast: lending fresh illustration to the doctrine that, in the order of nature, agriculture is the parent of manufactures.† Nor are the advantages a

* 'Économie rurale de Flandres,' p. 70.
† This principle, in its application to Ireland, has lately received a very important elucidation in an address, in many other respects deserv-

great industrial market confers on the farmer, so admirably expounded in M. de Lavergne's 'Rural Economy of Great Britain,' by any means smaller when they arise in the natural order, and the country has created the town. The agricultural question, he says, is nothing more than one of general prosperity : ' If you wish to encourage agriculture, develop manufactures and commerce, which multiply consumers; improve rapidly the means of communication, which bring con-

ing the attention of economists, by Mr. Mulholland to the Social Science Association, from which we take the following passages :—

'There are many reasons why Belfast is really more advantageously situated for this trade than any other town. The province of Ulster has been long celebrated for the growth of flax, and 40,000 or 50,000 tons of the raw material of a quality the most generally serviceable are produced annually within easy reach of the Belfast flax-spinners. . . . . Finally, there is an abundant supply of labour from a rural population that has acquired special aptitudes for the processes of manufacture from the habit of the congenial operations of flax preparation, hand-spinning, and hand-weaving, so long a part of the domestic life of the peasantry. The only point at which Belfast stands at a disadvantage is in its supply of coal. Coal forms only about 5 per cent. of the whole cost of linen. . . . . I conclude, therefore, that there is no reason to doubt that Belfast will continue to be the chief centre of the linen trade, and that its future depends upon the destinies of the trade itself. What is that prospective future ? I believe that it depends chiefly upon the supply of the raw material. The consumption of flax has latterly outgrown the supply. The prices of flax have been during the present year higher than during the worst excitement of the cotton famine. The position of the linen trade is, therefore, critical. Unless new fields can be opened for the extension of flax culture, the present rate of production cannot be maintained. . . . . One of the questions selected for discussion during the present congress has been, 'Can any measures be taken to develop and extend the manufactures of Ireland ? ' If it be possible to introduce any new industry into the south and west, the cultivation of flax would appear to offer the greatest probabilities of success, and it would be a useful step towards a preparation of the population for the more difficult processes of subsequent manufacture. In Ulster any extension of the growth is impossible. It has there been in many cases extended too far already.'

sumers and producers nearer to each other. There is only one law which admits of no exception, and which everywhere produces the same results,—that is, the Law of Markets.'

We should rather say that the Law of Security is the law which has no exceptions; that the manufacturing question is one of general prosperity; and if you wish to develop manufactures, secure to the cultivators of the soil the fruits of their industry, create a numerous and flourishing rural population. The peasant proprietor is, says Sismondi, of all cultivators, the one who gets most from the soil : ' Of all cultivators he is the richest, because he gets most from the soil.' The author of the admirable treatise on the 'Impediments to the Prosperity of Ireland' has pointed out that the prosperity of its agricultural population is important, not only because they are the largest class, but because the prosperity of the largest class in any country is the best foundation for the prosperity of the remainder : 'The condition of American tradesmen and servants, when compared with that of the same classes in England, shows how much more the value of this kind of labour depends on the general body of the population, than on the expenditure, however lavish, of wealthy landlords, merchants, and manufacturers. This same fact is established by the prosperity of trades which supply common articles of necessary use, and the precarious unhealthy state of the trades confined to the production of articles of luxury.'

Dr. Hancock's remark is well illustrated by the fact that the most unhealthy industry in Flanders, in every sense of the word, is the manufacture of lace for a rich class.*

To revert to a point of importance, wherever cultivation has begun the germ of manufactures is there too, and its growth follows the growth of the earlier industry. The old couplet—

> When Adam delved and Eve span,
> Who was then the gentleman?

indicates correctly the first historical step in the division of labour, and the natural relation of the needle, the wheel, and the shuttle to the spade and the plough. The frieze, flannel, and coarse linen woven in the cabin of the poor Irish peasant at this day exhibit the natural progress of industry in a state of arrested development. A statute of Edward III. makes mention of cloth called frieze as being manufactured in Ireland: 'At that time [says Macpherson] there were some considerable manufactures in Ireland. The stuffs called *sayes* made in that country were in such request that they were imitated by the manufacturers of Catalonia, who were in the practice of making the finest woollen goods of the kind. They were also esteemed in Italy.'

Ireland had those advantages of fertility, beauty, and climate which it was one of the best advantages of the early inhabitants of Flanders not to possess. Among the natural gifts which caught the poetic eye of Spenser were the 'goodly woods' of Ireland. Where

---

* 'Depuis que la vapeur a brisé l'antique symbole de l'industrie domestique, le rouet, la mère et les filles font de la dentelle, travail délicat et gracieux, mais trop peu rétribué, et surtout trop incertain, comme tous les travaux qui répondent aux besoins du luxe, et aux fantaisies de la mode.'—E. de Laveleye, *Économie rurale des Flandres*, p. 70.

are they now? 'There is no feature of an Irish landscape,' says the author of 'The Industrial Resources of Ireland,' 'more characteristic than the desert baldness of its hills, which, robbed of those sylvan honours that elsewhere diversify a rural prospect, present to every eye a type of the desolation which has overspread the land.'* What once were hideous morasses in Flanders are, on the contrary, now covered with those goodly woods which M. de Laveleye has described in the 'Pays de Waes.' It has been often said that Flemish agriculture had, from the earliest times, extraordinary advantages of maritime situation; but it would be nearer the truth to say that the greatest of all its advantages were great natural disadvantages. All the elements threatened the early cultivators with destruction, but they threatened the conqueror more. The swamp which gave way under the feet of his horsemen covered ground for the peasant to reclaim, and the very barrenness of the sands gave them fertility, because neither feudal lords nor mere serfs could wring anything from them. The peasant of Flanders was the securest, the freest, and the boldest of those times —'nunc ad aratra nunc ad arma gens promptissima,' says Giraldus Cambrensis—and the little farm and the loom flourished together in natural companionship; while the better situated regions of Belgium passed successively under the yoke of Roman and feudal

* Sir Robert Kane adds: 'Numerous localities in every part of Ireland derive their names from having been originally embowered in forests.' Some excellent remarks on the causes of the scarcity of trees in Ireland will be found in Dr. Hancocks's 'Impediments to the Prosperity of Ireland,' chaps. xxix.–xxxi.

domination, as their agriculture bears mark to this day. The industrial cities of Flanders rose under the same ægis; and the greatest advantage they conferred on the little farms that multiplied round them was not a market for their produce, but protection, independence, and commercial in place of feudal institutions.*

Great as is the stress which M. de Lavergne lays upon the proximity of manufacturing cities and great markets, as conducing to the prosperity and improvement of agriculture, that is not the principal or primary cause to which he ascribes its progress in England. The hereditary taste for country life, of its wealth and aristocracy is, according to him, the principal and primary cause. M. de Lavergne is indeed supposed to have written on England in something of the spirit of reflection on the institutions of his own country in which Tacitus, as some think, wrote upon Germany; but had he read M. de Laveleye's 'Rural Economy of Flanders,' of which he has since made an admirable report to the Institute of France, before writing his own 'Rural Economy of Great Britain,' we imagine that he would have seen in the love of a numerous peasantry for rural life a far more efficient and certain cause of the perfect cultivation of the soil. Early in the middle ages, peas, beans, cabbages, turnips, and all

---

* 'Tant que la Flandre jouit de son indépendance et de ses libertés locales, la culture ne cessa de s'y étendre et de s'y perfectionner, et en même temps de s'y diviser. Des digues furent construites, des terres submergées soustraites au retour des marées, des terres vaques soumises à la charrue, des forêts déboisées, des routes tracées, *les campagnes converties en une suite de jardins qui faisaient un contraste marqué avec celles des pays où dominait la féodalité.*'—*Économie rurale*, pp. 16, 17.

similar plants were commonly grown on the small farms of Flanders; while in England Hartlib, writing in 1650, states that men recollected 'the first gardener who came into Surrey to plant cabbages, cauliflowers, and to sow turnips, carrots and parsnips, pease, all which at that time were great wonders, we having few or none but what came from Holland and Flanders.' Even in 1850, while the sands of Flanders had long become one rich garden, Sir Robert Peel could thus describe the state of good land in England, in the immediate vicinity of good markets—the advantage on which M. de Lavergne lays so much stress, and under those large proprietors whose love of country life he conceives to be a source of constant improvement in agriculture: 'You will find immense tracts of good land, in counties with good roads, good markets, and a moist climate, that remain pretty nearly in a state of nature. Nothing has hitherto been effectual in awakening the proprietors to a sense of their own interests.' *

* This was in a letter to Mr. Caird at the beginning of his tour. The reader is begged to contrast with the results of peasant proprietorship in Flanders the following description by Mr. Caird of the results of great proprietorship in England: 'Oxfordshire. As a general rule the landlords of this county interest themselves very little in agriculture. Few of them are practically acquainted with or engaged in farming. And what is equally unfortunate as regards the improvement of the soil, and the welfare of the different classes engaged in its cultivation, they have not yet seen the necessity of making amends for their defective knowledge by the appointment of agents better qualified than themselves. In the majority of cases the agents or stewards are lawyers, who, without practical knowledge of the business of farming, in the endeavour to secure the landlord's apparent interests bind down the tenant with conditions most injurious to him, and with no corresponding benefit to the landlord. . . . . Essex. The landlords of Essex generally do not co-operate with their tenants in carrying out permanent improvements. With few exceptions, they have shown complete indifference to agricultural enter-

But let us quote M. de Lavergne's own description of the effects of the love of great proprietors for country life, and of the sort of 'happiness' of which he says it affords England long draughts:

'A wit travelling through England forty years ago said: "I would not advise the cottages here to rise against the castle, for the castles are twenty to one." He would say so much more at the present day, for the number of wealthy habitations has gone on increasing. The same observer remarked that in England the poor are swept like dirt in heaps into a corner (*en Angleterre on balaie les pauvres comme des ordures, pour les mettre en tas dans un coin*). The expression, coarse, but true to life, affords a perfect picture of the aspect of the country in England, where poverty rarely appears. It has been swept into the town—the corner in which

prise, neither laying out capital themselves, nor offering such security as would induce the tenant to do so. They impose restrictions and ill-considered covenants even on their most intelligent tenants, and preserve their hedgerow trenches with the utmost rigour. An explanation of all this suicidal and unaccountable mismanagement may be found in the fact that the landed property in the county is encumbered with mortgage debts and other liabilities to the extent of half its value, while the proprietors are nevertheless extremely tenacious of the influence which their position gives them over their tenants, and are afraid to entrust them with such security of tenure as might diminish that influence. These mortgages and embarrassments naturally throw the landlords into the hands of solicitors, who having themselves no practical knowledge of the subject, send down land valuers from London to fix the amount of rent to be charged. But that intelligent supervision which the personal knowledge of either the proprietor or a duly qualified resident agent should give is in such cases wholly wanting; and a tenantry who are encouraged neither by sympathy nor example, and who are positively obstructed in their voluntary efforts for improvement, soon lose the spirit of enterprise by which alone the difficulties of the clay-land cultivation can be overcome.'—*English Agriculture*, 1851-2. See as to the causes of this state of things a recent essay on 'The Land Laws of England in their Influence on Agriculture.' By C. Wren Hoskyns.

it is put. As in all other parts of the world care is paid to the finest quarters of great cities, the country is swept and garnished in England, everything that could offend the eye or the imagination is removed, they will have nothing there but pictures of peace and contentment. Travelling through the land one is struck at every step by the contrast in this respect between country and town. The largest cities are inhabited only by labourers and tradespeople, and the vast quarters they occupy present a melancholy and poverty-stricken appearance. . . . One would say that it was the infernal region at the gate of Paradise.'

M. de Lavergne appears to have been almost unconscious of the irony of his own description of the manner in which the country is swept and garnished in England. The peasant seems, after the old saying, to have been out of sight out of mind, with him. We may remind him of the maxim of another distinguished economist of his country, 'Ce qu'on voit et ce qu'on ne voit pas.' He saw the magnificent palaces and parks of great nobles throughout the country, but he did not see the villages into which the peasantry have been 'swept,' of which a Quarterly Reviewer has given by no means too dark a description.* 'The aspect of these villages is generally repulsive in the extreme. A small proprietor has found it a good speculation to

* 'Quarterly Review,' July 1867. The reviewer is, however, under a misconception as regards Spalding, which is the seat of a great corn trade, and is by no means inhabited almost altogether by labourers. It has many good houses of well-to-do inhabitants, and presents the appearance of a prosperous country town; singularly devoid of literature, however.

build houses for expelled cottagers and labourers who can procure no other home. The result is an aggregation of wretched hovels, the houses are low, the rents are high, and they afford the most miserable accommodation. These villages constitute what may be termed the penal settlements of the surrounding neighbourhood.'

About the same time that the tourist, whom M. de Lavergne quotes, travelled in England, a French traveller through Flanders gave the following description of the villages of Flanders, and the rural scenery and happiness created by the love of the peasant for country life: 'De Rousbrugge à Yprès l'odeur de l'aubépine en fleur qui clôture tous les champs embaume l'air. Belles et nombreuses plantations au bord de la route et des champs, pas un pouce de terrain perdu, les récoltes d'une beauté rare; tout ici annonce l'aisance, et le bel ordre des campagnes, et les bâtiments dans les villages, et la mise des habitants; c'est le jardin de l'Éden. . . . Sur cette route le nombre des villages, leur étendue, l'agrément des bâtiments neufs, leur riche population au milieu des sables humides, me paraissent un prodige. Partout se présente l'image du bonheur champêtre; tout semble le respirer—la physionomie des habitants, leur mise, leurs demeures. Comme ils sont nombreux les villages situés sur la route!'

M. de Lavergne must admit that, beside this, the sort of rural happiness he pictures in England looks like a whited sepulchre beside a neat Flemish cottage. And whereas in England the number of houses for the use of the peasantry has been decreasing, it has in Flanders steadily increased, while the quality of the houses has improved. In 1856, there were 100 houses to every 102 families in East Flanders, and to every 101 families in the western provinces. Even the pauper thinks existence insupportable without a separate cottage: 'Une vieille pauvresse [M. de Laveleye informs us] qui vit de charité me disait récemment, " *Plutôt mourir que d'avoir d'autres per sonnes dans ma maison.*"' There are, indeed, it is often contended in England, a great many paupers in Flanders. It is however worthy of remark that, twenty years ago, when pauperism was at its height from a combination of disasters, including the potato disease, and the failure of hand-spinning and the hand-loom, depriving the smaller cultivators not only of the subsidiary industry from which they derived half of their support, but also of a market for their flax; the number of cultivators reduced to indigence was comparatively trifling. Out of 191,264 *indigents* in East Flanders in 1848, only 3,183 were cultivators; while of female hand-spinners alone there were nearly 50,000. The truth is that the decline of manufactures in provinces in which production by steam has been slow to arise from the absence of iron and coal, and from which an ill-instructed and Flemish-speaking people could not emigrate, has been the great cause of extreme poverty of a large part of the population; and those who attribute it to *la petite culture* mistake the remedy for the disease. The peasant proprietor of a farm of even five acres is never in indigence; the farmer who rents five acres, at a very high rent, for very poor land, rarely ever : and among the labouring-classes it is those who cannot get a little plot, even a quarter of an acre, to cultivate, who are too frequently in the receipt of public relief. Nothwithstanding, moreover, the loss of the auxiliary industry which formerly contributed so much to their support, poverty has steadily decreased among the peasantry. M. de Laveleye, it is true, deplores the spare vegetable diet of the cultivator whose tiny farm is so richly productive; but he adds that he is always well dressed and well housed, and that in other respects his condition is improving. In the wild and thinly populated Ardenne, he says indeed, he visited the cave of 'la pauvre Geneviève'—'who thought herself beyond contradiction the most miserable being in the country; yet she had milk from a goat which it cost her nothing to feed on mountain herbs; the commune gave her firewood in winter, and let her two acres and a half of good land for six francs a-year. The food of this woman, who was pointed out to me as the type of extreme misery, was much more substantial than that of the little farmer in Flanders with a capital of seven thousand francs. Poor Geneviève lived better in her cave than the Flemish farmer in his spruce and tidy cottage amid the fields he has perfectly cultivated.'

But the peasant in England, cultivating a much richer soil, would not have those thousand francs, probably not the neat cottage, and certainly not the prospect of one day buying the farm on which he labours. What would be the condition of the Flemish peasantry, if the rural economy of England had existed in Flanders? Nor should it to be forgotten that the sparing diet of the Flemish peasant is in part economy rather than penury.* The diet of the English labourer, who spends all he gets upon food, is certainly not always better. M. de Lavergne indeed boldly declares: 'Consumption of milk under every form is enormous in England. Their habits in this respect are those of past ages. Cæsar said of them long ago, "Lacte et carne vivunt."'† Cæsar would certainly not say so now, were he to revisit our coasts. The English peasantry is, of all the peasantries in Europe, the one which is worst supplied with milk; and if the father of an agricultural family can get now and then a piece of cold fat bacon or mutton with his bread, it is a luxury which his wife and children are much more rarely afforded. We are far from denying that the *petit cultivateur* in Flanders, who does not own the little plot he farms, is very poor; but he would be much poorer without it. It is not the farm which makes him poor, but the natural sterility of a soil entailing a great outlay in labour and manure, which might otherwise form part of his income; secondly, the heavy deduction for rent in a district of the most limited extent, with a dense population, whose other chief industry has failed; and thirdly, the shortness of the customary lease, Malthus remarked that there is one error which landlords in

* 'So little are English travellers accustomed to consider it possible that a labourer should not spend all he earns, that they habitually mistake the signs of economy for those of poverty.'—J. S. Mill, *Pol. Economy*, book ii. chap. iv. Quoting from a writer on Flemish husbandry, Mr. Mill proceeds: 'Accordingly, they are gradually acquiring capital, and their great ambition is to have land of their own.'

† 'Rural Economy of Great Britain.'

all countries are prone to—namely, taking the highest rent they can get, and leaving the farmer no margin above minimum profit. The error is nowhere more common than in Flanders, being one into which very poor landlords are most likely to fall; but the bulk of its rural population have nevertheless a share either in land-rent or in agricultural profit; whereas, in England, the vast majority have neither. A writer, with special information on such subjects, says that the people of Brussels complain that the English demand for meat has doubled its price in the markets, adding himself: 'This demand arises from the land in England not being as carefully tilled as in Belgium. If it were as judiciously farmed, England would produce as much meat as she consumes, and would not require foreign supplies.'* But it is not the peasantry, at any rate, of Belgium who are the chief sufferers by a rural economy which leaves England, and still more Ireland, so imperfectly farmed. The English labourer has not the compensation for the high price he pays for a morsel of meat of receiving a high price for his cow or his butter, or of usually supplying his own consumption in good part, without resort to the market, as is commonly the case not only in Flanders, but in parts of Belgium where *la grande culture* is most prevalent: 'Hainaut and Brabant [says M. de Laveleye] are considered in Belgium as countries of *la grande culture*. However, little farms of less than a hectare are to be met quite as frequently here as in the Flemish provinces themselves. This is so because not only the agricultural

* 'The Food Supplies of Western Europe.' By Joseph Fisher.

labourers, but even the majority of the workmen employed in mining and manufactures like to have their bit of ground to grow a good part of the food they require for household consumption.'

In these provinces we are among Walloons, as in Ardenne; and in Walloon husbandry, diverse as it is in several respects from, and inferior for the most part to, that of the Flemings, we find conclusive testimony to the superior productiveness of *la petite* over *la grande culture*, as well as to its beneficial effects upon the habits of the peasantry. · Take, for instance, the region called Le Condroz, occupying the greater part of the provinces of Liége and Namur, where, relatively to advantages of soil and climate, husbandry is, according to M. de Laveleye, most backward in Flanders. The old triennial fallow is here practised; and M. de Laveleye, who, we should observe, has imbibed—certainly not from the best judge on the subject, Mr. Caird—the notion that *la grande culture* is the system which does best in England, asks what are the causes of the inferior farming of the Condroz?

'The Condroz,' he answers, 'is the region of Belgium which counts the greatest number of large farms; those which reach 250 acres, so rare in the Flemish provinces, being met here often enough. As soon as a farm is divided in Condroz the land is better cultivated, and the number of cattle increases. The small proprietors who farm their own five or six acres know no fallow; their crops are more varied and better kept; the produce is much larger; they raise beetroot, colza, and turnips; their corn is taller and carries more grain.' Thus, then, a too large size of the farms is one cause of the inferiority of the farming in Condroz.'

Another cause on which he lays stress is the shortness of the leases; but as they are equally short in Flanders, he seeks for a further explanation, which he finds partly in the density of the population of Flanders, compelling extraordinary efforts on the part of the cultivators, especially upon a soil so barren that it will yield nothing without copious manuring, and partly in an instinctive and peculiar love on the part of the Flemish population for agriculture. On this we may observe, that the density of the population is, in the point of view we are here concerned with, only another name for *la petite culture*. For it comes to this: that the farming is so good because the farms are so subdivided and small that the most must be made of every square inch. The reference to the love of the whole Flemish race for the cultivation of the soil corroborates what we have urged in commenting on the doctrine of M. de Lavergne, that the love of country life, which is the true source of agricultural prosperity, is the love of a whole rural population. M. de Laveleye's remark raises, however, a further question, which concerns not only Flemings and Walloons: 'Is the Flemish peasant's deeper love for agriculture an incident of difference of race? or is it not rather the result, partly of historical causes, partly of greater security for improvement at the present day, and partly of a longer and more general prevalence of very small farms, and by consequence, of a greater number of minds, with an especial genius for the industry, diffusing a taste for it?' The Fleming is no doubt a better spadesman and has a better spade than the Walloon; and it is a Flemish not a Walloon proverb that, 'De spa is de goudmyn der boeren'—the spade is the peasant's gold-mine. But the proverb has its counterpart among the small farmers of Italy in the saying, 'Se l' aratro ha il vomero di ferro, la vanga ha la punta d' oro '—if the plough has a share of iron, the spade has a point of gold. We might perhaps find sufficient historical causes of the superior love of farming of the Fleming in his ancient institutions, and the protection of numerous centres of civic life and liberty, during centuries in which the inhabitants of most other parts of Belgium were farther both from the busy mart and the vigorous republic. Even at this day we find traces of the superior security of the peasant farmer in Flanders in the fact, that the custom of compensation to an outgoing tenant for unexhausted improvements (of which the Flemish proverb says, 'Hoe hooger, hoe beter'—the higher the better) has no existence in the Hesbaye or the Condroz. That institutions of this kind and history, rather than race, explain the superior cultivation of the Fleming, is further confirmed by the fact that the farming is best in the districts of Flanders itself where the custom of tenant-right referred to is highest: namely, in the Pays de Waes, and between Gand and Termonde. Another cause, which we have suggested above, is the more general prevalence time out of mind of very small farms. The maxim of Carnot, respecting military talent, is of universal application: 'Supposing the abilities of the higher orders of society to be equal to those of the inferior, it is impossible that the former can ever produce as great a mass of talent as will emerge, on a free competition, from the numerous ranks of the humbler competitors. A hundred thousand men can never produce as many energetic characters as ten millions.' Every great revolution in farming, from the suppression of fallows to the introduction of intermediate crops—almost every plant known to the farmer, except the potato, we owe to the Flemings: but a wider and freer career for the agricultural genius of the race is a sufficient explanation. The saying of Montesquieu, which M. de Laveleye adopts,* that 'countries are not cultivated in proportion to their fertility, but in proportion to their liberty,' is as true of the fertility of the mind as that of the soil. And when we say liberty we mean security, of which, as Bentham explained, liberty is in fact only a part. But insecurity, like security, leaves long traces; and the economist may see the traces of both in the small kingdom of Belgium.

We may now turn to the two questions propounded by Mr. Harrison, the first of which is, 'Are small farms or large farms best?' It is not very clear whether this question relates to the perfection of farming, the

* Les progrès de la culture sont dus à trois causes principales : l'aptitude et le goût très-prononcé des habitants pour les travaux des champs, l'association intime de l'agriculture et de l'industrie, enfin la liberté et l'indépendance dont ont joui les populations. Quand on considère la nature ingrate du sol, et qu'on songe à quel point sa prospérité a dépendu de cette troisième cause de progrès, on se rappelle le mot si juste de Montesquieu, 'Les pays ne sont pas cultivés en raison de leur fertilité, mais en raison de leur liberté.'—E. de Laveleye, *Économie rurale de la Belgique*, p. 19.

welfare of the rural population, or the interests of landlords; but in each and all of these senses the critical questioner seems to have overlooked, that a most material datum is the ratio of land to population. The rural economy best suited to England is not that which would be best for America. Minute and elaborate tillage, with copious manure, would not be economical farming in a continent of boundless extent; it would not pay for the labour, not to speak of profit and rent. It is otherwise in old Europe; and a comparison alike of the farming and of—what is far more important—the peasantry of England and Flanders, demonstrates that it would have been well, not only for the peasantry, but for the landlords of the former, had the rural population never been converted wholesale, as it has been, into labourers for hire. Nevertheless, to Mr. Harrison's question—'Are small farms or large farms best?'—we answer, *Both* are best. Not only because there are in all countries, even in Flanders, places specially adapted for each, but also because the existence of both creates various experiments and improvements, which may be transferred from the one to the other, or which require different areas; and because it opens a career of promotion from the small to the large farm.

Next—'Does the peasant proprietor thrive?' We might ask in like manner, 'Does the sun shine?' Not everywhere: not where human obstacles intervene. By his own exceeding art the peasant proprietor thrives moderately even in the sands of La Campine; but he thrives better with less labour in the Bas Luxembourg, where M. de Laveleye portrays him in a picture such that we must follow the example set by M. de Lavergne, in his report to the Institute of France, of reproducing it in part:

'Afin de compléter l'étude des différentes régions de la Belgique, il nous reste à mentionner celle qui occupe le sud de la province du Luxembourg. La douceur de la température, la vigueur de la végétation, tout annonce qu'on approche de la zone plus favorisée de l'Europe centrale. Tous les fruits sont abondants. Avec son doux climat, ses gracieuses collines et ses beaux rochers, la zone du Bas-Luxembourg est sans contredit l'une de celles qu'on visitera en Belgique avec le plus de plaisir. Le sol, sans être trop morcelé, est divisé entre un nombre considérable de parts, presque toutes exploitées directement par les propriétaires. Chacun, pour ainsi dire, cultive son propre champ et peut s'asseoir à l'ombre de son noyer. Il en résulte pour tous une sorte d'aisance rustique qui dérive non de la possession de grands capitaux, mais de l'abondance de toutes les denrées. Une réelle égalité règne dans les conditions sociales; nul n'est assez riche pour atteindre à l'opulence et à l'oisiveté, nul non plus n'est assez pauvre pour connaître les extrémités de la misère.'

Even where the farming is good, the peasant proprietor's lot must depend something on the size of his little farm, the natural qualities of the climate and soil, and its situation. But the mere fact of proprietorship will not of necessity originate good farming on the part of a few isolated peasants, in a country shut out through all ages from every ray of light, improvement, and hope. The advocate of great estates and large farms in Ireland points to a squatter here and there who has cleared a piece of crown land, and become the fee-simple proprietor, yet farms no better and lives perhaps in more squalor than the neighbouring tenants-at-will. *La petite culture* is a difficult art, which will not grow spontaneously up from the ground as soon as a peasant is planted upon it as owner—the child of immemorial oppression and darkness, and surrounded by such, with the additional hardship in their case of being tenants-at-will. Such a peasant proprietor will probably not thrive; he will do as his fathers did, and as his neighbours do, with only the privilege of doing it more lazily. Improvement—civilisation in every-one of its forms—must be the work of many, and cannot be created by one hand in a desert. The eminent historian Heeren has observed that, but for the Mediterranean, which served as the medium between the inhabitants of three continents, their inhabitants would, beyond question, have continued as uncivilised as those of Central Africa, had the basin of the Mediterranean been a steppe like Mongolia. Flanders was originally such a steppe, but its inhabitants were not cut off from the light which Egypt, Tyre, Athens, Carthage, and Rome combined to shed upon the more favoured parts of modern Europe. Pieces of money of ancient workmanship, bearing the Phœnician palm, have been discovered near Gand, and idols of Isis and other gods found on the banks of Flemish rivers, show that, 'under names of old renown,' the arts of the ancient world had early wandered there.* The seeds of knowledge planted thus were fostered in the modern world by civic liberty and commerce; and the whole history of Flemish husbandry is, to borrow the language of a Flemish historian, 'bound up with resistance of the mercantile and industrial element to that armed territorial proprietorship which continued the barbarian conquest under the name of seignory.'

* A crew, who under names of old renown,
  With monstrous shape and sorceries abused
  Fanatic Egypt and her priests to seek
  Their wandering gods disguised in brutish forms.—*Paradise Lost.*

THE FARMS AND PEASANTRY OF BELGIUM, 1870.

AMONG the forms in which democracy,—not in the sense only of popular power, but also of a spirit in unison with popular requirements and feelings, and of respect for mankind—displays itself now throughout Europe, none is likely to affect more profoundly both English institutions and English philosophy than the growing interest in the condition and arrangements of other nations of which there is evidence. And it is remarkable in how many of the most prominent questions the experience of the youngest and almost the smallest state in Europe is appealed to. We turn to Belgium, not to Italy, to gauge the relative strength of ecclesiastical power and intellectual liberty; the sharp division of its people into two races or families, one speaking a German, the other a French tongue, marks it out as a field for the study of the race problem in its social and economic aspects; it was the first country in Europe to set the example of placing railways under the immediate control of the State; and in the agrarian controversies thickening around us, it is oftener referred to than any other part of the continent.

It is however its Flemish provinces only to which the last-mentioned controversies usually point, when Belgium is cited as an authority on rural economy; its other provinces, though eminent in mining and manufacturing enterprise, having but recently begun to attain distinction in agriculture. The former celebrity of the peasant farms of Flanders is on the other hand never disputed; the main question is, whether its ancient minuteness of both property and cultivation are found compatible with modern progress? To this inquiry a recent writer has returned an answer which has had wide circulation, and it is by no means the truth about Flanders alone which is at stake in the matter: 'The small proprietors may be found struggling with an ungrateful climate and hungry soil in the haunted valleys of the Ardennes, or the dreary swamps of Limbourg. In other countries, remote alike from commercial activity and the crowded markets of the world, not yet under the tyranny of competition, he still fulfils his humble mission; and by his very industry, rendering each day his little homestead more and more attractive, paves the way to his own extermination: in highly civilized countries he is daily becoming rarer. In the fertile plains of Flanders and Brabant he is almost extinct.'* Advancing another step the same writer affirms that 'in Flanders the peasant proprietor cultivating his own land has disappeared.' The plains of Flanders are assuredly not fertile, unless so far as they owe fertility to the peasant cultivator, and above all to the peasant cultivating his

* Letters to the 'Times.' By Mr. W. Mure.

own land. But as to the extinction of such cultivators, let us consult the report of M. de Ségur-Dupeyrac to the French Enquête Agricole, respecting East Flanders, the region most perfectly farmed. 'In East Flanders, of 88,300 cultivators of less than three hectares (less than seven acres and a half) 32,201 are proprietors, 37,283 are tenants under lease. Of cultivators of above three hectares, 12,346 are proprietors, against 11,481 tenants.'* On the 545,245 cultivated acres of East Flanders there are thus, according to this report, and exclusive of a great number of other small proprietors, more proprietors cultivating their own land than there were landowners on all the acres of England at the last census. And with respect to the conditions of perfect success on the part of the peasant proprietor's farming, M. de Ségur-Dupeyrac adds: 'Assuredly, these figures tend scarcely to prove that large property and large farms only can make the soil yield its utmost produce, since it is beyond dispute that in beauty of cultivation Flanders is one of the first countries in Europe. At the same time, if small property can reach the pitch of perfection beheld here, it is on the condition of finding itself surrounded by a considerable population, which adds a vast quantity of sewage to the manure the cattle-stalls yield; not to speak of tanneries, manufactures of animal black, refineries, distilleries, and breweries, which likewise by their refuse contribute largely to the amelioration of the soil, and to that uninterrupted succession of crops which here affords to the cultivator a comfortable

* 'Enquête Agricole. Documents recueillis à l'étranger,' i. 197.

subsistence.' In place then of expelling the peasant proprietor from his farm, it thus appears that 'commercial activity and crowded markets'—bring powerful auxiliaries to his aid. They do so too, not only in the manner M. de Ségur-Dupeyrac points out, by the fertilising agents they add, but also, and more so, by the new demand they create for his produce. The nearer the town comes and the larger it grows, not only the cheaper and the more plentiful is the small cultivator's supply of manures, but the higher are the prices of his milk, butter, and flax. The foreign trade which has brought him guano (the fertiliser most in esteem in East Flanders) is an excellent customer even for rabbits fed at no cost from the roadside ditch. The railway station which brings a new home market to his doors, is itself a new demand for his most profitable productions. The distilleries and breweries which enrich his sterile sands with their refuse afford him additional buyers. The large farmer himself who has a beet-sugar factory, becomes in the same manner one of his allies, both in the field and in the market.

Again, the change in comparative prices, consequent on commercial progress, which is one of the economic revolutions of our age, is a revolution in favour of small farming everywhere, but nowhere more so than in Flanders. Describing early in this century the farming of the Pays de Waes, the garden of Flanders, Sir John Sinclair remarked,* 'Indeed in the Pays de Waes, the sale or price of grain is considered only a secondary object; and it is not possible for a mere

* 'Hints respecting the Agriculture of the Netherlands.'

corn farmer to stand in competition with such rivals.' This is now more than ever the fundamental principle of Flemish husbandry; the chief part of the grain grown in rotation being used for domestic consumption, or in the shape of rye meal for the cattle. Rye is the principal grain crop; wheat, the market cereal, being grown to but a small extent. The market profit of the Flemish small farms comes almost entirely from butter or milk, and 'industrial' crops such as flax and tobacco; and the demand for all these market commodities of course grows with the trade population and wealth of the neighbourhood.

Let us now look at the effect of recent great changes in prices on this system of husbandry. Commenting on the tendency of the modern market to give the largest profit to productions requiring minute cultivation and care, Mr. Caird states: 'Every intelligent farmer ought to keep this steadily in view. Let him produce as much as he can of the articles which have shown a tendency to rise. The farms which eighty years ago yielded 100*l.* in meat, or in butter, would now produce 200*l.*, though neither the breed of stock nor the capabilities of the land had been improved. Those which yielded 100*l.* in wheat would yield no more now.' Thus the changes without in surrounding trade have been decidedly favourable to *la petite culture*; and science at the same time has come to its aid within. The progress of agricultural chemistry has brought with it corresponding improvement in a system of cultivation which depends for its profit, and almost for its existence, on raising a number of crops in succession without exhausting a naturally sterile soil. It is indeed sometimes said, that, far in advance of other countries as Flemish husbandry was fifty years ago, it has remained stationary since, and is consequently now in arrear of agricultural progress. The author might affirm that a considerable improvement has come under his own observation during the number of years he has known the country, and the frequent visits he has made to it. But the evidence of the French minister at Brussels, in a report to the Enquête Agricole, may be more to the purpose. Under the head of Progrès Agricoles, M. le comte de Comminges Guitaut, Ministre plénipotentiaire, says: 'Il est incontestable que de grands progrès ont été réalisés depuis l'année 1846. L'extension donnée à la culture de plantes et racines fourragères a permis au cultivateur d'augmenter la production et la qualité de ses engrais; grâce aux améliorations apportées aux instruments aratoires, principalement aux charrues, rouleaux, scarificateurs, le travail du sol s'est perfectionné; les labours sont plus profonds et exécutés avec plus de soin; le sarclage et le binage s'exécutent dans les champs sur une grande échelle. Dans les Flandres on ne trouve presque plus de terres improductives.' The minister adds a list of new manures which have come into common use, including, in addition to guano, animal black, superphosphate of lime, pulverised bones &c. The steam threshing-machine again has made great way even in the last four years. To the eye of an English large farmer, the simplicity of several of the implements in use may nevertheless fail to convey the idea of progress; for ornate as his culture is, the *petit cultivateur* does nothing for mere display. The wooden plough (as it is inaccurately called, for only the body is of wood) is everywhere still in vogue, more because it is light and saves needless labour, than for saving of original cost; though all saving of needless cost is of course of the essence of *la petite culture*, and one of the causes of its success in that competition which best tests the capacities of the two systems of farming. At a Belgian Agricultural Show, the large proprietor, who does things in an English style, and does so *for* style; who has the latest agricultural machines in the country, and the finest farm buildings; who does not look to profit or cost; and who has in one sense the model farm of the neighbourhood (although it would be folly for his neighbour to copy it) may carry off the first prize. But in the practical competition of the market it is the small cultivator who wins; and land passes more and more from the large to the small tenant who can give the highest rent, and from the larger owner to the peasant who can give the longest price. A writer referred to in a preceding page maintains that 'by an economic law in countries under the statutes of the code civil, the increase of competition does, inevitably, as time rolls on, force the cultivation of the soil into the hands of tenants.' It has been elsewhere shown by the author that this is not so in France;* and it is certainly not more true of Belgium, notwithstanding the law of succession. The success and extension of small

* 'The Land System of France.' Cobden Club Volume.

farms naturally carry along with them the success and extension of peasant proprietorship; and although the partitions effected by the law of succession must not unfrequently bring land into the possession of other than farmers, it often finds its way back in the end through the land-market to a farmer. In the Pays de Waes, for example, when a tradesman-proprietor dies, leaving land behind, a small farmer usually buys it up. That in spite of the distribution effected by the law of succession so much land remains the property of peasant farmers, and that the number of such properties gradually increases, is the strongest possible proof that the real tendency of 'economic law,' or in other words of agricultural progress and commerce combined, is to multiply peasant properties cultivated by their owners.

The case of Belgium is the more striking an example, since the peasant there has none of the special gifts which the skies of France bestow on la petite culture; the olive is not his, and the vine though it grows an indifferent vintage on a few slopes in the east and south of the kingdom, is nowhere to be met with in Flanders. The soil of Flanders, moreover, is so poor by nature, that even 'second' or intermediate crops (very unjustly called *cultures dérobées*, for they are certainly not *stolen* from the ground) require special manure; though as this is done by laying on double manure with the preceding crop, the language of M. de Laveleye on the subject may require explanation.[*]

[*] Sarrassin is the only crop grown by good farmers in Belgium without either separate manure, or double manure with the preceding crop.

The Pays de Waes, it should be observed, is not more fertile than the rest of the sandy regions, although it may appear so from the greater moisture of the soil, and its natural qualities were so far from attracting earlier cultivation than the rest of the province, that it was not reclaimed for centuries after the environs of Ghent. More manure to the acre is applied in it at this day than anywhere else, even in Flanders.

Although the Reports from Belgium to the French Enquête Agricole strongly corroborate the general testimony that there is a constant tendency towards the subdivision of landed property by purchases in small parcels in the Flemish provinces, it deserves attention that they also afford evidence of a different movement. Under a safe and simple system of land transfer by registration, there is, as there is in France, a double movement in the land market. Capital acquired in the trade and manufactures of towns seeks investment in the country along with small savings accumulated in the country itself. M. Leclerc, indeed, treats even the purchases of town capitalists as promoting the subdivision of land, because large proprietors are the sellers; the price of small lots and small farms being much too high to tempt capitalists. And while, for this reason, even the larger purchases encroach on the territory of *la grande*, not of *la petite propriété*, there is another class of capitalists whose transactions augment the territory of the latter. While men retiring from business are not unfrequently buyers, men investing in business are sellers; and sellers in small lots, because in pecuniary value the parts are more than the whole.

'The properties of merchants and manufactures,' says M. de Ségur-Dupeyrac, 'are subjects of frequent sales in small parcels, both involuntarily in consequence of commercial failures, and because the inheritors often prefer to realize their value in money, and add it to their capital. To realize all they can, they turn to account the habitual desire of the small cultivator to become a proprietor, and sell in extremely small lots.' Thus in yet another manner the progress of manufactures and trade tend naturally, not to the accumulation of land, but to its diffusion.

A fact mentioned by M. de Ségur-Dupeyrac respecting the *polders* of Flanders affords strong confirmation of the tendency of *la petite culture* to supersede la grande in the Flemish provinces; and the statement is the more deserving of notice from the observation he adds respecting the influence of small farms on wages. The polders are the rich alluvial lands reclaimed on the coast, and defended from the sea by dykes. Here the great natural fertility of the soil has permitted for a number of years of a very different description of farming from that by which the productiveness of the sands of the interior has been created and maintained; and the polders have been hitherto occupied by what are considered large farms in Belgium. The gradual exhaustion of their fertility, however, has begun to necessitate a change in the mode of cultivation and a subdivision of farms, which M. de Ségur-Dupeyrac refers to in his report under the head of wages, because of the tendency of the change to raise the price of labour through the increase of tillage and the greater competition of farmers. 'Dans les polders,' he states, 'pays de grande culture, bien qu'il s'y remarque une tendence à établir au lieu des exploitations de 15 à 20 hectares, existantes jusqu'ici, des fermes de 5 à 6 hectares seulement, la paye d'un premier valet est encore en ce moment, outre la nourriture, de 16 à 18 francs par mois, celle d'un second valet de 11 à 12 francs. Probablement la création de petites exploitations, en excitant la concurrence entre les fermiers, et en amenant la transformation des prairies naturelles en champs cultivables, aura pour résultat d'élever ces prix, et par suite sans doute, ceux de la main-d'œuvre.' *

Besides creating a demand for additional labour in this way, and stimulating competition among employers —whereas under the large farm system in England two or three farmers in a parish sometimes have the whole labour market to themselves—it cannot be too often repeated that a large proportion of the petits cultivateurs of Flanders, as of France and Germany, would under the English system be labourers only ; while under the Continental, they have a profit from their little farms in addition to their wages as labourers. And as every year a larger number of the labouring class become actual owners of small plots of ground, many add an equivalent to rent over and above profit to their wages ; not to speak of the comfort and independence of having a house and garden of their own, the resource for old age and slack times for work, and the means and motive of utilising the spare time which

* 'Documents recueillis à l'étranger,' i. 200.

the English labourer spends in the public house. Notwithstanding the decline of spinning and weaving by hand (which formerly contributed largely to their support) and the consequent increase in the competition for agricultural employment, the rural population of Flanders is decidedly better off now than it was when it had that subsidiary resource, and *la petite culture* has improved, its auxiliaries are more numerous, and the prices of its produce have greatly risen.

There is, nevertheless, an extraordinary difference between the rates of wages for agricultural labour in the Flemish as compared with the Walloon provinces. 'The line of division between high and low wages,' as M. de Laveleye states, ' closely corresponds with the line of division between the two races, the Flemish and the Walloon.' The Walloon farm labourer earns two francs in the day, and often more, while the Fleming earns but one. Does this difference, then, proceed from difference of race, and bread-earning capacity? It is, in the first place, matter of dispute whether there is a difference of race. The theory of the late Belgian scholar Moke was that there is none; but that the Walloons were thoroughly Romanised, like the neighbouring Gauls, by their conquerors, and thus acquired the Latin tongue; from which, as well as from complete subjugation, the Flemings were preserved by their morasses, and the unattractiveness of their infertile wastes. However the question of race may be resolved, the economic diversities which run with the difference of name and tongue, immense as they are, will be found on investigation to militate strongly against the bearing of race or blood (as distinguished from history, circumstances, tradition, and education), on industrial capacity.

The Flemings, as a general rule, may be said to occupy the northern region of the province; and a line of division from east to west, between the two tongues, and between high and low wages, corresponds in the main with two other divisions—namely (1), between the northern region of infertile sand, and the southern region of generally fertile loam, and (2), between a region without any mineral wealth, and one richly endowed with mines of iron and coal.

Now England itself exhibits a dividing line of wages remarkably analogous to one of the two just mentioned. Prefixed to Mr. Caird's 'English Agriculture,' is an 'outline map of England, showing the line of division between high and low wages; . . . the dotted line from east to west showing the line of wages.' This division is subsequently referred to and explained as follows: 'Taking the highest rate we have met with, 15s. in parts of Lancashire, and comparing it with the lowest, 6s. in South Wilts, and considering the facilities of the present day, it is surprising that so great a difference should continue. The line is distinctly drawn at the point where coal ceases to be found; to the south of which there is only one of the counties we visited in which the wages reach 10s. a-week, Sussex. The local circumstances of that county explain the cause of labour being there better remunerated; the wealthy population of Brighton and other places on the Sussex coast, affording an increased market for labour beyond the demands of agriculture.' A difference in local geological conditions is in like manner the proximate cause which makes the price of agricultural labour in the Walloon provinces double what it is in the Flemish; and the difference has an important bearing on the theory of wages propounded by Ricardo and M'Culloch.* What is particularly striking in the case of Belgium is the extreme sharpness of the division. A few miles north of Liége, the Flemish farm labourer earns hardly half what the Walloon does in the neighbourhood of the town; yet the Fleming is usually the better labourer of the two, and in fact does all kinds of work connected with the ground, much of a navvy's work for example, better than most of his French-tongued countryman. The Walloon on the other hand can reproach him that he displays small talent for manufacture, and that he has neither the wit to learn the French language, which would much enlarge his industrial sphere, nor the enterprise to double his wages as an agricultural labourer by migration. The Flemish provinces too are at no great distance from the mines of Liége and Hainaut, and might at small cost import all the coal and iron required for manufactures on a great scale. We must therefore look beyond mines for an explanation of the low value of the Fleming's spade work. What has been said of Lombardy, 'La Lombardie n'est pas tout-à-fait désespagnolisée,' is no less true of Flanders. Spanish oppression crushed its manufactures, trampled

* See further on the diversities of Wages in England, the Appendix to the present Volume, entitled 'Political Economy and the Rate of Wages.'

out most of its intellectual life, and left its peasantry under the dominion of a clergy who regard ignorance as much less dangerous than knowledge, and the industrial uses of the French language as too slight an advantage to compensate for the acquisition of new ideas. It is not race then that makes the Fleming at once an ill-paid labourer and a *cultivateur d'élite*, or the Walloon a manufacturer, with much less genius for farming, yet earning more by it; for the Fleming was once more famous in manufactures than the Walloon; and though now the least migratory of human beings, he was the great industrial emigrant of the middle ages, as English history attests. Nor, on the other hand, can he claim a complete monopoly of the art of husbandry, for there are parts of Hainaut now, where the farming rivals that of East Flanders. If, again, the doctrine be well founded that there was no original diversity of race, we may find in both Fleming and Walloon conclusive refutation of theories which trace the different industrial development of different nations to diversities of race. These theories mistake effects for causes, treating the effects of different histories, different laws, and different physical geography on different communities as manifestations of inherent and original diversity; and they ignore altogether the yet greater diversities exhibited by the same community at different periods of its career, and by its different classes at the same period. The doctrine of race as applied to interpret social or economic characteristics, is at best, in short, a mere speculation, which it is altogether unphilosophical to draw any positive conclusions from.

APPENDIX.

POLITICAL ECONOMY AND THE RATE OF WAGES.*

'THE premisses of the political economist,' says Mr. Senior, whose conception of the science is that of an influential school of economists, 'consist of a very few general propositions, the result of observation or consciousness, and scarcely requiring proof or even formal statement; and his inferences are, if he has reasoned correctly, as certain as his premisses.' According to this view, political economy not only is purely a deductive science, but its deductions follow from premisses obtained without labour of investigation, lying on the surface of the mind or of things; and they need no verification by comparison with facts; indeed Mr. Senior especially protested against its being considered by continental economists a science *avide de faits*. Considering how numerous and diverse are the things comprised under the denomination of wealth, how various the passions and motives relating to them, how numerous and complicated the conditions which control their production and distribution, it does appear to us amazing that it should ever have been thought possible to construct a science of such a subject with little or no inspection of the phenomena whose laws it aims to interpret. The shortest compass within which the ultimate problem of all science can be comprised, the fewest premisses with which the investigators ought to rest satisfied as complete, Mr. Mill

* Reprinted from *Fraser's Magazine*, July 1868.

defines thus : 'What are the fewest and simplest assumptions, which being granted, the whole existing order of nature would result? or, What are the fewest general propositions from which all uniformities which exist might be deduced?'* Every great advance in the progress of science is a step, Mr. Mill adds, towards the solution of this problem; and if this be a proper definition of the general problem of scientific investigation, and political economy be a branch of it, it surely follows that its fundamental laws ought to be obtained by careful induction, that assumptions from which an unreal order of things and unreal uniformities are deduced cannot be regarded as final or adequate; and that facts, instead of being irrelevant to the economist's reasoning, are the phenomena from which he must infer his general principles, and by which he ought constantly to verify his deductions.† The main object of this article is to examine the conditions which govern the great department of the production and distribution of wealth, indicated by the word wages; but it is hoped that the investigation may not only elicit some information on that special subject, but also afford evidence of the necessity of studying every economic problem in conformity with the universal canons of the logic of science—of accepting no assumptions as finally established without proof, none as adequate from which conclusions untrue as matters of fact are found to result, and no chains of deduction from hypothetical premises as possessing more than hypothetical truth, until verified by observation.

The theory of wages propounded by economic writers in general, though rejected by Mr. Thornton, and subjected to important practical modifications and corrections by Mr. Mill, Mr. Fawcett, and Mr. Waley, may be said to consist of two propositions. (1.) That there is a general wages fund,

---

* *System of Logic.* Book iii., chaps. 4 and 13.

† Mr. Mill's definition is: 'Writers on political economy profess to investigate the nature of wealth, and the laws of its production and distribution, including directly or remotely the operation of all the causes by which the condition of mankind or of any society of human beings in respect to this universal object of desire is made prosperous or the reverse.'—*Principles of Political Economy*; Preliminary Remarks.

POLITICAL ECONOMY AND THE RATE OF WAGES. 359

the proportion of which to the number of labourers fixes the average rate of individual earnings. (2.) That competition distributes this fund among the working classes according to the nature of their work, its difficulty, severity, unpleasantness, &c., so that allowing for differences in the quality of the labour there is an equality in the rates of wages in different employments. Mr. M'Culloch's treatise *On the Circumstances which determine the Rate of Wages,* states the first of these two propositions as follows (chapter i.): 'Wages depend at any particular period on the magnitude of the fund or capital appropriated to the payment of wages, compared with the number of labourers. . . . Let us suppose that the capital of a country annually appropriated to the payment of wages amounts to 30,000,000*l.* sterling. If there were two millions of labourers in that country, it is evident that the wages of each, reducing them all to the same common standard, would be 15*l.*; and it is further evident that this rate could not be increased otherwise than by increasing the amount of capital in a greater proportion than the number of labourers, or by diminishing the number of labourers in a greater proportion than the amount of capital. Every scheme for raising wages which is not bottomed on this principle, or which has not an increase of the ratio of capital to population for its ultimate object, must be nugatory and ineffectual.'

The second proposition is stated in the same treatise thus (chapter v.): 'Were all employments equally agreeable and healthy, the labour to be performed in each of the same intensity, and did they all require the same degree of dexterity and skill on the part of the labourer, it is evident, supposing industry to be quite free, that there could be no permanent or considerable difference in the wages paid to those engaged in them. . . . Hence the discrepancies that actually obtain in the rate of wages are confined within certain limits; increasing or diminishing it only so far as may be necessary to equalise the favourable or unfavourable circumstances attending any employment.'

We maintain in opposition to these propositions that no

funds are certainly appropriated by employers either collectively or individually to the hire of labourers; that the 'average rate of wages' is a phrase without practical meaning; that competition does not equalise wages; that the actual rates of wages are not determined solely by competition, or by any one general cause; and that the aggregate amount of wages is merely the arithmetical sum of the particular amounts of wages determined in each case by its own special conditions. We maintain too that the theory we controvert discredits political economy with the labouring class, and diverts the attention alike of labourers, employers, and economists from the investigation of means by which the wealth of the working classes might be increased and their relations with employers placed on a more satisfactory footing.

A remark which the first of Mr. M'Culloch's propositions might have suggested to his own mind at once is, that supposing it true that the average rate of wages depends on the proportion of an aggregate fund to the number of labourers, small light is nevertheless shed on the subject by the statement of the problem in that way. Has it ever been propounded as the theory of the rate of profit that it depends on the ratio of the aggregate amount of profit to the aggregate quantity of capital? or as the theory of rent that the average rent of an acre depends on the proportion of the total amount of rent to the total number of acres? Were M'Culloch's proposition true to the letter, the question put in a very instructive article in the *North British Review* would remain, ' How does the amount of the wages-fund happen to be what it is? What will make it rise or fall?'* By Mr. Dudley Baxter's estimate of the amount and distribution of the national income, 10,961,000 manual labourers have an aggregate income of 334,645,000*l*., while 2,759,000 persons in other classes have an income of 489,364,000*l*.; but Mr. Baxter does not pretend that these statistics afford an explanation of the facts they succinctly express, namely, that there is such a total national income, such a distribution of it, and such an aggregate amount of wages received by so many labourers. How is it

* *North British Review.* March 1868, p. 6.

POLITICAL ECONOMY AND THE RATE OF WAGES. 361

—it remains to be ascertained—that the many have so little while the few have so much? Why is it that both together have no more? Could any causes alter the total amount of the national income, or its distribution, or both, in favour of the labouring class; or, on the contrary, to their disadvantage? The doctrine of Mr. M'Culloch either means that the total revenue of the labouring class, 'the aggregate wages-fund,' is fixed and invariable in amount, or it does not. If it does not, if the working classes might earn more or less collectively than they actually do, the doctrine in question evidently leaves untouched the very problem it professes to solve, namely, what are the causes determining wages? If, on the other hand, it means that there is a fixed quantity of wealth appropriated exclusively and certainly to the labouring class, it must be seen in a moment to be false by any one who reflects that capital can emigrate, and that the place and manner of its employment depend on individual estimates of profit; that in husbandry there is the alternative of pasture or tillage; that in both manufactures and agriculture, machines, animals, and natural agents may be substituted for labourers; and that the amount of income, as well as of capital, expended on labour or service is as variable as the tastes and dispositions of different individuals and different periods. The successor to a large income may spend more or less than his predecessor in the hire of labourers or servants; moreover, as there will be occasion to notice more particularly hereafter, the expenditure of any given amount of income upon commodities causes a greater or less expenditure of capital upon labour according to the kind of commodities and their mode of production. Again, the same collective amount of capital and income expendible upon labour may yield very different rates of wages, according not to the number of labourers only, but to the number also of employers, and the manner in which the whole amount is divided among them. If engrossed chiefly by a few, they may fix wages by combination at a minimum; if very unequally shared among a large number of employers, the rate determined even by competition may be much lower than it would be upon an equal division, since the richer employers may get the pick of the market for a very little more than the poorer can pay. We may pass then to the second of Mr. M'Culloch's propositions, namely, that wages are equal, allowing for differences in the quantity and quality of work. So convinced was Mr. M'Culloch of the necessary truth of this proposition that he appended a note to Adam Smith's statement of the doctrine of wages, in which he affirmed that modern facilities of communication have brought the wages of labour 'much nearer to a common level than at the period of the *Wealth of Nations*;' and that they are 'nearly the same all over the country.' Now what are the facts? While Adam Smith was composing his treatise in Scotland, Arthur Young was collecting statistics of agricultural wages in England; and in the 26 counties he traversed, the lowest rate was then 6s. a week, in two counties only being so low; the highest rate was 8s. 6d., in one county only being so high; the rate varying generally between 6s. 6d. and 8s. Eighty years afterwards (in 1850 and 1851) Mr. Caird traversed the same counties and found the minimum rate still 6s., but the maximum raised to 16s. In Lancashire, again, wages had risen from 6s. 6d. to 15s.; but in Suffolk they had fallen from 7s. 11d. to 7s., though meat, butter, and milk had greatly risen, and cottage rents 100 per cent.* The real increase of inequality in wages in 1850, compared with 1770, was indeed considerably greater than the money rates show, for Adam Smith was altogether mistaken in supposing the prices of food to be nearly the same throughout the kingdom in his time, but they had become nearly the same in 1850. In 1860 they are still nearer a perfect equality, but the inequality in wages continues, as the following evidence proves:

'In the parish of Chester-le-Street, for example, a very large parish, with a population of more than 20,000 inhabitants, the rate of wages, whether from farmers or gentlemen, for an able-bodied agricultural labourer is at least 15s. a week, and for " hinds " about 19s. to 20s. with house free, and

* *English Agriculture in* 1850 *and* 1851; second edition, pp. 473, 510-515.

POLITICAL ECONOMY AND THE RATE OF WAGES. 363

very often coals also. I may mention also that the rate has never varied since I recollect looking into these matters, namely, from 1843; and I may say the same rate exists in the greater part of the county of Durham and the south part of the county of Northumberland. The labourers eat meat almost every day.

' With regard to Dorsetshire, where I am now living, wages are in many places now as they have been for thirty years, namely, from 7s. to 8s. a week; and out of this they have often to pay 4l. a year for a cottage, generally a wretched one. These labourers hardly know what meat is; they have perhaps a pig, but if so have to spin out the bacon; they live chiefly on cheese, bread, and potatoes. Occasionally they may have a small patch of land near their cottage, or a piece of allotment land for which they pay a small rent. Although the price of bread, meat, &c., has risen so much in late years, the rate of labour has not varied. There are no manufactories of any kind, and the labourers are a very unenterprising race, getting through much less work than a Northumbrian who has his 15s. to 18s. a week and eats meat.' *

Take next an intervening county between Northumberland and Dorsetshire, with intervening rates of wages. The rector of a parish in Northamptonshire writes :†

' Wages in Northamptonshire ranged in 1848 from 9s. to 10s. a week, 9s. being the most common rate ; in 1858 from 10s. to 12s., the latter prevailing generally near large towns. In 1868 I know of two parishes in the county where wages are only 11s. a week ; generally in the richest parts of the county they are about 12s. They rise as you get near the towns; being in my parish 14s. for ordinary agricultural labourers.

' The rate is ruled in this county chiefly by two causes, the price of wheat and the amount of competition. In the neighbourhood of railway works, for example, the farmers are obliged to keep their wages in fair proportion to their profits from prices ; and in such places, when a farmer gets good

---

* Communication from a landed proprietor, April 22, 1868.

† April 17, 1868.

prices, he generally raises the wages of his men spontaneously. For instance, in 1867, the farmers about here told their men they would raise wages from 12s. to 13s.; in 1868, from 13s. to 14s. In out of the way places, where there is no competition of other employments, I fear wages are kept at old rates of 11s. and 12s.; much too little for a labouring man at present prices. One woman in this parish showed her books lately, from which it seems that she paid 13s. 4d. each week this winter for bread and flour, her husband's wages being 15s.: not much left for rent and clothing, &c.! Harvest pulls them through.'

Political economists might many years ago have reformed the poor law, improved the cottages of the rural population in many counties, and done much to raise wages in the counties where they are lowest, if, instead of assuming a fictitious equality, they had applied themselves to discover the causes of a real inequality. But it is one of 'a profound kind of fallacies in the mind of man,' says Lord Bacon, that it 'doth usually assume and feign in nature a greater equality and uniformity than is in truth.' We have seen how far agricultural wages are from that equality and uniformity which Mr. M'Culloch assumed :* the following evidence, given before the Trade-Unions Commission, relates to wages in towns:

'Wages all over the country vary in a most unaccountable manner, as far as any reasons arising from the circumstances either of the trade or the locality would lead one to expect. For instance, masons' wages are at Chester $6\frac{3}{4}d.$ per hour, at Shrewsbury $5d.$ per hour; those are two towns which of course are very similarly situated as far as expense of living is concerned, and as far as other circumstances are concerned. At Clevedon they receive only $4d.$, at Penzance they receive $6d.$, at Exeter $4\frac{1}{2}d.$, at South Shields $7\frac{1}{4}d.$, at Newcastle-on-Tyne $5\frac{7}{8}d.$, at Preston $7\frac{3}{8}d.$, at Lancaster $6d.$ . . . . At Blackburn bricklayers' wages are $8d.$ per hour, at Liverpool

* The return of agricultural labourers' earnings for the quarter ended Michaelmas July 1869, just printed by order of the House of Commons, shows that weekly wages in the harvest quarter vary from 9s. to 21s.

$6\frac{1}{2}d.$, at Stafford $6\frac{1}{2}d.$, at Walsall $5\frac{1}{4}d.$, at Huddersfield $8d.$, at Barnsley $5\frac{3}{8}d.$; in different parts of England the wages vary from $8d.$ to $4\frac{1}{2}d.$ per hour. . . . . Carpenters and joiners at Chester get $6d.$ per hour, at Shrewsbury $4\frac{7}{8}d.$, at Southport $6\frac{3}{4}d.$, at Wigan $5\frac{5}{8}d.$; and wages vary from $8d.$ to $4\frac{5}{8}d.$ per hour. Plasterers' wages at Durham are $6\frac{1}{2}d.$ per hour, at Darlington $5\frac{3}{8}d.$, at Barrow-in-Furness $7\frac{1}{8}d.$, at Wigan $5\frac{5}{8}d.$, at Chester $5\frac{3}{4}d.$, in the Staffordshire Potteries $7\frac{1}{4}d.$, at Scarborough $7\frac{1}{4}d.$; and wages vary from $8d.$ to $4\frac{3}{4}d.$ per hour. As far as the plumbers, painters, and glaziers are concerned, it is difficult to institute a comparison; but as far as I can distinguish, they vary just as much as the other trades. Slaters' wages vary in different parts of England from $8d.$ to $4\frac{5}{8}d.$ per hour. Bricklayers' labourers' wages are at Chester $3\frac{1}{2}d.$ per hour, at Shrewsbury $3d.$, at Barrow-in-Furness $5\frac{3}{8}d.$, at Liverpool $4\frac{5}{8}d.$, at Preston $3\frac{1}{2}d.$, in London $5d.$, at Hereford $3\frac{1}{4}d.$, and at Gloucester $2\frac{3}{4}d.$; and wages vary from $5\frac{3}{8}d.$ to $2\frac{3}{4}d.$ in different parts of England.'

The secretary of the General Builders' Association, who gave the foregoing evidence, speaking on behalf of employers, attributed the striking inequality in wages he described to the disturbing influence of trade-unions. The secretary of the Amalgamated Society of Engineers, on the other hand, speaking on behalf of working men, though affirming in like manner that wages vary in quantity from town to town, maintained that the operations of the union tend to equalise them.* Whether this be so or not (and the information unions collect and the objects they have in view seem to tend to equalisation), the fact of great inequality remains. It is, moreover, much greater in the case of agricultural

---

* *Earl of Lichfield:* Have the operations of your society had the effect of equalising wages in different districts where you have branches?—They have had the effect of equalising wages to a very considerable extent, but have not made a uniform rate of wages.

Do they vary very much in different towns of the same district—say Lancashire, for instance?—Yes.

Do you mean more than the expense of living will account for?—I believe that the cost of living is pretty near the same, go where you will, if you live upon the same diet.

labourers, who have no unions, than of town operatives, who have; and the very existence of unionism is enough to disprove the theory that individual competition is the sole regulator of wages, and that labour naturally finds its own level, like water.

'The spirit quickeneth, but the letter killeth.' The followers of a philosopher owe him no literal sequence: they owe it, on the contrary, to his fame and example, and to the science or system of investigation which he establishes, to give it all possible correction as well as expansion; but in political economy it has been the fate of both Adam Smith and Mr. Mill that the letter of general propositions found in their pages has been pushed with pitiless logic to the utmost extreme, without even the qualifications in those very pages, as though a *reductio ad absurdum* of the master were the object of the disciple. Adam Smith, for example, laid it down as a general principle, that 'the whole of the advantages and disadvantages of different employments of labour must, *in the same neighbourhood*, be either perfectly equal or continually tending to equality, in a society *where every man was perfectly free to choose what occupation he thought proper, and to change it as often as he thought proper*.' But he was so far from treating this very limited proposition as true without exception, even within its specified limits, that he has expressly said: 'The wages of labour, it must be observed, cannot be ascertained very accurately anywhere, different prices being often paid at the same place and for the same sort of labour.' Yet his doctrine now commonly takes the form of an unqualified assumption that competition exactly adjusts payment in all cases to the quality and quantity of labour; that wages are equal in proportion to work all over the country; that the whole island is 'the same neighbourhood' to every man, like his parish; and that every man is able both to choose what occupation he pleases, and to change it as often as he pleases. Mr. Mill has been no less unfortunate than Adam Smith in the fate of his teaching. Instead of assuming that wages are equal, that free competition is the universal condition of the labour market, and that every disadvantage or difficulty is accordingly compensated by proportionate payment, Mr. Mill actually says, 'that wages are generally in an opposite direction to the equitable principle of compensation erroneously represented as the general law of the remuneration of labour. The really exhausting and the really repulsive labours, instead of being better paid than others, are almost invariably paid worst of all, *because performed by those who have no choice.*' In the employments of women, again, he observes that 'the remuneration is greatly below that of equal skill and equal disagreeableness in employments carried on by men;' the reason in some cases being, as he adds, that women's wages are not determined by competition but by custom, and, in all cases, their wages being lowered by their exclusion by men from many employments for which they are by nature eminently fitted. Speaking, on the other hand, of the effect of combination in some of the employments of men, Mr. Mill remarks that 'the journeymen typefounders are able, it is said, to keep up a rate of wages much beyond that which is usual in employments of equal hardness and skill; and even the tailors, a much more numerous class, are understood to have had to some extent a similar success.' Concurring, then, as we do with a critic of Mr. Mill's doctrine, as to the matters of fact in the following sentence, we maintain that they are matters of fact exactly analogous to those to which Mr. Mill has himself drawn pointed attention:

'How could the shoemakers compete with the tailors, or the blacksmiths with the glassblowers? . . . . So far as trade and competition are concerned in the matter, the capital applicable at any particular time for the employment of additional labourers in any particular trades in this country—such, for instance, as the iron trade or the watch trade—is far more accessible to the ironworkers of Belgium or the watchmakers of Geneva, than to any unfortunate members of our own population who, not being wanted in the trades for which they are skilled, are not skilled in the trades where the demand for labour is unsatisfied.'*

* *A Refutation of the Wage-Fund Theory of Modern Political Economy.* By Francis D. Longe.

In the case of cognate or similar trades, an interchange or migration from one to the other is not unusual. 'A man who was a ship-carpenter,' to take an example from the evidence collected by the Trade-Unions Commission, 'at the time the census was taken, very likely a month afterwards was a house carpenter, and *vice versâ* ; and such is the case with certain branches of the cabinet-making trade and carpenters.' Yet even between cognate trades there is often no migration; sometimes, no doubt, because of purely artificial and indefensible obstacles,* yet not the less real even then; sometimes because of natural differences in the work and the men; sometimes, again, because it is by no means easy to compare the relative advantages even of trades closely related. 'Take sashes and floors,' says Lord Elcho, 'the sash requires a more skilled workman than the floor?' 'Yes,' Mr. Potter replies; 'but the floor requires a stronger man.' Sashes and floors are sometimes made by the same men; but a classification and separation of workmen is sometimes founded even on this comparatively slight difference in the work and the qualities it requires; which illustrates the principle that there are, in the nature of things, obstacles to that perfectly free choice and change of occupations which many economists have assumed. The very division of labour creates, in its natural consequence of special skill, a barrier between one trade and another. Special skill, in fact, would possess no value, and would not be acquired, if it did not limit competition. Those who possess it are nevertheless liable to changes both in demand and in the modes of production; and wages are therefore by no means uniformly proportionate to skill, or to the labourer's cost of production; a point on which we must venture to differ from the theory of wages in a new *Manual of Political Economy* by Mr. Rogers. Besides, how is the workman to estimate the real earnings in every other trade in the country? It is by no

* In some parts of the country lathing is done by labourers, while in other parts of the country it is not. For instance, in London lathing is done by men who do nothing but lathing. I pointed out that in Liverpool plasterers and slaters went together, and in Manchester plasterers and painters. In Scarborough the plasterers tried to prevent the bricklayers from carrying on one part of that which they had been brought up to.—*Trade-Unions Commission*, 1 Rep. 3278.

means always easy to judge what the earnings are even in another branch of his own trade at the same spot. The secretary of the Sheffield United Joiners' Toolmakers, having stated to the Outrages Inquiry Commissioners that some of the branches of the trade were over-handed, was asked:

'Which of the four is the most highly paid branch?— That is a very disputed point. If I had to decide it, I should think the grinders were the best paid branch.

'And what would a grinder make per week?—Well, 2*l.* perhaps; but not being a grinder, I cannot speak exactly. Then he has heavier expenses than other men.'

The fact is, that the workman no more has a perfectly free choice of occupations than the barrister has a power of becoming whenever he pleases an editor, or the manager of a bank or a factory, or a Queen's messenger, or a clerk in the Admiralty. The impediments to the changes of occupation and the resulting inequalities in wages are partly, no doubt, unjust and pernicious, and so far as they are so, it is by detecting and not by ignoring them that the economist will really further equality; but they are also partly inherent and natural. There is, in fact, a much freer migration between some bordering grades of capital and labour than between different departments of labour; and the doctrine that a general tax upon profits must be borne by capitalists alone requires revision accordingly—a point which we notice as an example of the manifold errors resulting from reasoning on assumptions founded, not upon facts, but upon general terms. The line of demarcation in terms between 'capitalists' and 'labourers' no more separates the two orders impassably than the term 'competition' places all the members of each order in a position to compete with each other. The number of servants who become shopkeepers and lodging-house keepers in London is very considerable—even in the country we have known the same man become a butler, a grocer, and a butler again—and a heavy tax upon profits would thus fall partly on wages, by increasing the number of servants; while a carpenter or joiner rarely becomes a bricklayer or a mason, though the pay of the latter is in some places better.

The stickler for the doctrine of labour finding its level will probably answer that the level is found, not by old hands changing their trades, but either by a greater competition for the better paid trades on the part of new hands, or by a flow of capital into employments in which labour is abnormally cheap. But the answer, like the doctrine itself, is in conflict with facts, and therefore untrue. Four generations since Adam Smith and Arthur Young have widened the actual differences of wages in England. Mr. Mill's theory of international values, it is well to observe, is entirely based on the *fact* that 'there are still extraordinary differences both of wages and of profits in different parts of the world. Between all distant places in some degree, but especially between different countries, there may exist great inequalities in the earnings of labour and capital, without causing them to move one from the other in such quantities as to level those inequalities.' But it is evident that the economist who accepts this international theory cannot reasonably or logically disregard the fact that there *are* likewise extraordinary inequalities in wages in the same country without causing a movement of labourers such as to level these inequalities.

That instead of one common cause determining and equalising wages, different causes determine them in different cases, and produce the great inequalities found in fact to exist, is easily shown. In Northumberland and Durham good wages and good food make, as we saw, the farm labourer efficient, and his efficiency, along with the good market for his produce afforded by mines, enables the farmer to pay the high price for labour which the competition of the mines on the other hand compels him to pay. In Northamptonshire, near railway works and large towns, the competition of employers in other trades compels the farmer to raise wages when his own profits are high on the one hand from the prices of produce, and when, for the same reason, food is dear to the labourer on the other hand; but in retired parts of the country old rates of farm wages continue from the absence of all other employment. In Dorsetshire the agricultural labourer's earnings are determined mainly, not by the competition of employers, but by that tacit combination on their part not to raise wages above their actual rates, which Adam Smith declared in his time to be the constant and uniform practice.* Not many years ago, rates of wages even lower than in Dorsetshire were current in Wiltshire from the same cause. 'The wages of labour are lower on Salisbury Plain,' Mr. Caird wrote in his *Letters on Agriculture,* 'than in Dorsetshire, and lower than in the dairy and arable districts of North Wilts. An explanation of this may partly be found in the fact that the command of wages is altogether under the control of the large farmers, some of whom employ the whole labour of a parish. Six shillings a week was the amount given for ordinary labourers by the most extensive farmer in South Wilts, who holds nearly 5,000 acres of land, great part of which is his own property. Seven shillings however is the more common rate, and out of that the labourer has to pay one shilling a week for the rent of his cottage.' The truth is that instead of competition for labour being the universal condition of trade and the universal regulator of wages, there is rarely competition for labour on the part of employers *within* a trade in a particular place unless there be competition for it from *without*. And in the absence of competition for labour from without, what competition there is on the part of employers within a trade often tends to lower wages by lowering prices and diminishing the cost of production. ' If one single employer succeed in screwing down wages below the rate previously current, his fellow employers may have no alternative but to follow suit, or to see themselves undersold in the produce market.'† When indeed wages are thus screwed down to a minimum, the probable consequence doubtless is minimum work, and the labourer becomes worthy of little more than his hire. The selling value of the labourer's

---

* 'Whoever imagines that masters rarely combine is as ignorant of the world as of the subject. Masters are always and everywhere in a sort of tacit but constant and uniform combination not to raise wages above the actual rate. Masters, too, sometimes enter into particular combinations to sink wages below this actual rate.'

† Thornton on the Rate of Wages. *Fortnightly Review,* May 1867, p. 562.

work, it ought not to be forgotten by either employer or labourer, determines the maximum of wages; but it is seldom the sole consideration of the employer. 'How much can I give?' is his first consideration, but 'How much less can I make him take?' is generally his second. A great productiveness of labour and capital, high prices for the produce of both, security to reap a liberal profit on a liberal outlay, are the causes which enable employers to pay high rates of wages; but either competition for labour in other employments or places to which it can migrate, or the combination of labourers, is requisite for the most part to compel employers to pay labour either so as to make it highly efficient, or in proportion to its efficiency, if highly efficient. But competition for labour is not necessarily limited to competition on the part of employers. It affords an important illustration of the variety of the conditions determining wages, that in the United States land is a competitor for labour with capital because it offers the labourer an agreeable and lucrative employment, while in the United Kingdom land is not only out of the labourer's reach as an independent resource, but actually, under the system which prevails, often competes with labour instead of for it, by offering to capital employments which supersede labour, as for example, when arable land is converted into pasture or deer forest. The following evidence of an American employer respecting the influence of land upon wages in the States deserves the particular attention of the labouring classes of this kingdom:

'*Chairman*: Have you at all considered what is the reason of the fact that there is so much higher a rate in America?— Yes; it is a problem which faces us at every turn, because, in consequence of this difference in wages, you make iron in England a great deal lower than we can possibly make it. It comes into our country and undersells the iron of our manufacturers, and we are periodically ruined. And the sole cause that I know for that, is the ability of Great Britain to make iron at a less cost than we do, in consequence of the lower rates of labour in this country. You ask me the cause of this difference in the rates of labour. In the first place, there are what I should term the natural causes. We have a new country of immense extent, a very fertile soil, sparsely populated even in the populated parts, and to a very large extent unoccupied. Every enterprising man can, even near the centres of population, purchase land upon credit if he has not any capital ; or he may go west and have land for nothing, by simply filing his intention to occupy it with the registrar of the land office, and he has 160 acres under the homestead law for nothing. Of course the rate of wages is regulated substantially in our country by the profits which a man can get out of the soil, which has cost him little or nothing except the labour which he himself or his family have put upon it. That is the element which in my judgment determines the standard of wages in the United States which an ordinary labourer will derive, from the fact that the man who thinks that he is not getting enough takes to the land; and if he finds that the land does not yield him so much as he could get in some other branch of industry, he goes from the land back to that industry. Therefore the governing element in our country is the annual profit which a man can derive from land which has cost him nothing beyond the labour which he himself has put upon it. In other words, what you call rent to some extent enters into the question of the value of labour in our country. You add to what would be the ordinary value of labour in this country the element of the land, and you arrive nearly at the value of a day's labour in America.

' Your theory is, that as every man in America can hold 160 acres free as the gift of the State, a man is constantly making the experiment: "How do I get my subsistence out of that 160 acres ?—If I can get more by being a puddler in an iron manufactory, I will give up my 160 acres."—Yes.

' *Mr. Merivale* : I understand you to say that the natural rate of wages is fixed in America by the abundance of land, and cannot fall below that standard ?—Yes; on the average it is so.' *

* Second Report, Trade-Unions Commission, pp. 3, 5. Compare Seventh Report, p. 57.

In this country, on the contrary, instead of competing for labour, land offers to capital investments, whereby the demand for labour is diminished. It is among the unfortunate results of the almost exclusive attention of trade-unions to a single, and by no means invariably successful, mode of operating upon wages by combination, that the working classes bring nothing of their great political power and intellectual influence to bear on the liberation of land from restrictions which prevent its being within the reach of the labourer, and at once a competitor with capital for the use of his powers of production, and a powerful contributor to his welfare as a consumer as regards the cost both of his dwelling and of his food. The interests of the working classes as consumers, indeed their common interests of all kinds, seem hitherto to have obtained from them scarcely any attention. The whole 110,000,000*l.* of annual profit on capital divided among the 11,000,000 labourers of the United Kingdom would add but 10*l.* a year to each labourer's income, supposing capital to stay in the country on such terms; while money wages might be much more largely augmented, and their purchasing power perhaps doubled, by legal, financial, and administrative reforms, to which the labouring class give no heed. Among the considerations affecting their interests to which their attention seems never to be drawn, is that the aggregate amount of their revenue depends in a great measure on the modes of expenditure customary with all classes, including their own. They may, for example, spend a great part of their own earnings on things such as spirits and beer, the price of which consists chiefly of the profits of distillers, brewers, and publicans; or they may limit the bulk of their purchases to articles made mainly by labour and sold in co-operative stores. A good part of their income may thus either go back to other classes, or be redistributed among their own class, according to their own habits of consumption. An assailant of Mr. Mill's theory of wages referred to in a previous page has himself fallen into the same curious fallacy with Mr. Senior, that all the funds, expended upon commodities of whatever kind, are expended on labour.* Criticising Ricardo, Mr. Senior argued, 'Mr. Ricardo's theory is, that it is more beneficial to the labouring classes to be employed in the production of services than in the production of commodities; that it is better for them to be employed in standing behind chairs than in making chairs.' Mr. Longe, in like manner, ridicules the doctrine that the rich can make any addition to wages by diminishing their personal expenditure on commodities, and purchasing labour instead, 'a process,' Mr. Longe exclaims, 'very analogous to that of lengthening a stick by cutting off from the top a portion to be added at the bottom.' The error of both Mr. Senior and Mr. Longe lies in supposing that labourers get the whole price of all the things they contribute to produce, without any deduction for profit or rent. Take Mr. Senior's own instance of the price of a chair: part is the price of the wood, and this part is nearly all interest and rent —rent to the owner of the ground in which the tree grew, and interest to the planter, who had to wait for his money until his plantation grew up; part, and perhaps a very large part, is profit to the workman's employer; the remainder only, and it may be a very small remainder, is wages to the maker or workman himself. It is actually a very small remainder to the cabinet-maker in East London. 'The cabinet-makers at the East End, a very numerous body, are in what is called the slop trade, and are ground down by the dealers, who own what are called "slaughter houses," in which they take advantage of the small manufacturers, and compel them to sell their upholstery at little more than the cost of materials. Between dealers and want of work, I am told that numbers of the slop cabinet-makers are not earning 7s. 6d. a week.' †

Nearly two millions, that is, nearly one fifth of the entire number of labourers in the United Kingdom, are maintained directly as servants and labourers out of the incomes of the other classes of society, and probably their total receipts in wages and board may amount to forty millions a year. Does

* *A Refutation of the Wage-Fund Theory of Modern Political Economy.* By F. D. Longe.
† *National Expenditure.* By R. Dudley Baxter, p. 65.

Mr. Longe suppose that, if these forty millions were spent by employers on commodities, instead of on labour, the labouring classes as a whole would be nothing the poorer? The difference would be that other classes instead of labourers would get a good part of the forty millions' worth of commodities which servants and labourers now buy with their wages, or receive directly in board. We may add that Mr. Senior's theory that the average rate of wages depends on the quantity and quality of commodities appropriated to the use of labourers on the one hand, and their number on the other, confounds two perfectly distinct classes of causes —those which affect the labourer as a producer, and those which affect him as a consumer; those which determine the general value of his labour, and those which determine its specific value, that is to say, its purchasing power over the particular commodities which he consumes. The sale of his labour is one exchange; the purchase of the commodities he buys with the fruits of that sale—that is to say, with his wages—is another; and these two separate exchanges are subject to quite different laws or conditions. Reductions of taxation on tea and sugar, for example, improve the quantity and quality of some of the articles labourers consume without necessarily increasing their incomes as producers, or their purchasing powers over things in general. Thus it happens that a proceeding which benefits the labouring class, considered as producers, may possibly injure them as consumers; for instance, the conversion of sheep runs into deer forests in the highlands of Scotland. More men are employed as gamekeepers and gillies than would, in most cases, be employed as shepherds were the same land under sheep; but, on the other hand, labourers neither rent shooting grounds nor eat venison, while they do consume mutton, if its plenty and cheapness place it within their reach. Were the deer forests, however, restored to the spade and the plough, the labouring class would benefit both as producers and consumers; there would be both a greater demand for labour, and a greater production of the food which labourers use. We advert to such points, not only for whatever may be their special importance, but also to illustrate the great variety of the causes which affect the value of labour; and we do so, both because while employers commonly err in regarding competition as the labourer's only legitimate process, the labouring classes themselves err in laying almost exclusive stress upon combination.

Mr. Mill, Mr. Fawcett, Mr. Thornton, and Mr. Waley have demonstrated that without combination labourers would in some cases be completely at the mercy of employers. In the words of the first, 'How can they stand out for terms without organised concert? What chance would any labourer have who struck singly for an advance of wages? Associations of labourers of a nature similar to trade-unions, far from being a hindrance to a free market for labour, are the necessary instrumentality of that free market; the indispensable means of enabling the sellers of labour to take due care of their own interests under a system of competition.'* Accordingly when Mr. Jevons vindicates the right of labourers to combine to shorten the hours of labour, on the ground that 'the single workman, dependent for his living upon his week's wages, is utterly incompetent to enforce any concession from his wealthy employer,' † we think he must logically go further and admit that it may be as necessary for workmen to combine in order to get a fair price for their labour, as in order to shorten its hours. It is sometimes said that if the profits of a particular business are abnormally high, a consequent accumulation of capital resulting must raise wages in proportion; but there is nothing to compel the recipients of high profits to make that particular use of them. They may buy lands, or increase their personal expenditure, or speculate in other, it may be in foreign, investments. On the other hand, for labourers to rely exclusively on combination, seems to us a mischievous error. In many cases there is no room, in either profits or prices, for an increase of wages; ‡ and in

* *Principles of Political Economy.* By J. S. Mill. Book v. chap. 10, § 5.
† *A Lecture on Trades' Societies.* By W. Stanley Jevons, M.A.
‡ We cannot agree with the writer of the excellent article on Trade-Unions in the March number of the *North British Review*, before referred to, that

378 LAND SYSTEMS AND INDUSTRIAL ECONOMY.

at least one case of first rate importance, combination is in practice impossible. Increased powers of competition, rather than of combination—by education, by the collection of statistics of wages, and by the reform of the land laws—are the powers the working classes should seek to confer on the agricultural labourer.

But in all cases there are two questions to which both employers and employed should attend. One is, what is the utmost that can be made by capital and labour together? The other, how is the total produce of both to be divided between them? The mistake into which both employers and labourers commonly fall is, of attention only to the latter of the two questions: neither looking to the means by which the total amount to be divided may be raised to the utmost; both looking to extort the utmost possible share of the actual total;—neither treating the problem as one of production; both treating it as one only of distribution.

In submitting such considerations we venture to propound no universal rule respecting the conditions which do or which ought to regulate wages. In place of competition being the only condition by which the value of labour is determined as a matter of fact, we find competition, combination, and co-operation all active, and each in a variety of forms; nor dare we deny that there are cases to which each is the arrangement specially appropriate at present. Sometimes we see employers alone combining, and labourers competing; sometimes it is employers who compete and labourers who combine. In some cases each of the two classes combines against the other; in some, both combine against consumers. In some cases labour is not its own sole competitor, but machinery, animals, or natural agents compete with it and diminish its value; in other cases these agencies co-operate with it or compete for it, and add to its value. In some cases, instead of a conflict between labour and capital, there is co-operation, and

wages may be raised by means of a reduction of interest on borrowed capital. Its owners are under no necessity to make that investment of it, and will not accept a lower interest from employers of labour than they can obtain elsewhere.

that in various ways: for example, sometimes by arbitration of wages and sometimes by regular partnership in profits.

So various and variable being the causes which determine the rates of wages in particular cases, it is evident that wages in many cases might be different from what they are; that the result has been mistaken for the cause; and that the aggregate amount of wages is merely the total sum of the particular amounts in particular cases taken together; and that the average rate of wages is a phrase without practical meaning or relation to the actual earnings of labour. The investigation establishes likewise, we presume to affirm, Mr. Senior's protest notwithstanding, that political economy is, or ought to be, a science *avide de faits*. It has suffered much from that tendency towards mere abstract speculation of which Lord Bacon said: 'As for the philosophers, they make imaginary laws for imaginary commonwealths; and their discourses are as the stars which give little light because they are so high.' By no means concurring with all the criticisms of a powerful censor of the science, we cannot but join in his protest against its being put forward as one 'definite, distinct, and exact, the axioms of which are as universal and demonstrable as those of astronomy; the practical rules of which are as simple and familiar as those of arithmetic.' * Political economy must be content to take rank as an inductive, instead of a purely deductive science; and it will gain in utility, interest, and real truth, far more than a full compensation for the forfeiture of a fictitious title to mathematical exactness and certainty.

* *The Limits of Political Economy.* By F. Harrison. *Fortnightly Review*, June 15, 1865.